Constructions of Colonialism

Constructions of Colonialism

Perspectives on Eliza Fraser's Shipwreck

Edited by Ian J. McNiven,
Lynette Russell and Kay Schaffer

Leicester University Press
London and New York

Leicester University Press
A Cassell Imprint
Wellington House, 125 Strand, London WC2R 0BB
370 Lexington Avenue, New York, NY 10017-6550

First published 1998

British Library Cataloguing-in-Publication Data
A catalogue record for this book is available from the British Library.

ISBN 0-7185-0139-X (hardback)
0-7185-0171-3 (paperback)

Library of Congress Cataloging-in-Publication Data
Constructions of colonialism : perspectives on Eliza Fraser's
   shipwreck / edited by Ian J. McNiven, Lynette Russell, and Kay
   Schaffer.
      p.   cm.
   Includes bibliographical references and index.
   ISBN 0-7185-0139-X (hardcover). – ISBN 0-7185-0171-3 (pbk.)
   1. Fraser, Eliza Anne.   2. Shipwrecks–Australia–Queensland.
I. McNiven, Ian J.   II. Russell, Lynette.   III. Schaffer, Kay

   G530.F852C66   1998
   994.3–dc21   97–51839
                                                              CIP

Typeset by BookEns Ltd, Royston, Herts.
Printed and bound in Great Britain by
Biddles Ltd, Guildford and King's Lynn

Contents

Contents

Contributors

Jude Adams (Visual Arts, School of Art and Design, University of South Australia)

Barbara Blackman (Poet)

Elaine Brown (History, University of Queensland)

Jim Davidson (History, Victoria University of Technology)

Fiona Foley (Badtjala artist)

Sue Kossew (English, University of New South Wales)

Rod Macneil (J. Paul Getty Museum)

Ian J. McNiven (Classics and Archaeology, University of Melbourne)

Olga Miller (Butchulla Elder)

Lynette Russell (Museum Studies, Deakin University)

Kay Schaffer (Social Inquiry, University of Adelaide)

Gerry Turcotte (English Studies, University of Wollongong)

Acknowledgements

The editors would like to thank all the contributors and the University of Adelaide, Faculty of Arts, for supporting the symposium 'Post Colonial Fictions' which brought the contributors together for the first time. Callie Guerin was of great assistance in the initial editing of the papers. Taasha Coates' hard work was a key component of making the original symposium such a great success. Robert Iseman lent moral, physical and financial support. Linda Brainwood of the State Library of New South Wales went out of her way to assist in the locating of images for the volume. Research and publication were aided by ARC grants. Finally we would like to thank Janet Joyce and her staff at Cassell for their patience and assistance.

Introduction

Ian J. McNiven, Lynette Russell and Kay Schaffer

Off the Queensland coast lies the largest sand island in the world – Fraser Island. Long, sandy beaches and unspoilt beauty attract hundreds of thousands of tourists every year to this World Heritage listed icon of the Australian landscape. But to the crews of sailing ships that passed her shores last century before heading north through the treacherous Great Barrier Reef, Fraser Island was far from a tropical paradise. The island was the scene for the most famous shipwreck saga in the colonial history of Australia. In 1836, the *Stirling Castle* under the command of Captain Fraser sailed north up the Queensland coast bound for Singapore. After successfully missing the shoals of Sandy Cape at the northern tip of Fraser Island, then the most dangerous sailing obstacle on the east coast, the ship managed a further 250 km before hitting Swain Reefs at the southern end of the Great Barrier Reef. The ship was soon smashed to pieces but not before two groups of castaways managed to escape. For many weeks they floated adrift in the vast expanse and silence of the Coral Sea with little water and no rain. They had to contend with sharks, scorching heat, hunger and desperate thirst. When all seemed lost, one of the boats with Captain Fraser, his wife Eliza, and a number of crew found themselves fighting the roaring surf off Fraser Island's coast. Successfully beaching themselves, one by one the castaways stepped ashore and soon realized they were being watched.

Fraser Island was the home of the Badtjala people – a large group of coastal hunter-gatherers who had harvested the resources of their seas and lands for many thousands of years. But to the *Stirling Castle* castaways, these 'Aborigines' were savages and cannibals, living a hostile life in a hostile land. The Badtjala soon played host to the castaways who had stepped into their backyard. For a while, tensions were eased by exchanges of food and water for European curiosities such as clothing. Soon, however, the castaways had to fend for themselves and help with the daily activities of food gathering and firewood collection. Misunderstandings led to confrontation, and soon Eliza Fraser found herself alone and naked, her husband speared to death and other crew members gone missing. A month or so later, Mrs Fraser presented a ravaged spectacle to Lieutenant Otter and his rescue party.

In the year after Mrs Fraser's return to England, events surrounding the rescue of the castaways from their Aboriginal captors, in particular Eliza Fraser, received international media attention. Newspaper articles on the shipwreck saga sent shivers down the spines of readers in Europe and colonies across the globe. Capitalizing on this interest, journalist John Curtis published a lengthy account of the saga in his 1838 book *Shipwreck of the Stirling Castle*. Curtis, a court reporter in London who had covered the Lord Mayor's Inquiry into Mrs Fraser's captivity, noted that he wrote his version of the loss of the *Stirling Castle* and the sufferings of the castaways in order to set the record straight, his intention being to resurrect the reputation of Mrs Fraser who had been profoundly maligned in the popular presses. Towards this end Curtis documented what he believed to be a factual account of the experiences of Eliza Fraser and the shipwrecked crew members. His narrative was, he maintained, confirmed 'by unquestionable corroborative testimony both oral and documentary'. The book proved to be immensely popular, and was reprinted by American publishers in 1841. These early sensationalized and popular reports of this event represent Mrs Fraser as an innocent white victim of colonialism and her Aboriginal hosts as barbarous savages. These 'first contact' narratives of the white woman and her Aboriginal 'captors' impacted significantly upon England and the politics of Empire at an early stage in Australia's colonial history. These two key themes – the representation of Eliza Fraser and the representation of the Badtjala people – are explored in *Constructions of Colonialism*.

Part 1 concerns historical representations of the Eliza Fraser saga from a range of historical and cultural vantage points. Despite an extensive archive dealing with events of the saga, many of the events of the shipwreck and the activities of Eliza Fraser remain curiously vexatious. Elaine Brown (Chapter 1) sets the historical scene and provides an all-important backdrop to the volume with a critical look at events from a reconstructive historical perspective. Western historical observers can never really know the ultimate fate of Eliza; her body is lost to us, her resting place is unknown. How does a woman of such notoriety disappear from history? Eliza's bones, like those of her husband somewhere in the sands of Fraser Island, remain lost. For the indigenous people of Fraser Island her fate is less mysterious. Olga

Miller (Chapter 2) is an elder of the Badtjala (or Butchulla) people of Fraser Island. Her chapter presents the first Aboriginal voice in the saga based on oral history passed down by those living on the other side of the colonial frontier. In keeping with these traditions, Mrs Miller relayed her chapter orally. The fundamentally different historical narrative presented by Mrs Miller reiterates a clash of ideas that echoes the cultural clash experienced by her ancestors and the *Stirling Castle* castaways some 160 years ago. History is as much about facts as it is about vantage points. Olga Miller's chapter tells us that, from an Aboriginal perspective, Eliza Fraser's body is not lost and her fate is known.

Lost historical remains are the domain of archaeology, and the *Stirling Castle* archive has proved invaluable in archaeological reconstructions of Fraser Island's Aboriginal past. Ian McNiven explores these reconstructions in Chapter 3 and discovers another frontier in terms of Euro-Australian and Aboriginal constructions of identity. Despite the importance of the *Stirling Castle* archive as an unparalleled ethnohistorical source on 'traditional' Badtjala lifeways, it is all but ignored by the Badtjala in their own reconstructions of their history. Here again the interplay of historical reality and vantage point takes place in the post-colonial arena. Are some colonial narratives so tainted that they cannot be salvaged? The Eliza Fraser saga gained its strength by juxtaposing civilization and savagery, good and evil. Perhaps the Badtjala have no interest in playing the game of redeeming the actions of their ancestors by revealing to Europeans what are, to them, obvious and gross distortions of their culture in the *Stirling Castle* archive. The Badtjala approach is one of exorcizing Eliza from history not exercising academic discourse in her honour. The paintings by Badtjala artist Fiona Foley showing a decapitated Eliza seem to suggest this.

In Chapter 4, Lynette Russell explores notions of otherness and the construction of 'savages' within the Eliza Fraser saga. In doing so, Russell elaborates several theoretical positions and demonstrates how an exploration of the Eliza Fraser saga can contribute to post-colonial studies elsewhere. In 1836 the *Sydney Gazette* reported that the Aboriginal people involved were 'savages' who had inflicted 'severe miseries' upon Mrs Fraser and the other castaways. Two years later in the Curtis volume, the indigenes had become 'demons in human form'. Russell considers the textual representations of Aboriginal people in nineteenth-century descriptions of the Eliza Fraser saga. Three interconnected and interwoven themes course through the texts. The first of these is the silence and anonymity of the Aborigines. Rarely in these depictions does the reader hear the native voice. The second issue is the polarity of the representations of Aboriginal people. Throughout the nineteenth century the *Stirling Castle* narratives depicted Aboriginal people as either pernicious savages or poor, afflicted creatures. Both types of native beseeched the intervention of the settlers who were charged with bringing enlightenment and civilization. The final theme detected by Russell in the nineteenth-century texts is the perception that Australia exhibited a homogeneous Australian Aboriginal culture.

Rod Macneil's exploration of visual imagery in Chapter 5 further develops notions of post-coloniality. This chapter deals with notions of otherness, identity and Empire as depicted in the visual imagery of the *Stirling Castle* shipwreck. The resonance of the Eliza Fraser story lies partly in the effectiveness with which it allegorizes the confrontation with the uncolonized. The hapless castaways battle not only for their physical survival, but also for the survival of their identity. The struggle is for the preservation of difference – for those tangible signs of cultural divergence that signify not merely their physical, but their moral difference from their (uncivilized) Aboriginal captors. In this most unsympathetic and contrary of environments, the castaways struggle to maintain those social and cultural tenets fundamental to their self-identification as European/civilized. Their sense of self must depend entirely upon those cultural signifiers salvaged from the wreck and those they are able to muster from within themselves. Mrs Fraser's embodiment of the values of the Empire, her preservation of cultural difference, and the way in which this endorses the colonial mission, are all paramount to the transcendence of the Eliza Fraser story from historical narrative into myth.

It is the movement from historical narrative to myth, from definite to indefinite, which dominates Part 1 of *Constructions of Colonialism*. The authors explore the nineteenth-century representations of Eliza Fraser and the wreck of the *Stirling Castle* and ask what these tell us about the writers and artists of the time. Through the minutiae of these representations we explore the meanings, the agendas and the processes of the colonial settler culture and its need to reconcile the issues of 'race', class, gender and nation. These are issues which Part 2 of the book takes up as the twentieth-century representations of Eliza and her saga reinvigorate the myth.

By the mid-nineteenth century, Eliza Fraser's name and her tale of survival were known in America, Great Britain and her colonies, as well as in Australia. The story of Eliza Fraser and the shipwreck of the *Stirling Castle* was all but forgotten by the late nineteenth-century and the early decades of the twentieth century. She rose from the ashes of the historical past, however, to attain an almost legendary status, at least in Australia, in the 1970s. Since that time Mrs Fraser has become a figure of note within an Australian nationalist mythology and an internationalist post-colonial arena. Kay Schaffer has studied the materials extensively in her book *In the Wake of First Contact: The Eliza Fraser Stories*.[1] She argues that the saga has been amenable to colonial and national histories for over 160 years in an international context because of the many oppositional aspects of the story: the conflicts between indigenous and non-indigenous peoples, the captain and his recalcitrant crew, the colonial administrators and the convicts, working-class and middle-class people, women and men. Writers and audiences continue to be fascinated by the motif of the white woman as captive among indigenous peoples. In Chapter 6, Kay Schaffer traces the fascination with the story in twentieth-century Australia. She demonstrates how, within modernist nationalist and post-colonial contexts, modern retellings of the tale focus on Mrs Fraser's sexuality and her rescue by Bracefell, a runaway convict who becomes, at least for contemporary Australian audiences, the Australian underdog hero. In this way the story, in its many variants, has continued to nurture shifting national agendas. It also enables artists to reconstruct the categories of race, class and gender throughout the Western neo- to post-colonial world.

The late twentieth-century adaptations of the Eliza Fraser story bear little relation to their nineteenth-century variants and have only the most tenuous links to the 1836 report of the shipwreck. They represent new transformations in radically different historical contexts. The ambivalences and anxieties of white Australian artists in the twentieth century revolve not so much around issues of race, but around sexuality, difference and identity. The legend which evolved in Australia focuses on these issues. It has been of interest to many of the nation's most revered creative artists including the painter Sir Sidney Nolan, novelist Patrick White, playwright David Williamson, poet Barbara Blackman, composer Peter Sculthorpe, and film directors Tim Burstall and Gillian Coote. Their reconstructions and revisions of the Eliza Fraser legend, taken collectively, celebrate many aspects of Australian nationalism and mythology. This stands in stark contrast with the work of Badtjala artist Fiona Foley, who offers a different approach to the saga. Her retelling, through a series of paintings and installations, looks with bemused irony at the attention, bordering on mystical, which has been bestowed on this one white woman by Australia's Eurocentric population.

Much of Mrs Fraser's contemporary fame derives from the creative mythologizing of the revered Australian painter, Sir Sidney Nolan. She is the subject of a series of his paintings which he began in 1947 and returned to frequently until his death in 1992. Nolan's paintings became familiar to an international audience after his retrospective exhibition in London in 1956 which featured a number of paintings from his 'Mrs Fraser' series. It resulted in the publication of a Thames & Hudson monograph of the artist's work, *Sidney Nolan: Landscapes and Legends*.[2] The monograph caught the attention of a number of overseas writers, as will be discussed by some contributors to the anthology. In the book, Mrs Fraser's ordeal is described thus:

> Mrs Fraser was a Scottish lady who was shipwrecked on what is now Fraser Island, off the Queensland coast. She lived for 6 months among the aborigines, rapidly losing her clothes, until she was discovered by one Bracefell, a deserting convict who himself had hidden for 10 years among the primitive Australians. The lady asked the criminal to restore her to civilisation, which he agreed to do if she would promise to intercede for his free pardon from the Governor. The bargain was sealed, and the couple set off inland.
>
> At first sight of European settlement, Mrs Fraser rounded on her benefactor and threatened to deliver him up to justice if he did not immediately decamp. Bracefell returned disillusioned to the hospitable bush, and Mrs Fraser's adventures aroused such admiring interest that on her return to Europe she was able to exhibit herself at 6d a showing in Hyde Park.

This legendary retelling contains the key motifs which lay the foundation for future versions of the story. In it, Mrs Fraser's time on the island has increased from six weeks to six months and she is rescued not by John Graham, as the official rescue reports maintain, but by a runaway convict David Bracefell, with whom (it is imagined) she had a romance and whom she eventually betrays. In addition, the account makes almost no mention of the Aboriginal actors in the event; it ends with an evocation of an image of Mrs Fraser as a spectacle/exhibition in Hyde Park for which there is little evidence.

Jude Adams (Chapter 7) focuses on the treatment of the figure of Eliza Fraser, the representation of the landscape, and the role of myth within the works of Foley and Nolan. She argues that, as with the characters of the Eliza Fraser story, Nolan and Foley can be seen to inhabit structures of opposition. Nolan is celebrated, male and Anglo-Irish. Foley is young, female and Aboriginal. Foley's work speaks from a position of post- or anti-colonialism, whereas Nolan's work is inextricably tied to modernism and neo-colonialism. His work is expressive; its meaning universalized. In contrast, Foley's work is minimal, abstract, quotational. Nolan's own fantasies are projected on to an essentialized Australian landscape. Foley's landscape is located and known; her story is political. Nolan speaks from outside. In regard to the Eliza Fraser story, however, his is the controlling gaze. Foley can be seen to speak from inside, from the traditional position of silenced, exotic otherness. In examining these relations of opposition and coincidence in Foley's and Nolan's work, Jude Adams investigates how the reading together of these works can extend our understanding of different cultural meanings and relevances of the Eliza Fraser story.

In Chapter 8, Jim Davidson sets out to place the mythologization of Mrs Fraser against a broader canvas of archetype and myth. He asks, 'What have been the changing circumstances in Australia that have led, over the past thirty years, to an upsurge in interest in her? What shifts in perspective have taken place so that a shipwrecked woman, presumably regarded as vulnerable and representing (for white Australia) an extreme form of exposure, should now be regarded as an archetypal figure?' The chapter also investigates similar narratives located elsewhere in Australia, and discusses how the South African novelist, André Brink, took up the theme and reinterpreted it by relocating it to the Cape in the eighteenth-century. It also considers the Greek variant myth about the fate of Iphigenia in Tauris, and discusses the ways in which that too can shed light on the aspects of the Mrs Fraser story which have resonance for us.

André Brink, like the London-based dramatist Gabriel Josipovici and the Sri Lankan-born but Canadian-based writer Michael Ondaatje, all maintain that they were introduced to the Mrs Fraser story through the Thames & Hudson *Sidney Nolan* publication. The paintings and legend it contained spurred their interest and led to their respective adaptations: the novel *An Instant in the Wind* (1976), the play *Dreams of Mrs Fraser* (1972), and the long poem *the man with seven toes* (1976). In Chapter 9, Sue Kossew presents a detailed analysis of Brink's version of the Eliza Fraser story. She argues that it is not merely coincidental that a 'dissident' white South African writer of Afrikaner heritage, André Brink, should choose to rewrite a myth of encounter between a settler woman and Aboriginal people in his novel. It is an encounter that has been figured in various ways in a number of South African myths and one that embodies the ultimate 'Thou shalt not' – a relationship between white woman and black man. While initially attracted by the Sidney Nolan paintings of Eliza Fraser's shipwreck, Brink reinterprets the Australian version in the context of South African history (and its suppression and manipulation by the apartheid government) and the specifics of the South African colonial encounter. Brink writes the story of the encounter between Elisabeth Larssen and Adam Mantoor essentially as a romance. His text counteracts the propaganda of revulsion disseminated by the nationalist government as indicative/characteristic of any contact between white woman and black man. By envisaging the possibility of a relationship of equality, albeit a temporary one, he is also resisting the basic tenets of the apartheid system. Kossew examines the specifically South African contexts and issues which Brink's text raises and provides some comparison with Australian versions. What is of particular interest is the number of intersecting post-colonial concerns within these two settler colonies, South Africa and Australia, like the issue of history as a legitimizing narrative; the shared colonization of woman and the indigenous other; the problematic notion of finding a settler language with which to speak; the importance of landscape; and the metaphor of mapping which seeks to impose Western textuality and rationality on the supposedly blank page of *terra nullius*.

The versions by Gabriel Josipovici and Michael Ondaatje imagine the captive white woman as a spectacle – an object of fear and desire. Her excessive sexuality, and her spectacular body, are invoked as a locus for otherness, one that provides an erotic investment in the dilemma of nationalism in white settler societies. In Chapter 10, Gerry Turcotte addresses this fear of primitive otherness in relation to race in Michael Ondaatje's long poem *the man with seven toes*. This work is among the least known works of Ondaatje's oeuvre, and certainly of the Eliza Fraser stories. Along with the Barbara Blackman libretto 'Eliza Surviva', and Gabriel Josipovici's play *Dreams of Mrs Fraser*, *seven toes* has been displaced by more famous accounts produced by writers such as André Brink, Patrick White and Sidney Nolan. And yet the poem is as resonant, as misleading and as provocative as any of the better-known accounts, and it yields fascinating insights into the way myth-making (sexual, racial, national) is manipulated. Turcotte begins by tracing the imaginative occlusion of nation and gender at the heart of the poem, but he focuses primarily on the way indigenity is manipulated and exposed to re-confirm existing stereotypes of the primitive 'other'. This racist construct is particularly surprising in the works of a writer who has otherwise challenged such representations and may explain his own reluctance to allow the work to be reprinted. It remains an odd contribution to his œuvre, one which benefits from Turcotte's scrutiny.

The long poem by Michael Ondaatje, published in Canada, spurred Canadian interest in the tale. The Canadian Lyric Arts Trio ensemble commissioned Australian poet Barbara Blackman and composer Peter Sculthorpe to produce a musical piece on the theme which was performed as music theatre in 1977–78 under the title 'Eliza Fraser Sings'. This piece, too, features themes of sexuality, difference and identity but it is one of the few instances where a woman takes up the tale. In Chapter 11, Barbara Blackman provides some personal background to her involvement with the story, including her memories as a child growing up in Brisbane, of the ways in which Eliza Fraser had entered popular myth. In her childhood Blackman's family moved to the bush and lived for many years within Aboriginal communities. In later life Barbara, who was married to the Australian painter Charles Blackman, befriended Sidney and Cynthia Nolan, as well as Patrick

White. Through her memoir she provides a very grounded, living memory of the geography of the area, as well as the artists who came to take up the Eliza Fraser story. It is followed by a republication of her libretto, 'Eliza Surviva', created for the Blackman/Sculthorpe collaboration 'Eliza Fraser Sings'. In the libretto we have a rare account of the saga from a female perspective, where Mrs Fraser traverses the boundaries between sanity and madness. The poem dramatises her ordeal in a lyrical and dramatic fashion and asks how it is possible to maintain one's own sanity during such an alienating and traumatic experience.

More recently, Mrs Fraser's story has been revived and critiqued within Australia for its inherent racism, its silencing of Aboriginal voices and fates. In this, the most recent approaches to the Eliza Fraser story by artists in the 1990s in Australia give evidence of significant changes in attitudes and beliefs about what it means to be an Australian. The latest reincarnations of 'Eliza' by Allan Marett, in his Japanese Noh Play *Eliza*, and Gillian Coote in her television documentary *Island of Lies* (1991), both of which are discussed in Kay Schaffer's earlier chapter, re-contextualize the story again, this time in keeping with shifting political forces within Australia and new global economic realities which tie Australia to the Asian Pacific region. Marett and Coote explore Australia's racist past and the hidden history of frontier violence bordering on genocide which the popular versions of the Eliza Fraser story obscure. They provide oppositional readings and a new ethical and moral stance for Eurocentric, white Australians to consider in relation to their blindness to the history of racial oppression and genocide within the country.

As a story of first contact with a trajectory of white conquest which eventually resulted in the virtual extinction of Aborigines from the Great Sandy Region of Queensland, it is of renewed political interest to land rights activists and the contemporary Badtjala people of Fraser Island. In the 1990s, Aboriginal people are publicly contesting dominant legends and mythologies. Fiona Foley, a Badtjala artist with ancestral links to Fraser Island, is one such artist/activist. Her artwork invites the viewer to look at and to think again about Australia's racist past and to recognize the different histories, contexts, political agendas and realities which constitute the state of the nation. In Chapter 12, Foley begins by telling of her travel to Berlin as an international guest at an Eliza Fraser symposium sponsored by the German government. There she visits the Leipzig collection of artefacts and skeletal remains of eight Queensland Aborigines. The visit prompts her to reflect on the 'nouveau colonization' which goes on today – not of bodies but of indigenous intellects. Her essay juxtaposes cultural knowledge about the 'lionized' Mrs Fraser with the little-known lives of often nameless

Aboriginal heroines whose brave deeds have been silenced, their lives unknown, their cultures unrecorded in the white histories of nation, and the ways in which Aboriginal artists have begun to address this history and to pay tribute to their shamefully neglected heritage. In Foley's final words in the collection she returns the gaze of Aboriginal Australia back on to what she sees as a guilty and awkward nation.

Notes

1 K. Schaffer, *In the Wake of First Contact: The Eliza Fraser Stories* (Cambridge: Cambridge University Press, 1995).
2 K. Clark, C. MacInnes and B. Robertson (eds), *Sidney Nolan* (London: Thames and Hudson, 1961).

PART 1

Historical Representations

Chapter 1

Eliza Fraser: an historical record

Elaine Brown

It is May 1836 – as Europeans measure time. Off the coast of north-eastern Australia the weather is fine, the winds are fair. In swelling seas, the *Stirling Castle*, a large, two-masted sailing ship, is making headway north from Sydney, bound for London.

The ship's Captain, James Fraser, intends to dock at Singapore to take on cargo. The Captain suffers from a stomach complaint; so, seven months before, his wife Eliza agreed to accompany him on this voyage to Australia in order to minister to his health. Their daughter and two sons were left at home in the Orkney Islands in Scotland in the care of the Presbyterian minister at Stromness. Eliza is now advanced in pregnancy.

Somewhere in the waters of the Great Barrier Reef (see Figure 1.1) – it might be, as the Second Mate John Baxter later tells the authorities, at latitude 24 degrees south, longitude 155 degrees 12 minutes east, while the ship is steering north-west by north half north at 7.5 knots (or it might not) – at about half-past eight on the evening of Saturday 21 May, the *Stirling Castle* unexpectedly strikes a coral reef, which holes her hull and breaks her back.[1]

And so begins our story, the foundation of legend and myth ...

Before continuing this reconstruction, which I have made by analysing documents and exploring the area where events took place, I wish to make a point about the use of historical records.

Good history is written from primary sources. One of the problems with this story is that the eyewitness and contemporary accounts of the shipwreck of the *Stirling Castle* and the rescue of survivors were for a century hidden in the archives of New South Wales, while more accessible and increasingly contradictory hearsay accounts were selectively repeated, embellished, distorted and possibly fabricated – leading to the popular idea that no one could ever arrive at the historical 'truth' about Eliza Fraser's experiences.

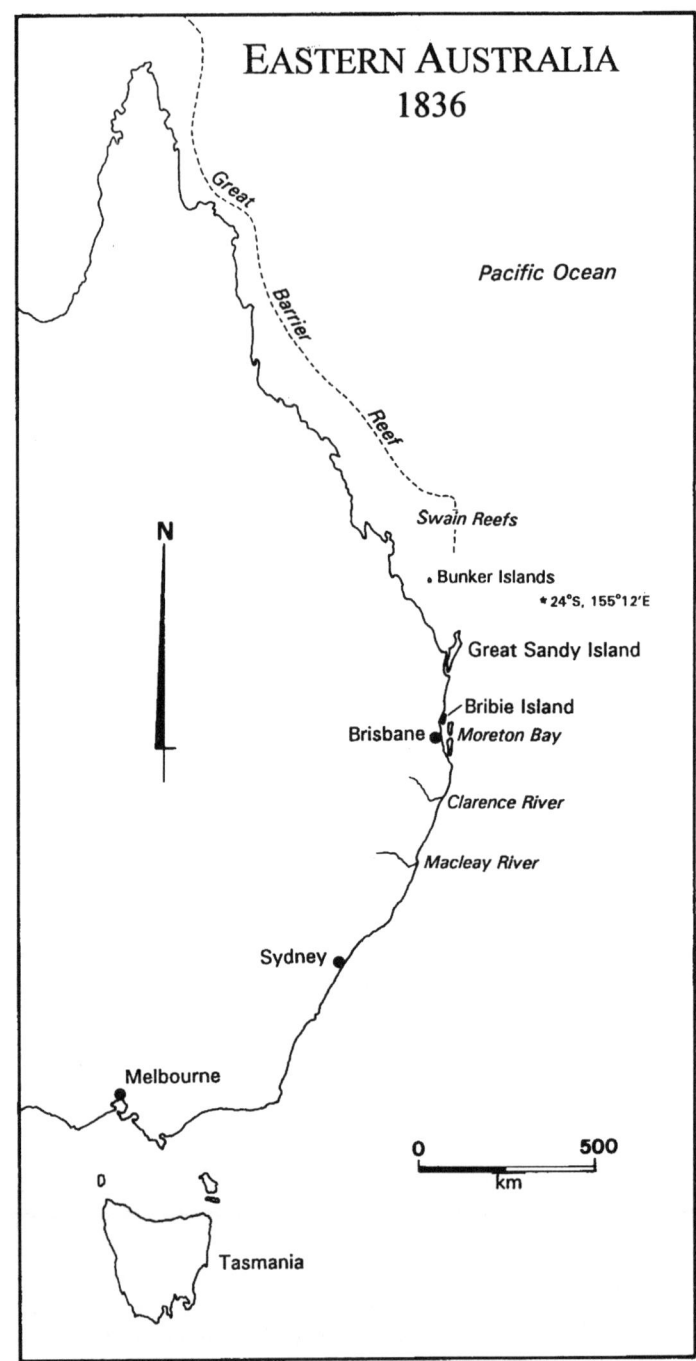

Figure 1.1 Map of Eastern Australia, 1836

Looking back over the 160 years since the shipwreck of the *Stirling Castle*, it is possible to detect many examples where potent images from dubious later or secondary versions of the story have contributed to a conclusion or 'truth' that simply perpetuated ignorance or served the interests of some person or group. There follow two examples to whet your appetite.

First fallacious image: Second Mate Charles Brown, tied to a stake, being burnt to death. Conclusion: the Aborigines of Fraser Island were exceptionally cruel savages. Who benefits? Perhaps the people who are invading Australia and need to feel superior to the people whom they are dispossessing.

Second fallacious image: Eliza Fraser in a side-show tent in Hyde Park, London, showing her scars to all comers. Conclusion: Eliza Fraser was an exhibitionist – a woman with severe character defects. Who benefits? I'm not sure, so I'll leave you to work it out, just telling you that the origin of this image is the often unreliable Henry Stuart Russell, an English immigrant, who recalled, in memoirs written in 1888, a placard he had seen in London fifty years earlier. (He never claimed to have seen the show.)[2]

As an historian it is important to be open, honest and discriminating in your use of records. In the case of Eliza Fraser, you need first to gather as many historical and fictional materials as possible, and then to approach each document with scepticism, asking which sources, primary and secondary, that writer had access to.

Second, you need to arrange the sources in the order in which they were created. Understanding the chronology of the documents or versions helps you to see where and when (and sometimes even why) distortions and embellishments were introduced.

Third, you need to compare the sources very carefully and consider them in context. By context I mean their background in place and period. The story of the shipwreck of the *Stirling Castle* is so powerful in its own right that it has been easy to overlook its context. Writers have capitalized on the story's dramatic qualities – conflict, tragedy, pathos; its setting on an exotic, unexplored Pacific shore; and its cast of stereotyped characters – the mutinous crew of a merchant ship, the Captain's lady, cruel savages, redcoated soldiers and an heroic runaway convict.

Some writers, like Michael Alexander in *Mrs Fraser on the Fatal Shore*,[3] have attempted to come to terms with the social backgrounds of the castaways, though I believe a great deal more could be revealed by studying events against the broad backdrop of colonial Australia and parent Europe in the 1830s. But two aspects of the story's background which are essential to a fuller understanding of its significance – the particular natural environment into which the *Stirling Castle* survivors were cast and the culture of the Aboriginal people who received them – have, for over 150 years, been blissfully ignored. This neglect has led to some very unsatisfactory interpretations and representations.

I wish I could take you to Fraser Island and let you experience its spirit of place. The people who have lived there – from the Aborigines, who clung to their land as long as they could, to the timber-getters, fishermen and holiday-makers who supplanted them – have been among the most privileged of human beings. Whenever I visit, I consider it an honour to be able to do so.

I remember an occasion a few years ago when we had as our guest on Fraser Island a teacher from Tianjin, in drab and dusty northern China. We had walked in to Lake Wabby (see Figure 1.2) and returned to the beach in the late afternoon. It was just after the eruption of Mount Pinatubu in the Philippines, and atmospheric dust coloured the sky over the Pacific Ocean in the palest pastel shades of yellow, pink and blue. Our friend moved away from us and stood alone, soaking in beauty of a kind she had never before experienced. I'm not surprised that Sidney Nolan and Patrick White were moved by their visits to Fraser Island to produce great works of art and literature. I doubt, however, that Eliza Fraser would share my opinion in this. Given her very different circumstances, I don't think she saw much beauty in the place.

Let me take you back to the deck of the *Stirling Castle*, where chaos reigns no matter who tells the story. There are four eyewitness accounts of the shipwreck. At Moreton Bay soon after their rescue, Eliza Fraser and Second Mate John Baxter dictate their experiences to a scribe for the official record that is sent to Sydney.[4] In her recollection, Eliza sides with her husband in a confrontation with the seamen over effecting a suitable response to their dangerous situation. Baxter, an officer and Fraser's nephew, also sees events from the Captain's point of view, but his own considerable powers of observation are reflected in the clarity and detail of his narrative.

Two of the seamen, Robert Hodge and Harry Youlden, also leave accounts of the shipwreck. After his quite separate rescue, Hodge speaks to a journalist from the *Sydney Gazette*, and his account is immediately put through the filter of a journalist's desire for a good story.[5] Youlden's account, the longest, most vivid and most personal recollection, is to appear as an article entitled 'Shipwreck in Australia' in the American magazine *Knickerbocker* – but not for another seventeen years, not until 1853, when, because of gold discoveries in New South Wales and Victoria, world interest focuses on these previously unimportant British colonies.[6] This account, apart from some questionable details which can be explained as deliberate attempts to portray his own actions in a favourable light or as lapses of memory due to the long interval between the events and their recall,

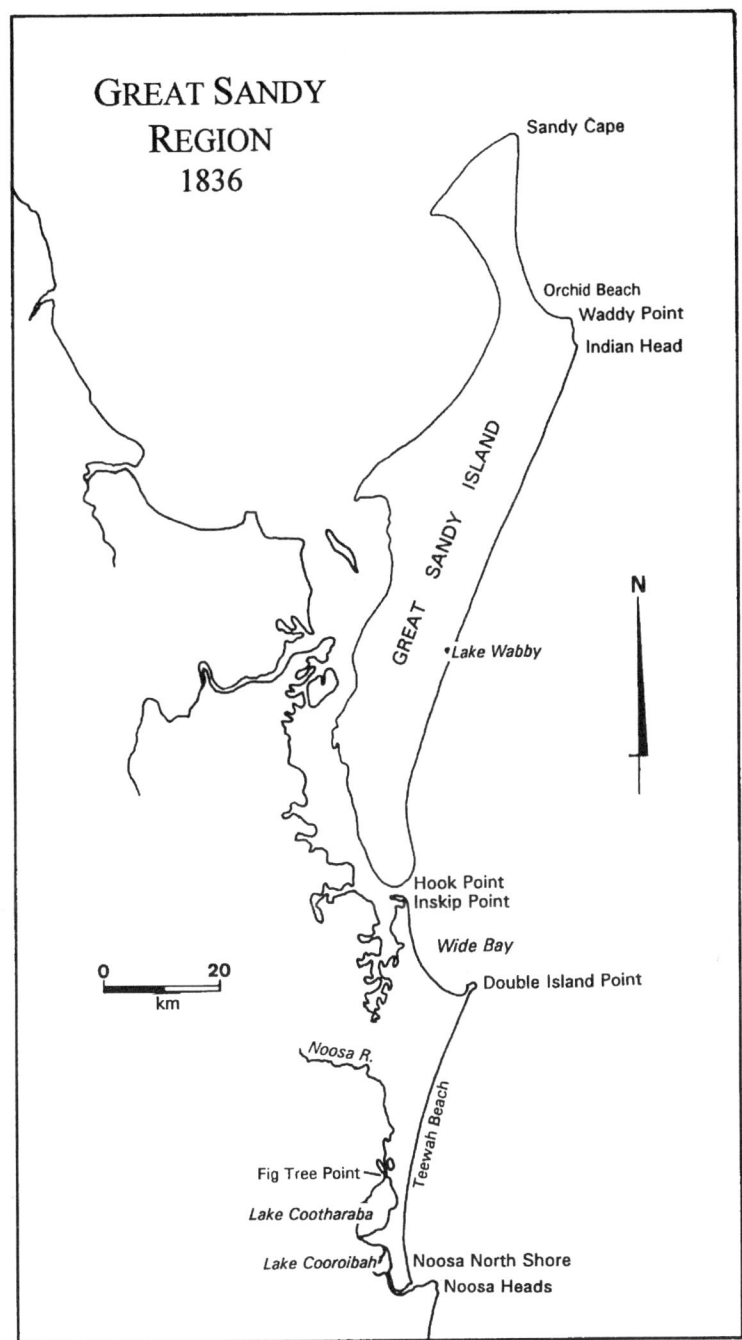

GREAT SANDY
REGION
1836

Sandy Cape

Orchid Beach
Waddy Point
Indian Head

GREAT SANDY ISLAND

N

•Lake Wabby

Hook Point
Inskip Point

Wide Bay

0   20
km

Double Island Point

Noosa R.

Teewah Beach

Fig Tree Point

Lake Cootharaba

Lake Cooroibah

Noosa North Shore
Noosa Heads

Figure 1.2   Map showing Great Sandy Region, 1836

fits well with the accounts of other survivors and appears to be authentic.

All accounts agree that the *Stirling Castle* is doomed to break up on the reef, so the two remaining lifeboats, a longboat and a pinnace, are roughly repaired and fitted out with whatever can be salvaged from a hull filled with water. On the day after the wreck, Sunday 22 May, the survivors, with some difficulty, lower the boats over the ship's side and push off into the unknown. The Captain has a chart and instruments of navigation. He knows he has to sail first towards the mainland, then southwards to the penal settlement at Moreton Bay. He is determined to avoid landing on the coast for fear of falling into the hands of hostile Aborigines, so they visit only a few offshore islands.

Here I must introduce another source of information who will define this story but who does not yet even know about it. His name is John Curtis. A year from now, he will attend a hearing in London where Eliza Fraser, John Baxter and another seaman, Robert Darge, far removed in time and place from the scene of their sufferings, will describe their experiences for public consumption. Filtered through Curtis' ears and eyes and reconstructed around his perceptions, the story will be reported in the London *Times* in 1837 and then published in Curtis' book, *The Shipwreck of the Stirling Castle*, in 1838.[7]

I mention Curtis here because, among the events of the five weeks after the shipwreck, as the two lifeboats make their way slowly and tortuously southwards, landing on barren islands, needing frequent repairs, being caught in winds and high seas, a significant event is mentioned only by him. This is the birth and death of Eliza's baby, which takes place four or five days after the boats leave the wreck. So many of Curtis' reports are doubtful that some commentators have wondered whether this event was later added to gain extra sympathy for Eliza. Personally I have no problem imagining why the painful and distressing scene in the longboat might have been passed over by the survivors at Moreton Bay and later by Eliza in the drawing-rooms of polite society in Sydney. Only very recently have such scenes become acceptable in literature and films in our culture. So I ask you to keep an open mind on this until later, when we'll consider Aboriginal reactions to Eliza's body.

In about mid-June the longboat and the pinnace part company. The eyewitness accounts simply record this fact, but those on board the longboat harbour a suspicion that those on board the pinnace, which was in better repair and a faster sailer than the longboat, might have deliberately given them the slip. This allegation is later denied by Robert Hodge, the only survivor from the pinnace, but by the time John Curtis deals with it the event is set in concrete. He reports that

Edward Stone, the boatswain, pretended to search for water in the pinnace and sailed away.[8]

I might now dispose of the crew of the pinnace by recounting Hodge's version of what happens to them. Sent off to find water, the pinnace misses the longboat in the night and pursues a course southwards, bypassing Moreton Bay and coming ashore somewhere in what is now northern New South Wales (see Figure 1.1). Five men and two boys set off to walk south along the shore. John Fraser, a midshipman and the Captain's nephew, is drowned when washed off a rock while gathering oysters. One seaman is burnt to death while sleeping in a hut; another is drowned attempting to cross a river. The boatswain and carpenter are left on an island in the Clarence River after a dispute with some Aborigines. The cook sinks exhausted as he and Hodge near the Macleay River, and only Hodge survives to be picked up and taken to Sydney on a small vessel owned by cedar-getters.

When the revenue cutter *Prince George* sails to Moreton Bay to pick up Eliza and the other *Stirling Castle* survivors, Hodge travels with the Captain to check for other survivors of the pinnace. They find a burnt body in a hut but no sign of anyone else.[9] Of course, this part of the story arouses speculation among those who love tales of cannibalism, and the legend develops that, as in some documented cases among escaped convicts, the crew of the pinnace have eaten one another, starting with the boys.

On that cheerful note we return to the eleven survivors in the leaking longboat. They steer slowly southwards in bad weather until, about the end of June, they sight the bare, high dunes at the northern tip of Great Sandy Island, which will later be renamed Fraser Island after their luckless Captain[10] (not, as tourists are often told, after his wife). Captain Fraser knows they are nearing Moreton Bay and wants to keep going, but the seamen are hungry, thirsty and desperate and insist on landing 'about twenty miles south of Sandy Cape' in the sheltered bay on the northern side of Waddy Point, where fishing boats are launched today.[11]

The best description of the landing is the dramatic account by Harry Youlden:

> As we approached, we could see a number of black, naked natives, armed with clubs and spears, moving in the direction of the point to which we were steering. The sea was breaking with terrible force upon the beach ... With throbbing hearts we were tossed over that disturbed ocean, to be cast ... into the very jaws of destruction. There was a solemn stillness in the boat; not a word was spoken. We were soon in the midst of the breakers. The poor, shattered, hard-pressed bark shivered

and staggered in the boiling surge, struggling for very life in the agony. A sea dark as night came rolling in, and covering us with spray, dashed us high up on the beach. To spring out and cling to the sides with all our energies, to prevent her being washed away by the undertow, was the instinctive thought and act of all of us.[12]

Near the spot where they land, the castaways find fresh water trickling down a rock. Aborigines, shy at first and wary of the party's firearms, eventually come forward and show they are willing to trade fish for such novelties as clothing and nautical instruments.

For the next few days the castaways rest to recover from their ordeal. They turn the boat over and try to repair it. Captain Fraser is anxious to put to sea again, but the crew want to walk to Moreton Bay. After attempts to launch the boat into the prevailing south-easterly wind fail, five of the seamen – Darge, Youlden, Dayman, Elliot and Carey – take weapons and bags of materials for trading with the natives and set off southwards along the beach. Those who remain – Captain Fraser, Brown, Baxter, Corallis, Doyle and Eliza – finding themselves too weak to handle the boat and soon becoming aware that their smaller numbers are making the Aborigines more aggressive, leave under cover of darkness and, walking in the surf to avoid detection, slowly follow the others.

Four of the survivors – Darge and Youlden from the first party and Eliza and Baxter from the second – leave accounts of the 100 kilometre walk down the beach.[13] All report similar experiences. As they walk, the only food they eat are berries and the fruit of the pandanus, which, having a 'relaxing tendency', gives them an 'attack of the flux' and undermines the recovery begun after their landing.[14] Both parties are met by groups of Aboriginal men, who appropriate their material possessions and encourage them to keep moving. Finally, to add to their discomfiture, one group of Aborigines remove their clothes and examine their bodies. Baxter later reports that Eliza is left with 'an article of underdress' on this occasion.[15] Once they lose their clothing and blankets it is difficult to sleep or keep warm in the showery weather conditions.

By the time the Captain's party nears Hook Point at the southern end of the island the survivors are strung out along the beach, with Brown struggling at the rear. In the 'disagreeable chilliness'[16] of midwinter they are exhausted, hungry and cold, and the Captain and Brown are showing signs of illness. At Hook Point they can go no further – a mile-wide, swiftly flowing stretch of water lies between them and the mainland. It is up to the Aborigines who are camped there to do something about them.

We will need to be sensitive to the differing viewpoints of the participants in the encounter that follows. The castaways will claim that the Aborigines 'captured' them and, giving each person a 'master', forced them into 'slavery'. This language reflects a preoccupation of their generation. They belong to a period when slavery, a reality in many British colonies until its abolition in 1833, is the subject of moral condemnation and earnest political debate.

The Aborigines, who know nothing of the concept of slavery, face a practical problem: how to cope with the arrival of a dozen extra mouths to feed. White people, whom they believe to be the returning spirits of their own dead relatives, have come among them before – from the sea or from the south – but these are the most difficult 'ghosts' they have ever had to deal with.[17] Their solution is to allocate each person to a family group and allow them to make a contribution to daily subsistence activities. For the more able-bodied men, this means fishing and hunting. For the weakened Captain Fraser and Charles Brown, it means at least gathering firewood, a constant chore because fires are kept burning day and night. John Baxter and Harry Youlden both express surprise that the first act of their 'captors' is to give them food and drink.

Eliza poses a different problem. She is left sitting on the beach until a group of women arrive and take her in hand. First, they throw salt sand over her to cleanse her body, which she finds excruciatingly painful because of the sunburn from which her newly exposed skin is suffering. Later they rub her skin with charcoal and grease to keep her warm, and decorate her body with colour and her hair with feathers. She does not understand the role she is expected to play and resents the menial tasks they require her to do: nursing children, digging fern roots, fetching firewood and climbing trees to rob bees' nests for honey. She carries out these activities with such ineptness and reluctance that the women begin to goad and torment her. Fed on scraps because of her inability to contribute much in the way of food and kept separate from the other castaways, she begins to despair.

Unable to communicate with the women except by signs, Eliza has no way of understanding the social system of which she is now a part. She does not know that among the males female blood is feared, so that menstruating women and women giving birth temporarily live apart from the rest of the group.[18] She cannot guess that the physical evidence of her recent childbirth may have caused the men who stripped her of her clothing to leave her with that item of underdress and to abandon her to the care of the women.

Accounts of the events that take place at Hook Point grow more melodramatic with each retelling, so it is helpful to start with the account Eliza gave to the Moreton Bay Commandant soon after her rescue, which is direct, detailed, and backed up by other references, and then note where changes occur. Captain Fraser's death, for example:

> In consequence of these hardships my husband soon became so much weakened as to be totally incapable of doing the work that was required of him, and being on one occasion unable through debility to carry a large log of wood one of the natives threw a spear at him which entered his shoulder a little below the blade-bone. Of this event he never recovered and being soon after seized with a spitting of blood he gradually pined away until his death which took place eight or nine days afterwards. During this time when he was laying on the ground incapable of moving, I was always prevented from approaching him or rendering him any assistance. When he died they dragged him away by the legs and buried him.

The death of Brown:

> The first mate Mr Brown having likewise become too weak to carry wood the natives burnt his legs and back in the most dreadful manner by rubbing them with firebrands. Three days after my husband's death one of the natives put Mr Brown and myself over to the mainland in a canoe – Mr Baxter the second mate being too weak to accompany us. Three or four days after we had crossed, Mr Brown died from the frightful injuries he had undergone. For some days he had been unable to walk as the flesh had fallen from his feet and the bones of his knees protruded through his skin. He was left without any sort of assistance and on one occasion when I endeavoured to take a few cockles to him, some of the natives came up, and taking them from me, they knocked me down and dragged me along the ground. After this I saw him no more.[19]

The report of Brown's death in the *Sydney Gazette* five weeks later illustrates what can happen to a story that is retold, filtered, mixed and spiced with a little interpretation:

> In eight days from this brutal affair [i.e. the death of the Captain] the same cannibals also killed Mr Brown, the chief officer, by holding firebrands to his legs, and so burning him upwards! The cause of their destroying Mr B., was in consequence of his showing some signs of dissatisfaction in the death of his Captain.[20]

Let us move on to John Curtis' report of what Baxter tells the London inquiry a year later. Baxter is still on the island when Brown dies on the mainland, so he can only be repeating what Eliza tells him after the rescue. According to Baxter, Brown is 'inhumanly tied to a stake and, a slow fire being placed under him, his body, after the most excruciating sufferings, [is] reduced to ashes'.[21]

This is the image I referred to earlier, the one that sticks in the collective mind and influences the attitudes of generations of white Australians towards the Aborigines of Fraser Island. Brown's death is undoubtedly agonizing, but I believe it has been misinterpreted. There is a clue in one of Eliza's statements. She reports that the natives were friendly towards Brown in the days before his death, but interprets this as evidence of their treachery. It does not occur to her that the application of heat to his back and legs may have been an attempt to treat his condition rather than a deliberate form of torture.

An Aboriginal account of the treatment of open wounds describes how the wounds were cleaned, sprinkled with charcoal, covered with downy feathers and poulticed in white clay, which was then 'exposed to the heat of a small fire' until the clay was seen to steam. This caused a great deal of pain and the patient had to be forcibly restrained while the treatment was being carried out.[22]

As well as the Captain and Brown, two seamen perish near Hook Point. William Elliot and Michael Doyle, frustrated by their inability to reach the mainland, try to swim across the strait, but, when about a quarter of the way, begin to struggle violently and sink from sight.

The other seamen – Darge, Youlden, Dayman and Carey – and the steward, Corralis, bide their time and in due course cross to the mainland with the families to whom they are attached. Darge and Youlden will later give accounts of their walk south, passing from one group of Aborigines to the next, confident they will reach Moreton Bay because Baxter has assured them no other wide stretches of water will impede their way.

Thus it happens that, on the afternoon of Tuesday 8 August, while Lieutenant Charles Otter, an officer of the garrison guarding the Moreton Bay settlement, is taking his recreation shooting game on Bribie Island, he is surprised to encounter two 'black and perfectly naked' men.[23] Introducing themselves as Corralis and Darge, they ask that Youlden, who is resting his torn feet at an Aboriginal camp some distance behind them, be assisted to safety.

Back in Brisbane the Commandant, Foster Fyans, acts quickly. Within twenty-four hours he has an expedition of volunteers – three soldiers and fourteen convicts – ready to set out to rescue the remaining *Stirling Castle* survivors. The expedition is to be led by Charles Otter and guided by John Graham, a small Irish convict who desperately wants the promised pardon. (Graham absconded from the penal settlement in 1829, stayed with the Aborigines of Wide Bay for the remaining six years of his sentence, then returned, only to find the rules had been changed in his absence and he was still required to serve his time.) Fortunately for us, both Otter and Graham are to leave eyewitness accounts of their experiences from which we can reconstruct the actions of the rescue party.[24] It is clear that the complete success of this operation depended on the relationship of trust between these two men.

Meanwhile, Dayman and Carey have managed to reach the western shore of Lake Cooroibah on the Noosa River (see Figure 1.2). They are the first to be rescued by John Graham when, on the night of Saturday 13 August, as an emissary from Otter, he discovers their whereabouts from friendly Aborigines on the Noosa North Shore. Brought across the lake in canoes and assisted to the beach along a track by the light of bark torches, the naked 'unhappy youths' are in an 'abject state'.[25]

Informed that the Captain and Brown are dead but that Baxter is still on the island and Mrs Fraser somewhere on the beach in Wide Bay, Otter proceeds the next day to a camp at Double Island Point, from where Graham can gain further intelligence. Walking north to Inskip Point, Graham crosses to Fraser Island in a canoe at slack water and finds the tottering Baxter in a camp near Hook Point. Describing a beached whale he has seen at Double Island Point, Graham persuades the suspicious Aborigines to help him transport the starving castaway across to Inskip Point. Here he feeds Baxter with fish and keeps him warm during the night by pressing a firebrand to his heart. Early next morning he checks a women's camp for signs of Eliza, but is assured that she has been taken by the men to a place further south where she can be shown to their friends.

Late on Tuesday 16 August, with Baxter safe at Double Island Point and the Aborigines rewarded for their help, Graham sets off on the most difficult part of his mission. Proceeding south along Teewah Beach, he spends a disturbed night in a gully in the broken cliffs. At dawn he marks in the sand the spot where he wants Otter's party to wait, and turns inland. Crossing the low dunes and the swamp around Lake Cootharaba, he then wades around the lake's shallow north-eastern shore to the eastern bank of the Noosa River. Here he meets a man and a woman fishing from a canoe. Travelling with them saves a swim across the river and gives him the opportunity to test the reception he might expect at the camp at Fig Tree Point (see Figure 1.2).

A large gathering of Aborigines from coastal and inland groups is camped at the site. Eliza is here, an 'unhappy lady',[26] wandering around the huts. In the manner of Aboriginal decision-making a long discussion follows, during which Graham exercises his oratorical powers and makes promises he has no intention of keeping. Supported by the coastal people with whom he spent six years as a runaway, Graham claims Eliza as the ghost of his Aboriginal wife, and persuades the assembly to release her into his care. On the pretext of taking her to his land on Teewah Beach, where he can catch fish to feed her, he and four of his 'relatives' convey her across the lake in two canoes and walk her across to the beach. Near the end of the track, he leaves her by a waterhole while he fetches the clothing that Lieutenant Otter has brought for her. To the delight of Otter, who has arrived at the marked spot only half an hour earlier, Graham proudly produces his prize.

At this point, two vivid descriptions of Eliza are available, one from Graham and one from Otter. Graham notes her 'lacerated feet' and 'sunburnt shoulders where the tender skin hung in scales' and describes her appearance:

> On her head was a Southwester, the smell of the paint kept the blacks from taking it. Around her loins were part of the legs and waistband of a pair of Trousers, which covered part of her thighs, wound round with Vines twenty fold as well for delicacy as the preservation of her marriage and Ear rings which she concealed under the Vines.[27]

Otter describes his first view of her thus:

> You never saw such an object. Although only 38 years of age, she looked like an old woman of 70, perfectly black and dreadfully crippled from the sufferings she had undergone. I went to meet her and she caught my hand and burst into tears and sunk down quite exhausted. She was a mere skeleton, skin literally hanging on her bones, while her legs were a mass of sores, where the savages had tortured her with fire-brands.[28]

During the afternoon the rescue party, again assisted by Graham's 'relatives', sets out for Double Island Point. Eliza's debility makes the walk slow and they do not reach camp until the early hours of next morning. A south-easterly wind makes it impossible to leave for Brisbane immediately, but after several days' rest and some minor skirmishes with the now hostile Aborigines, the two boats, containing a jubilant rescue party and four relieved survivors, round the Point and return directly to Brisbane on Monday 21 August, after an absence of twelve days.

After resting for two months in Brisbane, where they make satisfactory recoveries from their ordeal, Eliza and the six male survivors return to Sydney. In mid-October the *Sydney Gazette* publishes reports from Eliza and John Baxter, in which the first variations from their official statements can be detected.

A house guest of the Colonial Secretary, Eliza is encouraged to repeat her story at social gatherings. She is the object of considerable sympathy, receives a large sum of money raised by public subscription and seems secure for life.

Then, on 3 February 1837, defying the social convention that makes remarriage unacceptable for a widow within a year of her husband's death, she secretly marries Captain Alexander John Greene, on whose ship, the *Mediterranean Packet*, she returns to England, arriving in Liverpool on 16 July to begin the next episode of her story.

Notes

1 This information is taken from two sources – Baxter's report to Foster Fyans at Moreton Bay on 6 September 1836 (AONSW SZ976, COD 183) and Baxter's story in the *Sydney Gazette* on 17 October 1836.

2 H.S. Russell, *Genesis of Queensland* (Sydney: Turner & Henderson, 1888), 250.

3 M. Alexander, *Mrs Fraser on the Fatal Shore* (London: Michael Joseph, 1971).

4 Both these documents are in the file AONSW SZ976, COD 183.

5 *Sydney Gazette*, 13 September 1836.

6 H. Youlden, 'Shipwreck in Australia', *Knickerbocker* 41.4 (1853).

7 J. Curtis, *The Shipwreck of the Stirling Castle* (London: George Virtue, 1838).

8 Ibid., 31.

9 *Sydney Gazette*, 13 September and 17 October 1836.

10 C.C. Petrie, *Tom Petrie's Reminiscences of Early Queensland* (Brisbane: Watson, Ferguson & Co., 1904), 260.

11 Eliza Fraser's sense of time and place was generally hazy, but this statement from her earliest account is surprisingly accurate.

12 Youlden.

13 Robert Darge gave evidence to the London inquiry in 1837. His evidence appears in the chapter 'The Narrative of Robert Darge' in Curtis (220–40) and in the chapter 'Darge's Testimony' in Alexander (134–41). See also Youlden. Eliza Fraser's first account, in 1836, was detailed and clear. In later accounts, such as those in the *Sydney Gazette*, Curtis and other published sources attributed to her, some details differed. John Baxter's 1836 account stops at the point where the seamen desert the Captain. His account of what happened after that was given in London in 1837 and published by Curtis in 1838.

14 Baxter, 6 September 1836 (AONSW SZ976, COD 183).

15 Ibid.

16 Ibid.

17 J. Graham, A Memorandum of the Real Facts, 4 January 1837, AONSW 4/2325.4, in J.G. Steele, *Brisbane Town in Convict Days: 1824–1842* (St Lucia: University of Queensland Press, 1987), 235.

18 J. Mathew, *Two Representative Tribes of Queensland* (London: Unwin, 1910), 178.

19 Eliza Fraser 1836 (AONSW SZ976, COD 183).

20 *Sydney Gazette*, 17 October 1836.

21 Curtis, 79.

22 G. Langevad, *Some Original Views Around Kilcoy: Book 1. The Aboriginal Perspective* (Queensland: Archaeology Branch, 1982), 83.

23 Charles Otter, 27 August 1836 (AONSW SZ976, COD 183).

24 Otter's first account is part of the AONSW file. Similar information is given in his letter to a cousin in England which was published in Curtis, 181. Graham also gave two accounts, at Moreton Bay on 6 September 1836, and in a Memorandum on 4 January 1837 at Sydney.

25 Graham (AONSW SZ976, COD 183).
26 Ibid.
27 Ibid.
28 Otter in Curtis (186).

Chapter 2

K'gari, Mrs Fraser and Butchulla oral tradition

Olga Miller

It is a common factor throughout Aboriginal Australia that all important sacred information could not be passed on until the recipient was judged worthy of receiving that information. This was arrived at by completion of appropriate initiation ceremonies by both males and females. If people had not passed the initiation ceremonies the information was not passed on, and the uninitiated person held the status of a child. Unfortunately on the eastern seaboard, there are no initiation ceremonies carried out, so any information about the inner structure of our people I cannot pass on to my people because they are not initiated (I have been partially initiated). However, they worked on a system of 'need to know' – if you need to know it you are told. For example, a 5-year-old child is only taught what a 5-year-old child should know; it is not taught what a 14-year-old or a 16-year-old needs to know. This went on right up the chain, and the legends were not just stories, they were not just for entertainment, they were for teaching. Because there were legends for every age group, so at my age I would have been learning how to die. Because if you are taught how to live, you must be taught how to die with dignity so you do not bring dishonour on your people. I feel that with this symposium, and I was very pleased to hear that it was taking place. I feel there are some things that *you* need to know. Now because you are not Aboriginal people, you don't have to be initiated.

The map that has been distributed to you (Figure 2.1) was done many years ago for a book which I haven't yet written. I've been struggling to write it and it's called *Hidden History*.

So, the Butchulla people. In the bottom left-hand corner you will see Mt Bauple and a dotted line up to Burrum River and down to Double Island Point. This is the genesis story of the Butchulla.

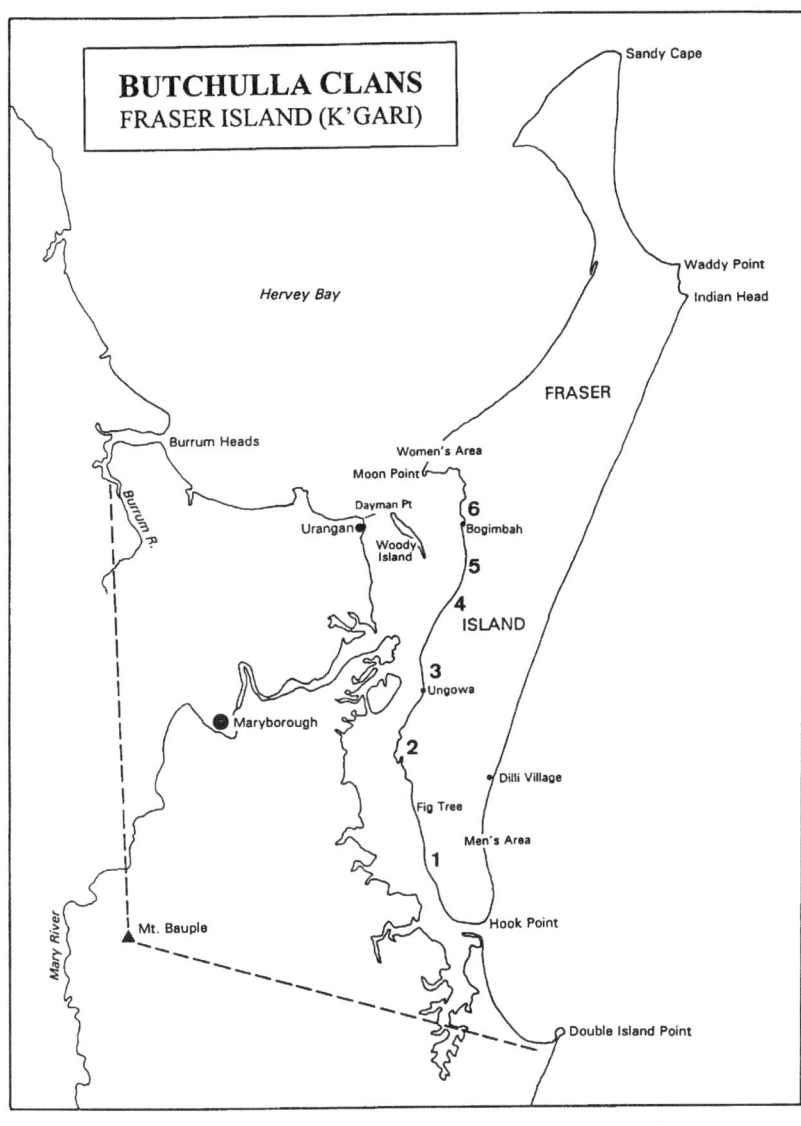

Figure 2.1 Map showing the distribution of the Butchulla clans on Fraser Island (K'gari)

Way way back in the First Time, Beeral the God who lived in the sky – the Rainbow God – sent down his messenger Yindingie to make the land, and with him he had a helper, and she was a beautiful white spirit, and her name was K'gari (pronounced 'Gurri'). She worked very hard with Yindingie and they made all the beautiful land coming down the coast, from as far as you can see up that way, to as far as you could see down the other way. When they reached Hervey Bay, Yindingie said to K'gari, 'Oh you've been working very hard.' He said, 'I think you should go and have a rest, otherwise you'll get too tired.' He said, 'Go and lie on those rocks over there, in the water.' So she did. She lay down on these rocks and soon she went to sleep. And when she woke up, Yindingie had finished making all this beautiful land – lovely, lovely white beaches and little islands. In the distance there was a beautiful mountain and a big river. K'gari woke up and said to Yindingie, 'Oh what a beautiful place, I think this is the nicest place you've made so far.' She said, 'I'd like to stay here.' He said, 'You can't do that.' And she said, 'Why?' And he said, 'Because you are a spirit, you've got to go back to the spirit world.' Anyway, she had really fallen in love with this area. So she pleaded and coaxed, and at last Yindingie relented. He said, 'All right, all right.' He said, 'But you can't stay here as a spirit.' He said, 'I'll have to change you into something else.' He said, 'You go and lie on those rocks again.' So she did, just laid down on the rocks. And he changed her into a beautiful island. He covered her with trees and shrubs, beautiful flowers and ferns. He gave her some lakes to be her eyes, and as she lay there she could look up and see her friends. And then he made some creatures, animals and birds. And lastly he made some people. And he gathered them all at a place called Mooen, which is today known as Moon Point. He took them all around the island; showed them where they could live; brought them back again; and then he stepped across to the mainland to a place called now Dayman Point. And then he took another step up into this mountain in the distance, and we call that mountain Bauple Mountain. And he turned around, he put out his left hand and put out his right hand, and he looked at all the land in between his hands, and he said, 'Know this is your land, but you have to look after it, and I'll give you some laws.' And he did – he gave them three laws, which are: (1) What is good for the Land comes first; (2) Do not touch or take anything that does not belong to you; and (3) If you have plenty you must share.

Thus, on the map, you will see where his left hand pointed to the Burrum Heads and his right hand pointed to Double Island Point. These people were named the Butchullas and they had the six clans starting from Hook Point: one, two, three, four, five, six. Then you'll see the Women's Area at Moon Point, and down in the south, roughly where Dilli Village is, you'll see the Men's Area. Each of these clans had a job to do. It's just the same as any society.

Number One, the Wunapinga, were the ones who taught all about hunting and the making of weapons and things like that.

The next one up, Number Two, were the fishermen, and they taught all about making canoes and fishing lines, and nets and fish traps.

Number Three, the clan of the Clever Man, was the central figure in this life of the society.

Number Four was my family – the Wondunna family, and the head man here was the Wise Man. We've got the clever man, we've got the Wise Man. From this family comes the Caboonya – the Keeper of Records – which I happen to be today. It's a very difficult job, even today with the use of printed material to keep a record of everything that is happening, not only in our own land. If you live near our area you will know that I make a nuisance of myself, particularly with developers, they say 'Oh! watch out for Olga Miller.' But I want to know what is going on. I'm not interested in money. I just have to look after the land.

Number Five were the clan which looked after all the arts. They were the song writers, the dancers, and they kept a record of the history in their songs and dances.

Number Six was the Clever Woman. When the children were about 10 years old (they practised segregation right through), little girls went with the Clever Woman and the single girls, and the boys went with the Clever Man and the single men. This segregation was very very important because the Number 2 law was: do not touch or take anything that doesn't belong to you – and that covered all crime. And rape was their worst crime. If a girl was raped she was killed immediately, even though she was the innocent victim. They were very superstitious and they believed in spirits, both bad spirits and good spirits; and they believed that because rape was an evil act the baby would be full of evil spirits. So the girl was killed. And that's why they kept very much apart.

Approximately seventy people would be in a clan, so there would be about 500 Butchulla people altogether on the island in pre-contact days. There are reports of thousands of people, especially on the Back Beach, which is the eastern beach. Now those gatherings on the Back Beach, when there could be as many as 4000 people, were for the Feast of the Tailor Fish (seasonal). And there was also another time in the bay when there was the Feast of the Winter Mullet (seasonal). And at these times the land was made open to everyone. No one was refused admittance to come and share in the harvest of these fish. That accounts for a big explosion of the population at certain times and explains the Number 3 law.

It has been recorded that the Butchulla people were always fighting among themselves, especially on the Back Beach where there seemed to be four miles of Aborigines just fighting. I asked my grandfather about this, and he said 'Oh, you can't fish all the time'; he said, 'What about when the tide goes out', he said, 'You've gotta do something.' And so they would pit their young warriors against each other. Each area would put up their champion men and this one would fight that one, and the winners would fight somebody else. And so it was like an elimination system of winner fighting somebody else in these mock battles. And the reason I asked about this was because every winter my grandfather would come around and he had rheumatism (we call it arthritis today). And I'd rub his leg and knee (he had a terrible scar) with linament. And I said to him 'How'd you get this?' So he told me about these mock battles. And I said to him, 'Why did you have these mock battles if you could get speared in the knee?' And he got very huffy. He said 'Humf – Why do white fellas play football?' So it was the same thing, it was a sport. But it was recorded in the *Maryborough Chronicle* that they were fighting among themselves. And they were too, but it was a sport. So there you are – distortion of facts.

In 1897, Archibald Meston was the then Protector of Aborigines, and he gathered up all the Aboriginal fringe dwellers who were upsetting the settlers and he took them over to Beer-rill-bee (on Fraser Island) which is our homeland number four – my homeland. It is today called McKenzies, because this firm from Sydney, McKenzies, had a sawmill at Coffs Harbour, and then they built a mill at Beer-rill-bee. The old jetty is still standing there. It was also the site of the quarantine station and Meston used this old building as part of his Mission. Then he was moved up to Bogimbah. McKenzies had originally owned the land at Bogimbah and they did a deal with the government and got the land at Beer-rill-bee, and the Mission went up to Bogimbah.

Archibald Meston actually advocated genocide. When he started his Mission, in his own report he said he had gathered up people from 26 *different areas*, besides the fringe dwellers. He took them over to the island and they had to live with each other, even though they were bitter enemies and had different religious beliefs, but they had to live together. In 1865, long before this, he had advocated this genocide business. He said, 'When an Aborigine ceases to speak his own language and make and use his own weapons it is time for him to leave this planet, because he's of no use to the anthropologist, the ethnologist, and the general public' (or words to that effect). And if *that's* not genocide I don't know what genocide is. However, with his Mission, firstly at McKenzies or North White Cliffs, moving down to Bogimbah, by that time he had gathered up more and more people. And by 1900 there was a lot of dissatisfaction with the way he was running the Mission, and to make a long story longer, the government asked the Church of England to take over the mission.

Everybody's got two grandfathers. I was lucky as I had an Aboriginal one and a non-Aboriginal one. So that is why I know both sides of the story. J.B. Gribble, who was my mother's father, was born in Redruth, Cornwall, and her mother, the Honourable Mary Bulmer, was born in Hull, in Yorkshire. Grandfather Gribble founded Yarrabah, but he contracted malaria and was sent by ship to Sydney and died – he was only 43. Uncle Ern (Ernest Gribble) took over.

So we come to 1900. Uncle Ern is at Bogimbah briefly to take over. Grandma's there, my mother's there – a single woman. Because when the Church asked about taking over the Mission at Bogimbah, the only thing Uncle Ern could do was to send Grandma and my mum down there. Uncle Ern went back and he and Auntie Milli (his wife) ran Yarrabah. Bogimbah was an awful place.

These Aboriginal people at the Mission were on the island from 1897 to 1904. They had been gathered up from all around the place, but they had only been there for seven years. The point is it lasted only four years with the Church. It was terrible soil. And when grandma wrote to the ABM (which was the only department in existence then that looked after the welfare of Aboriginal people), that was the Australian Board of Missions, and asked for some more money to go towards buying fruit and vegetables, she got the answer back, 'Do what you have done on your other missions – grow them.' Well, you couldn't grow anything there, not even the weeds would grow. So then it was decided to take the people back to Yarrabah where there was more food and a better climate.

At some time between 1900 and 1904, my grandmother and mother had come to identify the real Fraser Island people – the Butchulla people. You see, they were not in the group that was gathered up by Meston. All they had to do was stay on the Back Beach. But as Mum said, they were very cunning, and they seemed to know when all the grocery orders were coming down. So suddenly there'd be a few more Aboriginal people at the end of the queue at the Mission. So they'd come over then, get their share of tobacco and tea and sugar, then go back. But then Grandma got to know them and there were a few things she wanted to know about the Butchulla people, not the other people. She asked the old women about Mrs Fraser. Remember now, they didn't know Mrs Fraser from a bar of soap. But they said yes. There was a man, a woman and a baby found dead on the beach. Now this is where I'm going to throw the cat among the pigeons. You all see the women's area and Number 6: Bogimbah. See Woody Island marked there (Figure 2.1). Well, that little bump at the end of Woody Island goes straight across to Number 6 and draw a line and that's Bogimbah. Now that's on the land of the Clever Woman. No men were ever allowed to go around there from Urang Creek right around to Coongal Creek. That was definitely a women's only area. So anyway, the women said yes, they had found the bodies of a man, a woman and a child. And they had buried them. Of course, Grandma was very religious and she said to my mother, 'What a wonderful Christian act, God had entered the spirits of these people and they'd given this man, woman and baby a Christian burial.' My mum thought differently and she said to these old women, 'How come, what was it that prompted you to bury these people?' And Mum said the old women looked at each other and had a bit of a talk among themselves, and one of them said, 'Well if we hadn't they would have stunk the beach.' Their logic was simple logic. As children they were taught, 'If you put your hand in the water it will get wet, if you put your hand in the fire it will get burnt.' And that's to show the difference of obeying something and disobeying.

So that's what they said. Now you may be wondering why we've never written this down. We simply weren't interested. We had known about all these things that Elaine Brown had brought up and written about (see Chapter 1), but to us Mrs Fraser was never a very important person because she knew she was a big waterhole, and that means you're a big fibber.

Now when Grandma was talking to these women – the *Stirling Castle* was wrecked in 1836 – she must have been talking to them somewhere between 1900 and 1904. As I said, the little girls were segregated at the age of 10. From 1836 to 1900 is 64 years. If they were 10 at the time they would have seen what happened and they would have been between 74 years and 78 years old at the time they were telling my grandmother. And my mother said, 'They never said "We were told". They just said, "We buried them".' They must have been there. They must have seen it happen. It's feasible, because I'm 75, and I'm still yapping. So it's quite feasible that they had been there.

Now as the conversation went on, they referred to this other woman they found on the beach, and they said she was 'brundy'. Brundy means 'not all there'. But she was affected by the sun, very sunburnt. And the women only referred to her as a white lubra. Now a lubra is a young woman, a young single woman, a woman who has never borne a child. A matron or a woman who has borne a child is called a gin, G – I – N (pronounced gin as in begin). A gin is a mature Aboriginal woman who's had children. Gin, G – I – N (pronounced jin), is a white man's drink. The single girl is the lubra. They called her a lubra, Mum said, because they could tell by her figure that she'd never borne a child. She tore the clothes off herself simply because she was in a terrible state of sunburn, and of course you could imagine the hysteria of being in a strange place with no one to help her. You can't blame her for going 'brundy'. Now the women said that she was rubbed with ointments and things. They did rub her with ointments and things that were their own medicines, and that was for her sunburn.

The women were uncertain as to what to do with this white lubra, so the Clever Woman decided it was better to take her down to where the men were at Nungowa (now called Ungowa). It was here that the Clever Man lived and the men were gathered there at that time to listen to him and his teachings. The men were not at all pleased with the arrival of the women with the stranger. However, the women insisted that they did not want the stranger to stay with them. The Wise Man sent messengers to locate Durrumboi, with instructions to meet them at a point at Maroon, opposite a spot on the island now known as Fig Tree. The women had marked the 'stranger' with 'ochre signs' which read 'let this woman through' and 'do not harm this woman'. Durrumboi (an escaped convict) and his party took charge of her and proceeded south, for the 'Boorie grapevine' had news of a party of white men out looking for a missing woman.

This party met up with another party of Aborigines – my brother Wilfred and I could only surmise that they were Goomboorian people as their land was neighbouring the Freeway or road south.

I do not know if it has ever been recorded by European writers, but there was an instance spoken of by our local men of those days. It seems 'the woman stranger' did not realize that she had to help gather firewood as her contribution towards being fed. One man of the group who had joined Durrumboi's party pushed and shoved her angrily. In no time, he was impaled with several Butchulla spears. The signs the Butchulla women had marked on her had to be obeyed.

When Durrumboi and his party came within close proximity to the official rescue party, he told the 'woman stranger' to go to the camp of the rescue party, as it was not far away. She left and Durrumboi and his party, free of the responsibility of escorting the woman, hurried away to return to their own area, which was at the foot of the Gunalda Range. Some time later, when on the island for a visit, Durrumboi was taken to task by the Men's Council of Elders who had been told that the 'white woman' had complained to the rescue party that Durrumboi had raped her. Durrumboi's answer to the charges was that he had never touched her at all.

While still a student at the Maryborough Girls' Grammar School (1935), I was puzzled by Eliza Fraser's appearances at country fairs. On a visit to Hervey Bay and a meeting with our grandfather, Willie Wondunna, my sister and I brought up this subject. My sister asked what were the marks made by the Butchulla women on Eliza Fraser. I asked if the marks were 'cuts' (cicatrices). Our grandfather replied that the marks had been made with ochre. I then asked, 'How long would these ochre marks stay on her?' He replied, 'Until she had a good, hot, soapy bath.' It was then that my sister and I lost all interest in the story of Eliza Fraser. To have appeared at country fairs displaying the 'marks' put on her by 'the black cannibals' after such a long period of time branded her, to us, as an untruthful person.

A further curious 'fact' concerning 'Eliza' is that at no time did she return to the Orkneys to visit her three children.

During the World War Two years, about the end of 1944, I was invited to go on a day's fishing trip with Mr and Mrs Fred Ross (they were Aboriginal people – Mrs Ross being a Butchulla woman). Fred Ross was a professional fisherman and had a very good fishing boat. It was a Sunday, and as the commercial fishing week did not start until sundown on Sundays, the purpose of the day's outing was to get live bait and also some seafood for the family Christmas season. We fished off Moon Point for a while and then moved to a spot off the eastern side of the south end of Big Woody Island. It was intended then to return to the Urangan area to 'beat the gutters' at low tide. We were anchored over a spot called 'Boge's Hole', only found accurately on the outgoing tide. It was a pleasant day, and as we sat in the stern of the boat with our lines out, gazing across to Fraser Island, Mrs Ross said, 'See that big tree over there, sticking up high?' She was pointing across towards Bogimbah. My gaze followed her pointing finger. 'Yes,' I said. 'Well,' said Mrs Ross, 'There's a "whin-middi" and her "piccanin" buried there' (a 'whin-middi' is a white woman and a 'piccanin' is a new-born baby). 'Oh,' I said, 'Someone from the Mission?' 'No,' she replied, 'Long before that'. 'Who was it?' I asked. 'I don't know,' said Mrs Ross, 'But our "old people" say it was Mrs Fraser and her baby!'

Chapter 3

Shipwreck saga as archaeological text: reconstructing Fraser Island's Aboriginal past

Ian J. McNiven

The development of the discipline of archaeology over the last 150 years has had a profound impact upon the way human history is both constructed and perceived. In most cases, representations of the past based on archaeological information have proved extremely important in the way we view not only our own culture but also other cultures. We only have to think of the ancient monuments of Egypt, Greece and Mexico to see this process in action.[1]

In settler colonial contexts such as Australia and North America, the role of archaeological research in the construction and representation of the heritage of local indigenous peoples has taken on new meaning. Archaeological research, as an academic pursuit, invariably draws on Western scientific methodologies and is almost always undertaken by non-indigenous archaeologists. Although archaeologists may differ in their paradigmatic leanings, most agree with the fundamental tenet that archaeological research allows a more plausible and reliable reconstruction of people's pasts. This tenet immediately presupposes that the 'real' past of people is an archaeologically presented past and indigenous presentations of the past, whether through oral tradition or expressed through ceremony or myth, are somehow less 'real'.

In recent years, increasing dialogue between archaeologists and indigenous peoples has resulted in a greater understanding of the legitimacy and relative values of differing approaches to the past.[2] In Australia, central to the acceptance of archaeological research by many Aboriginal people has been a range of work practice changes which in effect help to decolonize archaeological research. These changes include increased consultation with custodians and respect for the social and spiritual significance of cultural materials by archaeologists. Both changes have taken place alongside an increased use of archaeological research in the preservation of Aboriginal cultural heritage.[3]

This chapter investigates another dimension of the decolonizing process in Australian archaeology by examining how the actual form of archaeological narrative presented by archaeologists can dramatically affect its acceptability by Aboriginal people. During the 1970s, detailed archaeological research on Fraser Island provided the first reconstructions of 'traditional' Aboriginal society at the time of European contact and in 'prehistoric' times. It is in this regard that the Eliza Fraser saga played a key role for two important reasons. First, the 1838 text *The Shipwreck of the Stirling Castle* by John Curtis and statements by castaways and members of the 'rescue' party represent the earliest and most detailed European 'archive' of information on 'traditional' Aboriginal lifeways on Fraser Island. Second, and as a result of the first point, the *Stirling Castle* archive has proved significant in archaeological reconstructions of past Aboriginal lifeways on Fraser Island. However, while these archaeological insights and the story of Eliza Fraser have been given prominence in local history books written by Euro-Australians, both historical narratives have failed to rate a single mention in texts written by local Aboriginal people. I explore this issue here and examine whether or not the use of this colonialist archive in archaeological reconstructions of past Aboriginal life on Fraser Island inadvertently tainted the appeal of this research to local Aboriginal people. Conclusions drawn have relevance for archaeological researchers working on the pasts of indigenous peoples in (ex-)colonial contexts.

A past with Eliza: archaeology meets the *Stirling Castle* archive

Archaeology came late to Fraser Island. In 1975, the Australian Federal Government established the Fraser Island Environmental Inquiry to assess the impact of sand mining on the island and to determine whether or not mining should be banned.[4] An important part of the inquiry was to assess the potential impact of mining on Aboriginal archaeological sites. Towards this end, John Sinclair and his conservation group – the Fraser Island Defence Organisation (better known as FIDO) – employed Peter Lauer (then Curator of the Anthropology Museum at the University of Queensland) to undertake a reconnaissance survey to determine the potential scope and significance of archaeological sites. The survey cost $1000 and was funded by the famous novelist Patrick White. According to his biographer David Marr,[5] White was frustrated by the lack of available knowledge on the island's Aboriginal past and wanted to be actively involved in the anti-mining struggle. In his report to the inquiry, Lauer[6] noted that some stone tools such as microliths may be 'some 5000 years old' while others such as 'core scrapers' belonged to an earlier tradition up to 30,000 years old.

Inspired by the survey results, Lauer obtained research funding to undertake further archaeological investigations of Fraser Island. He noted that the primary research aim was to 'reconstruct lifeways of the Aboriginal population'.[7] In only two seasons of fieldwork, he managed to record over 200 archaeological sites revealing physical evidence of past Aboriginal activity.[8] Essentially, all these sites were represented by two types. First, shell middens located within sand-dunes fronting the eastern surf beach, and second, scatters of stone artefacts with microliths and other implements located on the surface of sandblows (bare sand-dunes) located around 1.5 km from the sea.[9] To provide an interpretive framework for these sites, Lauer examined historical references to Fraser Island Aboriginal culture during the eighteenth and nineteenth centuries. These references included fleeting observations by navigators such as James Cook[10] and Matthew Flinders,[11] and the abbreviated accounts of government officials,[12] anthropologists[13] and the escaped convict David Bracewell.[14] However, the single most referenced source, representing one-third of the hundred or so referenced observations to Aboriginal culture, was the *Stirling Castle* archive – especially the 1838 Curtis book. Clearly, the *Stirling Castle* archive featured prominently in Lauer's reconstructions of 'Badtjala' culture.

For the purposes of Lauer's archaeological interpretation, the most important Curtis references were those relating to Aboriginal subsistence, campsite location and campsite activities. In terms of subsistence, the numerous references to fish clearly identified it as an important food item. For example, John Baxter, Second Officer of the *Stirling Castle*, informed Curtis that:

> On the third day after their arrival at this inhospitable coast, a regular system of barter commenced between the party and the natives, who at first came down about ten in number, which gradually increased rapidly until more than 150 would appear at one time. The principal article they brought were a fish called mullet, which is extremely delicious.[15]

As Lauer rightly concluded, 'the Islanders were indeed expert fisher-men'.[16] As a result, he associated fishing with the extensive shell middens along the coast which he saw as focal points for specialized, marine-based subsistence activities.

Lauer provided a different 'economic' interpretation for the numerous sandblow stone artefact scatters located further inland.

These sites he called 'campsites' to distinguish them from 'middens' located along the adjacent beach. It was at these campsites that Lauer believed Fraser Island Aboriginal people actually spent most of their time while using the eastern sections of the Island:

> Away from the wind-swept heath country [on the coast] which affords little shelter, the camps were thus located amongst shade giving trees and gently undulating land which provided immediate access to pursuits of hunting and gathering in the dune lands as well as to shell fish collecting near the sea. At the same time access to raw materials like bark and wood would also be readily facilitated.[17]

Lauer's interpretation clearly derived from his reading of the Curtis text. Baxter noted a campsite located 'about the distance of a mile' from the coast.[18] Lauer made much of Baxter's observation, for it became *the* ethnographic exemplar of his archaeological campsites which were similarly located '1.5 km' from the sea.[19] To corroborate this inference, Lauer[20] suggested that the sandblows which now surround archaeological campsites resulted from the long-term effects of Aboriginal vegetation disturbance such as firewood and bark collection documented by Curtis.[21] All these inferences were consistent with Lauer's calculation that at least one of the archaeological campsites may have been created only 40 or so years before the *Stirling Castle* saga based on contemporary observations of rates of sand erosion.[22]

A past with dates: the radiocarbon challenge from Cooloola

Although Lauer obtained a number of radiocarbon dates for shell middens (see below), he never obtained radiocarbon dates from the inland campsites to test his hypothesis that both sets of sites were used in recent times. Subsequent research on midden sites and sandblow sites in the broader Great Sandy Region strongly suggest that Lauer's chronological interpretations are open to major reassessment. My archaeological research on the adjacent mainland region of Cooloola revealed sites almost identical to that recorded by Lauer on Fraser Island. The eastern sections of Cooloola exhibit numerous shell middens eroding from dunes fronting the beach while large sandblows located a kilometre or so inland contain stone artefact scatters complete with microliths. As with Lauer, it seemed obvious to me that the middens were not very old, as many were eroding from dunes that had clearly formed in the last 500 years. Like Lauer, I too associated these middens with coastal fishing as documented by the *Stirling Castle* archive.[23]

My interpretation of inland sandblow sites (stone artefact scatters) differed radically from that put forward by Lauer. By comparing the types of stone tools found in the coastal middens and those found in the inland sandblow sites, it became apparent that the sandblow sites contained artefact forms such as microliths that research in other parts of Australia had shown were at least 1000 and possibly 5000 years old. In addition, at the same time I was undertaking my research at Cooloola, new information on sand-dune formation in the region became available.[24] The geomorphological evidence indicated that the inland stone artefact scatters were eroding from the surface of old sand-dunes that had been buried by more recent sand deposits. It was only by removal of these overlying deposits by massive wind erosion and sandblow formation that these older dunes and artefacts became re-exposed on the ground surface. As a result, I hypothesized that the coastal middens and inland sandblow sites represented not different elements of a single lifeway (as Lauer's research indicated) but elements of two entirely different chronological phases of Aboriginal occupation of the Great Sandy Region.

Subsequent radiocarbon dating confirmed the existence of two chronological phases. In the case of shell middens, results indicated recent ages of less than 200 years.[25] Like Lauer on Fraser Island, I felt that the Cooloola midden sites could be associated with my reconstructions of 'traditional' Aboriginal lifeways based on nineteenth-century European records such as the *Stirling Castle* archive.[26] In terms of the inland sandblow sites, much older dates of at least 2300 years were obtained. Further excavations in the region confirmed that the types of artefacts found in sandblow sites belong to an early phase of occupation which was between 2000 and possibly up to 5500 years old.[27] Clearly, inland sandblow sites across Fraser Island and Cooloola were much older than shell middens on the adjacent coastline and both sets of sites represented the remains of two major and different phases of Aboriginal occupation of the Great Sandy Region.

Lauer's reinterpretation of sandblow artefact scatters as contemporary with ethnographic times is curious in light of his initial speculations that such sites could be up to 5000 years old.[28] Indeed, Lauer abandoned the long-term time-scale indicated by the archaeological evidence in favour of the short-term and recent chronological framework offered by historical evidence in Curtis' text. In this light it can be seen how the archaeological record of Fraser Island became subsumed within the historical narrative of the *Stirling Castle*, and the shipwreck saga became, somewhat ironically, the archaeological text through which the island's Aboriginal past could be read. This approach essentially quashed any potential for elucidating long-term changes in the archaeological record and ensured that the island's Aboriginal past remained ahistorical and time-locked to the nineteenth century.

A past without history: European public presentations of Fraser Island archaeology

To investigate how Lauer's archaeological insights were picked up and presented by the popular press, I use the two best-known writers of Fraser Island history – Fred Williams and internationally acclaimed environmentalist John Sinclair. In 1982, Williams' history of Fraser Island entitled *Written in Sand* was published. It remains the only single text devoted to the island's Aboriginal and European history and its popularity is indicated by subsequent reprints in 1986 and 1989. Although written as a popular text, Williams uses a wide range of previously unpublished textual and oral information and synthesizes them into a detailed, semi-scholarly book. In 1990, Sinclair released a coffee-table book on the natural and human history of the region entitled *Fraser Island and Cooloola*. In 1994, Sinclair's autobiography *Fighting for Fraser Island* was published and it too contains much interesting information on the island's past.

In *Written in Sand* it is clear that Williams was most impressed with Lauer's work which he featured in the opening two chapters on traditional Aboriginal lifeways. Indeed, a central theme running through the book is how Europeans managed to turn the 'paradise' of the Aboriginal people into a 'paradise lost' through attempted cultural 'genocide' and environmental vandalism.[29] The high regard Williams had for Lauer is further evidenced by the fact that Lauer wrote the foreword for the book.

Despite the just praise for much of Lauer's archaeological research, *Written in Sand* actually highlights and compounds the chronological limitations of his archaeological research. Wherever Williams makes reference to the possible antiquity of Aboriginal occupation of Fraser Island, he simply states that it must have been in the order of 'thousands' of years.[30] For example, in one instance, he notes that Aboriginal people have lived on the island 'over many, many thousands of years',[31] while in another he suggests 'It is possible that there were Aborigines on the island as long as 30,000 years ago'.[32] In terms of what Aboriginal people may have been doing 1000, 5000 or 30,000 years ago is never made clear. The reader is left to assume that such activities must have been similar, if not the same, as the 'traditional' marine-based lifeways recorded last century. The fact that Fraser Island only became an island around 6000 years ago after sea-level rise flooded the continental shelf seems to have been forgotten altogether.

Williams' explicit ahistorical view of Fraser Island's Aboriginal past is a direct reflection of Lauer's synchronic reconstructions. Neither Lauer nor Williams provide any chronological insights into past Aboriginal use of Fraser Island beyond Captain Cook's first sighting in

1770. This situation is all the more remarkable given that Lauer's opening sentence to Williams' book reads 'For many of us the history of our continent still begins in 1788.' I would argue that despite references to the possible antiquity of Aboriginal occupation of Fraser Island, Williams' book actually reinforces the view that Fraser Island Aboriginal history begins with the coming of Europeans to the island.

Not surprisingly, Sinclair repeats the ahistorical view of Fraser Island's Aboriginal past seen in Williams' book. *Fraser Island and Cooloola* also draws explicitly on Lauer's archaeological findings and lists his academic publications. As a backdrop to a section in the book titled 'Traditional Aboriginal Society', Sinclair noted:

> The first human tenure of the region probably occurred early in the Aboriginal settlement of Australia, about 40,000 years ago. Through their rich oral history the Aborigines recorded events such as the interglacial periods when the sea levels were high and the times when the sea receded during the ice ages. They were healthy vigorous people whose culture was based on the sea and its harvest. Evidence for this is still found in the numerous middens of oyster shells and the shells of a bivalve mollusc which they called *ah-wong*.[33]

Sinclair's assertion that Aboriginal people have been on the island for 40,000 years harps back to Lauer's initial comments at the 1975 Fraser Island Environmental Inquiry. In his 1994 autobiography, Sinclair goes one step further and states that 'the period of their undisputed occupation [is] perhaps 100,000 years'.[34] Again, no attempt is made to outline what Aboriginal people may have been doing throughout this long history, although the reader is left to assume that their activities were in line with 'traditional' lifeways as recorded last century. Again, Fraser Island Aboriginal people are pictured in an ahistorical light with an unchanging and seemingly amorphous past.

From a European perspective, ahistorical perspectives on Australia's Aboriginal past can be seen to fall within the broader context of colonial attitudes towards Aboriginal Australians. The European settlement of Australia was aided by colonial notions which attempted to delegitimate Aboriginal associations with their land by negating the existence of their cultural landscapes and their unique historical pasts. In terms of the latter, the history of Australia was seen to begin only in 1788 and all Aboriginal activity prior to that date simply did not count.[35] Although not the intention of either Lauer, Williams or Sinclair, their ahistorical presentations of Fraser Island's Aboriginal past runs dangerously close to perpetuating colonial mentalities. It presents the pre-European Aboriginal history of Fraser Island as a homogeneous mass lacking change, dynamism, and ultimately a substantive reality beyond that recorded by Europeans last century.

Fraser Islanders are presented as a static people, the paradigmatic 'unchanging people, living in an unchanging environment'.[36]

A past without Eliza: Aboriginal presentations of their history

How do Badtjala people view Fraser Island's Aboriginal past? For the most part I am in no position to answer this question, for I am not a Badtjala person. My answer is therefore limited to Badtjala presentations of their past where the intended audience is primarily non-Aboriginal. The first of these presentations was the 1964 book *The Legends of Moonie Jarl* by Olga Miller and her brother Wilf Reeves.[37] The text was the first book published by Badtjala people and revealed to Europeans for the first time many of the creation legends of the Badtjala.[38] A revised version of the book entitled *Fraser Island Legends* was released by Olga Miller in 1993. Both books in essence present a Badtjala view of events prior to the coming of Europeans. Interestingly, neither archaeology nor the *Stirling Castle* saga feature in these books.

The second Badtjala presentation is a paper given by Shirley Foley at the 1990 COMA Conference held at the University of Queensland, Brisbane, which was subsequently reproduced in a major Badtjala submission to a commission of inquiry into the future management and impending nomination of Fraser Island to the World Heritage list. Shirley Foley suggested that the pre-European Badtjala had a

> unique, rewarding, plentiful lifestyle. Richness was to be found in all aspects of our culture. Our lives were to be governed by environmental conditions, the moon, the sun, the seasons, the availability of natural resources and our social structure and belief system. There existed a complete fabric of society. For at least 40,000 years, most probably more, the sovereign nation of Badtjala people exists with well established laws, customs and boundaries.

Except for the reference to '40,000 years', no reference to archaeological research is provided.

The third and most formal presentation of Badtjala history and culture is Shawn Foley's 1994 book entitled *The Badtjala People*. Commenting on how long Aboriginal people have been on Fraser Island, Foley made a passing, albeit important, note: 'They have always been there, ever since the time this land was created and shaped by our ancestral beings.'[39] From a European perspective, one could be lured into tying Foley's statement directly in with the static, ahistorical perspective presented by Williams and Sinclair. That is, instead of saying Aboriginal people have been on Fraser Island for 30,000 or 100,000 years, the antiquity has simply been extended to 'always'. Such a view, however, would miss the fundamentally important point that

Foley's view of the pre-European Aboriginal past is both dynamic and filled with historical events. Foley makes reference to the creative powers of ancestral beings:

> There are many Badtjala creation beliefs which explain and answer many fundamental questions about the landscape, the birds, the animals and how things came to be. These creation beliefs also embody Badtjala law, and explanation of right and wrong expressed through oral traditions.[40]

Significantly, Foley makes no reference to Lauer's archaeological research results, despite his knowledge on these matters.[41]

The lack of reference to archaeological research by Shirley Foley (1991), Olga Miller (1993) and Shawn Foley (1994) is not due to ignorance, as all three writers know Lauer and are familiar with his research. Such a situation would seem to suggest that archaeological research is of little interest to Badtjala people in the construction of their past. However, all three Badtjala writers have a deep interest in archaeological sites on Fraser Island and have spent considerable time undertaking activities to help manage and protect such sites. The significance of such sites is revealed by Shawn Foley where the caption to a photograph of a large shell midden reads: 'A significant Aboriginal shell midden on Fraser Island, a physical testimony to Badtjala People's resource gathering and family occupation within the coastal landscape.'[42]

The interest of Badtjala people in archaeological sites suggests that their lack of reference to archaeological reconstructions of their past says more about the nature of archaeological research than about archaeological remains themselves. I suggest that two factors may have contributed to this situation. First, the static, ahistorical perspective on the pre-European Badtjala past presented by past archaeological research failed to strike an accord with Badtjala people, particularly in light of their own creation beliefs which gave form and dynamism to their past. Second, and perhaps most importantly, reconstructions of 'traditional' Badtjala culture offered by Europeans are rejected by many Badtjala people because they draw heavily on the *Stirling Castle* saga which to many Badtjala people represents a distorted and offensive aspect of their contact history.[43] The significance of this latter point is illustrated well by Shirley Foley and Shawn Foley. Both writers, despite documenting nineteenth-century Badtjala contact history in some detail, make not a single reference to what in European eyes is considered the most significant event in local contact history – the *Stirling Castle* saga.[44] Badtjala resentment of European constructions of Badtjala history is corroborated by the following comment by Shirley Foley:

For too long people have abused our culture. They have raped our culture, and they have used it to their best advantage, so I think it's about time now that we turned the clock around saying, well, we're the indigenous people; we'll tell our story the way it was told to us. You learn our culture from us, not from anyone [else].[45]

Conclusion

In this chapter I have shown how the *Stirling Castle* archive has been treated variously by European archaeologists and Badtjala people. From an archaeological perspective, this archive has provided a valuable source of information and it is in this connection that the *Stirling Castle* saga takes on great power, as its associated archive has been used extensively in European reconstructions of 'traditional' Aboriginal society. However, the static, ahistorical perspective of Fraser Island's pre-European Aboriginal past which was created by initial applications of the *Stirling Castle* archive led to the situation where all of Badtjala history was presented as time-locked to the nineteenth-century. As such, the pre-European Aboriginal past of Fraser Island was in a sense infiltrated by the *Stirling Castle* castaways, and the voice of Eliza Fraser could be heard echoing throughout the island's distant Aboriginal past while the voices of the Badtjala remained mute.[46] The shipwreck saga had become the archaeological text which provided the window into Fraser Island's Aboriginal past.

The implications of this use of ethnographic analogy in archaeological interpretation extend well beyond the well-recognized theoretical problems of imposing an ethnographic resolution and reality to an archaeological record which may represent a palimpsest of activities from hundreds and possibly thousands of years. Archaeological research in the Great Sandy Region reveals the hidden power of historical texts to overwrite mute archaeological remains. Ironically, such an approach can suppress the temporal depth and variability of the archaeological record to an ethnographic instant and expand the temporal specificity of historical events such as the *Stirling Castle* saga to millennia. For areas where European historical records misrepresent the cultural values of indigenous peoples, local archaeological research may be rejected by contemporary descendants of those people as misguided, insulting and irrelevant, as it signifies and perpetuates the hegemonic assault on their culture. In other words, archaeological research may be seen by many Aboriginal people as a form of colonizing activity which transcends the temporal bounds of accepted colonial history to engulf their deep past or (pre)history. For Fraser Island, archaeological research may have inadvertently created a situation where the Badtjala captured Eliza Fraser for less than two months, but she ended up capturing Badtjala history for eternity.

Issues surrounding the relevance of archaeological research to Badtjala people ties into the broader issues of colonialism and archaeology. In previous discussion of this topic, Lynette Russell and I have examined how early archaeological research in Australia was aimed at appropriating the Aboriginal past as a dimension of European cultural heritage.[47] In these discussions, the issue concerned how archaeology and anthropology, as colonialist pursuits, had explicitly attempted to distance Aboriginal Australians from their own cultural heritage by representing their archaeological sites as the result of more advanced non-Aboriginal immigrants such as Palaeolithic Europeans. The Fraser Island study reveals that Aboriginal people may perceive contemporary archaeological research as similarly charged with colonialist tenets if it uses historical records, such as the *Stirling Castle* archive, which misrepresent Aboriginal actions and cultural values.

Badtjala treatment of archaeological research on their island also reveals that Aboriginal concerns over archaeological research cannot be resolved simply by Aboriginal people and archaeologists accepting that each other's view of the past is different but valid. The problem is more than a clash of belief systems – it is a clash of powers to control constructions of identity. Making archaeological research more relevant and acceptable to Aboriginal people requires a nuanced understanding of the colonialist tenets of archaeological research. Use of colonial texts such as those associated with a shipwreck saga to aid archaeological interpretation may seem a straightforward attempt at extending the knowledge frontier. However, from an Aboriginal perspective, use of such documents may be offensive and achieve little except an extension of the colonial frontier back into the deep past.

Notes

1 For example, G. Daniel, *A Short History of Archaeology* (London: Thames and Hudson, 1981); J. Malina and Z. Vasicek, *Archaeology Yesterday and Today* (Cambridge: Cambridge University Press, 1990); B.G. Trigger, *A History of Archaeological Thought* (Cambridge: Cambridge University Press, 1989).

2 For an extended discussion of this topic see R. Layton (ed.), *Who Needs the Past? Indigenous Values and Archaeology*, One World Archaeology 5 (London: Unwin Hyman, 1989).

3 For example, I. Davidson, C. Lovell-Jones and R. Bancroft, *Archaeologists and Aborigines Working Together* (Armidale: University of New England Press, 1995).

4 *Australian Fraser Island Environmental Inquiry – Final Report* (Canberra: Australian Government Publishing Service, 1976), x.

5 D. Marr, *Patrick White A Life* (Sydney: Vintage, 1992), 551.

6 P.K. Lauer, 'Ethnohistorical Observations on Fraser Island', ms. submitted to the Fraser Island Environmental Inquiry, Exhibit No. 543 (Australian Archives, Canberra, A3911 Series, 1975).

7 P.K. Lauer, 'The Museum's Role in Fieldwork: The Fraser Island Study', *University of Queensland, Anthropology Museum, Occasional Papers in Anthropology* 9 (1979), 32.

8 P.K. Lauer, 'Report on a Preliminary Ethnohistorical and Archaeological Survey of Fraser Island', *University of Queensland, Anthropology Museum, Occasional Papers in Anthropology* 1 (1977); 'The Museum's Role in Fieldwork: The Fraser Island Study'; see also J. Devitt, 'Fraser Island: Aboriginal Resources and Settlement Pattern', unpublished BA (Hons.) thesis, University of Queensland, 1979.

9 Lauer, 'Report on a Preliminary Ethnohistorical and Archaeological Survey of Fraser Island', 34.

10 W.J.L. Wharton (ed.), *Captain Cook's Journal During His First Voyage Round the World Made in H.M. Bark 'Endeavour' 1768–71. A literal transcription of the original MSS.* (London: Elliot Stock, 1893).

11 M. Flinders, *A Voyage to Terra Australis 1801, 1802, 1803. Three Vols.* (London: G. & W. Nichol, 1814).

12 For example, A. Meston, *Report on Fraser Island* (Queensland Legislative Assembly, 1905).

13 E.M. Curr, 'Great Sandy or Fraser Island', *The Australian Race*, Vol. 3. (Melbourne: Government Printer, 1887), 144–9.

14 Cited in S. Simpson, Narrative of David Bracewell. Enclosure with letter to Colonial Secretary dated 30 May 1842, in G. Langevad (ed.), 'Some original views around Kilcoy: Book 1: The Aboriginal Perspective', *Queensland Ethnohistory Transcripts* 1.1.

15 J. Curtis, *The Shipwreck of the Stirling Castle* (London: George Virtue, 1838), 43–4.

16 Lauer, 'Report on a Preliminary Ethnohistorical and Archaeological Survey of Fraser Island', 17.

17 Lauer, 'The Museum's Role in Fieldwork: The Fraser Island Study', 55.

18 Curtis, 61.

19 Lauer, 'Report on a Preliminary Ethnohistorical and Archaeological Survey of Fraser Island', 12, 34.

20 Lauer, 'The Museum's Role in Fieldwork: The Fraser Island Study', 56, 65.

21 Curtis, 145, 153–4.

22 Lauer, 'The Museum's Role in Fieldwork: The Fraser Island Study', 56.

23 I.J. McNiven, 'Teewah Beach: New Evidence for Holocene Coastal Occupation in Southeast Queensland', *Australian Archaeology* 33 (1991): 41–27; McNiven, 'Ethnohistorical Reconstructions of Aboriginal Lifeways along the Cooloola Coast, Southeast Queensland', *Proceedings of the Royal Society of Queensland* 102 (1992): 5–24; McNiven, 'Shell Middens

and Mobility: The Use of Off-site Faunal Remains, Queensland, Australia', *Journal of Field Archaeology* 19.4 (1992): 495–508.

24 For example, C.H. Thompson and A.W. Moore, 'Studies in Landscape Dynamics in the Cooloola-Noosa River Area, Queensland. 1. Introduction, General Descriptions and Research Approach', *CSIRO Division of Soils, Divisional Report* 73 (1984).

25 I.J. McNiven, 'Prehistoric Aboriginal Settlement and Subsistence in the Cooloola Region, Southeast Queensland', unpublished PhD thesis, The University of Queensland, 1990.

26 I.J. McNiven, 'Ethnohistorical Reconstructions of Aboriginal Lifeways along the Cooloola Coast, Southeast Queensland'.

27 K. Frankland, 'Booral: Preliminary Investigation of an Archaeological Site in the Great Sandy Strait Region, Southeast Queensland.', unpublished BA (Hons.) thesis, The University of Queensland 1990; McNiven, 'Teewah Beach: New Evidence for Holocene Coastal Occupation in Southeast Queensland'.

28 Lauer, 'Ethnohistorical Observations on Fraser Island'.

29 F. Williams, *Written in Sand: A History of Fraser Island* (Brisbane: Jacaranda Press, 1982), ix, 4.

30 For example, ibid., ix, xi, 2, 16.

31 Ibid., xi.

32 Ibid., 2.

33 J. Sinclair, *Fraser Island and Cooloola* (Willoughby: Weldon, 1990), 45.

34 J. Sinclair and P. Corris, *Fighting for Fraser Island: A Man and an Island* (Alexandria: Kerr, 1994), 51.

35 I.J. McNiven, *'Relics of a By-gone Race'? Managing Aboriginal Sites in the Great Sandy Region*, Ngulaig Vol. 12 (St Lucia: Aboriginal and Torres Strait Islander Studies Unit, The University of Queensland, 1994).

36 R.H. Pulleine, 'The Tasmanians and Their Stone-Culture'. *Report of the Nineteenth Meeting of the Australasian Association for the Advancement of Science (Australia and New Zealand)*, ed. C.E. Lord (Hobart: Government Printer, 1929), 310.

37 W. Reeves, and O. Miller, *The Legends of Moonie Jarl* (Brisbane: Jacaranda Press, 1964).

38 See also O. Miller, *Fraser Island Legends* (Brisbane: Jacaranda Press, 1993).

39 S. Foley, *The Badtjala People* (Hervey Bay: Thoorgine Educational and Cultural Centre Aboriginal Corporation Inc, 1994), 7.

40 Ibid., 10.

41 Personal commentary, 1993.

42 Foley, 4.

43 See Olga Miller (Chapter 2) and Fiona Foley (Chapter 12), this volume.

44 See R. Evans and J. Walker, ' "These strangers, where are they going?" ' Aboriginal–European Relations in the Fraser Island and Wide Bay Region 1770–1905', *University of Queensland, Anthropology Museum, Occasional Papers in Anthropology* 8 (1977), 39–105; K. Schaffer, *In The Wake of First Contact: The Eliza Fraser Stories* (Cambridge: Cambridge University Press, 1995).

45 Cited in Foley, 19.
46 See Chapter 4 by Lynette Russell, this volume.
47 I.J. McNiven and L. Russell, ' "Strange Paintings" and "Mystery Races": Kimberley Rock Art, Diffusionism and Colonialist Constructions of Australia's Aboriginal Past', *Antiquity*, 71 (1997): 801-9; L. Russell and I.J. McNiven, 'Monumental Colonialism: Megaliths and the Appropriation of Australia's Aboriginal Past', *Journal of Material Culture*, 3.3 (1998).

Chapter 4

'Mere trifles and faint representations': the representations of savage life offered by Eliza Fraser

Lynette Russell

When European colonialists and explorers encountered native peoples for the first time there arose a need to reconcile preconceived expectations with actual observations.[1] The indigenous people of the new and recently colonized world became the 'ethnographic Other'. Through the processes of colonialism and exploration the Other came to be defined through a series of binary oppositions. These dichotomies, manifested in descriptions of the Other in terms like noble savages, cannibals and natural slaves, distinguished the Europeans as superior and indigenous cultures as inferior and weak. The Other was also perfidious, treacherous and untrustworthy; capable of being childlike and deserving of paternal care but also able to behave with utter contempt for European authority. This unpredictability was perceived partly as the result of their state of savagery and immaturity which stood in stark contrast to the sophistication of the civilized Europeans.

The ethnographic observations of the world's recently located indigenes provided an empirical base for debates over a number of issues which had been articulated initially in the works of Enlightenment scholars, Hobbes, Rousseau, Voltaire and Condorcet among others.[2] A vital aspect of these debates included attempts to draw comparisons between modern 'savages' and the ancestors of modern Europeans. Within this context the Australian experience, recordings and observations were indispensable. The commonly held belief was that indigenous Australians represented the lowest form of humanity, possibly sharing this dubious position with the Tierra del Fuegians. Whether this questionable honour meant that the Europeans should attempt to bring salvation and civilization or adopt a teleological perspective which would ensure a swift but humane extinction was the subject of extensive colonial debate.

When the *Stirling Castle* was wrecked off the Queensland coast in 1836 the Captain, his wife and crew members were described as being held captive by primitive savages who in time murdered the Captain and several crew members. Mrs Eliza Fraser somehow survived despite the treatment she received from the Aborigines who were described as 'demons in human form' who had inflicted upon her 'severe miseries'. In this chapter I examine the textual representations of Aboriginal people in nineteenth-century descriptions of the Eliza Fraser saga. I do so not because I want to understand the Badtjala people whom she encountered or believe that this would be possible through a close reading of these texts; rather I wish to look at the castaways' constructions of the Badtjala, as these provide a key to understanding the Europeans, their fears and their motivations. I have detected and will discuss three interconnected and interwoven themes which course through these texts. The first of these is the silence and anonymity of the Aborigines. Rarely in these castaway stories does the reader hear the native voice. Silence is a powerful and effective technique for subordinating the colonized and, when coupled with anonymity, the indigenes become a homogeneous, indistinct mass. The second issue with which I deal is polarity. The Eliza Fraser narrative, like so many colonial stories, depends on a polarization between savagery and civilization. This is a polarity that supports and nurtures the colonial enterprise. The *Stirling Castle* narratives also offered a polarized view of the Aboriginal people – they were either pernicious, vicious savages or poor, afflicted creatures. These depictions ensured a two-way loss for the Badtjala as both types of native pleaded for the intervention of the settlers who were charged with bringing enlightenment and civilization. The final theme detected in the nineteenth-century texts is the perception that Australia exhibited a homogeneous Aboriginal culture. In exploring the connections and disjunctures among these three themes I argue that these representations tell us more about the intruders and their society than the natives the text purports to describe.

In *The Order of Things*, Michel Foucault argued that histories constructed for the Other and the self necessarily implicate each other.[3] As the European invaders wrote of the Aborigines in Australia, they wrote also of themselves. The definition of the Aborigines was a product of the colonial discourse, and the ontological status of the

Aborigines is only ever stipulated in terms of an antithetical relationship. Later they would be defined as an oppositional element in the process of constructing a sense of national identity. Within this discourse of self and Other, the idea of the primitive Other is a deliberate and intractable invention that is ultimately more informative about the observers than the observed.[4] Within the genre of early to mid-nineteenth-century Australian explorer and castaway observations the primitive Other takes on the guise of a fiendish foe. In the Eliza Fraser story the native people literally personified the dangers of the Australian landscape.

The journalist John Curtis noted that he wrote his version of the loss of the *Stirling Castle* and the sufferings of the castaways in order to set the record straight, his intention being to resurrect the reputation of Mrs Fraser who had been criticized widely in the popular press.[5] Towards this end Curtis documented what he believed to be a factual account of the experiences of Eliza Fraser and the shipwrecked crew members. His narrative was, he maintained, confirmed 'by unquestionable corroborative testimony, both oral and documentary'.[6] His assertion that his text contained an absolute truth is a premise which we need to keep in mind as we consider the details of the narrative.

To be detained, to be held captive or to live among the Aborigines was a fate few colonists were prepared to contemplate. The popular imagination sustained a belief that associating with Australia's natives would degrade the European intruders. Yet ironically the early colonists also knew that interaction with the Aborigines could be a source of great knowledge, especially in terms of the land, its uses and resources. This ambiguity was originally articulated by first fleeter David Collins who, when discussing a female convict generally thought to have been living with the 'natives', remarked: 'how much information must it have been in her power to afford! But humanity shuddered at the idea of purchasing it at so dear a price.'[7]

A deafening silence and anonymity

As I noted above, the evocation of silence is a powerful and effective technique for subjecting and suppressing the colonized. Within the Australian context this silence was extended to include both the indigenes and the landscape itself. The landscape was silent until the ringing of the axe heralded the European presence. The Aborigines were silent in part because of the Europeans' failure to understand their complex languages, but also because of their ability to negotiate their way around the landscape silently. Paul Carter in *The Sound In-Between* has analysed the misunderstanding, the mimicry and the animation of early European–Aboriginal encounters.[8] He asserts that the Europeans and Aborigines never really understood one another, for their mutually unintelligible languages ensured that to each the Other remained silent. My use of the term silence follows that of Carter, in that by silence I do not mean the absence of sound but rather the textual representation of an absence of intelligible sound.

Within the Eliza Fraser narrative, as documented in the Curtis text, the Aboriginal people of the Great Sandy Region are depicted as both anonymous and silent. Except for the occasional yell, shriek or 'coohee' the Badtjala are described as communicating essentially without the aid of language. There is a sense of babbling rabble when Curtis describes the Aborigines as 'engaged in an affray with each other, all parties being much excited'.[9] To convey meaning, according to the Europeans, the Aborigines gesticulated, they poked and they prodded. In an exchange which took place on the beach shortly after the landing, Curtis outlines this non-verbal communication: 'The natives then by signs of a very significant kind, expressed a desire to possess themselves of the clothes worn by the captives.'[10] Although he does not state explicitly as much, it is clear that these supposedly silent and incomprehensible exchanges were well understood by both parties. Understood or otherwise for the reading audience, the portrayals of silence subtly suggested a native muteness that acted as an eloquent form of primitivism.

The only European in the shipwreck narrative who conversed with and was understood by the Aborigines of the Great Sandy Region was John Graham, an escaped convict. Graham's social status within European society was considerably beneath that of the genteel Mrs Fraser and was even below that of the *Stirling Castle* crew. The ease with which Graham was able to communicate and understand the indigenes nourishes and sustains the divide between the classes. The primitive and debased can communicate with one another, while the delicate and civilized are incapable of descending to such a level.

Perhaps the only time the audience hears the native voice is when crying out 'coohee'. The text articulates the actual sound and for a brief moment the silence is shattered. The Aboriginal use of 'coohee' was initially described as 'a friendly salutation', but later Curtis notes that the captives discovered coohee was really a rejoicing, especially, in the death or capture of a 'white man'.[11] The use of 'coohee' was perceived by the captives to be an ominous proclamation. When first the Badtjala came upon the castaways on the beach they began 'to coohee in most fearful and boisterous manner'.[12] Paul Carter has suggested that the Aboriginal use of 'coohee' was often a mimicking response to European usage.[13] He notes that 'coohee' was almost certainly not a universal pan-continental Aboriginal word. We may never know if the cry on Fraser Island was in response to the Europeans or a traditional exclamation. What we can be sure about, however, is that its use in the Curtis text strategically links the Badtjala to the rest of Australia as part of a homogeneous cultural tradition. This is a point that I will develop below.

Through the portrayal of Aboriginal Australia as a silent, unintelligible space, Curtis and his narrators homogenized Australian Aboriginal society. The reading audience was denied access to the Badtjala and their particular cultural formations. Aboriginal Australians were presented as all the same; all were anonymous and silent. Such images naturalized Aboriginal people as features of the landscape and reinforced the colonial notion that native peoples were a 'natural' phenomenon, whose presence in the landscape required no comment or explanation. The unquestioned association of Aboriginal people and the environment is a common characteristic of nineteenth-century first contact representations. The simplicity of this naturalized association undermined the complexity of the relationship of Aboriginal people to their land. Portrayals of Aborigines as a product of the natural landscape emphasized notions of primitivity, implying that traditional Aboriginal society was conservative, constrained by natural forces and reluctant to change.

Within the Eliza Fraser narratives the silence of the Aboriginal people was coupled with anonymity, by which I mean there was a general failure to individualize the group members. These otherwise anonymous representations of the Great Sandy Region Aborigines were, however, gender specific. These specifications would have been familiar to the European audience as these quite clearly relate to the Western categories of masculinity and femininity. The gender specific descriptions included men as the perpetrators of cruel acts of savagery. The women were portrayed as less hostile, though just as uncivilized and primitive. After Mrs Fraser was taken 'captive' and placed in the custody of the women, she was saved the barbarity of physical beatings. Curtis notes that the 'women did not maltreat her by any further act of violence'.[14] They did, however, ensure that she worked extremely hard, often collecting firewood for lengthy periods without rest.

The anonymity of the Badtjala was ruptured only twice in the Curtis text. Mrs Fraser chose to record the name of only one of the women with whom she spent her time. This was a young woman who was afflicted with ulcerous sores and suffered in silence, whom Mrs Fraser named Robina. Robina was a derivation from Robin Red Breast, as the young woman reminded Mrs Fraser of a nursery rhyme she had read as a child. This choice which related to an infantile nursery rhyme places Robina in the role of child to Mrs Fraser's role of mother. The only Aboriginal man to escape anonymity was named Gormondy by the convict Graham on account of his ravenous appetite.[15] As I noted earlier, Graham's familiarity with the natives and his own inferior status as a convict distanced him from the other European characters in the narrative and at the same time connected him to the Badtjala.

The general failure to individualize the Badtjala continued into the post-contact and mission periods. Official mission records for the earlier part of the twentieth century confirm that a limited number of European names were bestowed upon the mission inmates. In order to avoid confusion people were differentiated by numbers. This resulted in the mission records noting that there were Georges 1, 2 and 3, and Charlies 1, 2 and 3, while there were six Rosies.[16] The general reticence to record the individuality of the Fraser Island Aborigines fostered the perception that the indigenes were an undifferentiated mass. Such a representational technique is familiar to readers of Edward Said's critique of Orientalism.[17] Said argues that it is the failure to record individuality and variations within the Orientalist discourse that assures the native is perceived as a primitive and singular Other.

Representations and cannibalism

Aboriginal people described in the Curtis text and other contemporary documents were either wantonly pernicious – 'demons in human form'[18] – or pitifully pathetic. The pitifully pathetic were exemplified by Mrs Fraser's Robina. Incidents of barbarity were numerous and described in colourful detail. Curtis suggested that the castaways were subjected to violent and unmerciful beatings and that the Aborigines took 'savage pleasure [in taking] the captives out into the sea and let[ting] them swim back to shore'.[19] In their 'horrible captivity'[20] Mrs Fraser and the others constantly feared cannibalism. Gannath Obeyesekre has observed that from the late eighteenth-century onwards the English reading public was fascinated by the notion of eating human flesh.[21] Cannibalism was considered to be the defining characteristic of the savage. Within the Eliza Fraser narrative the possibility of cannibalism was a constant concern. Curtis described the traditional Aboriginal corroboree as 'a merry making, and consists of dancing in a circle round a miserable captive, whose flesh they would presently greedily devour'.[22]

Notions of cannibalism and human sacrifice continued to underwrite European references to the Aborigines of the Great Sandy Region throughout the nineteenth century. Long-time resident of the Great Sandy Region, and anthropologist Alfred Howitt's informant, Harry Aldridge, remarked that ritual cannibalism was practised but the idea that the Aborigines had sacrificed and consumed people was a 'pure fiction'.[23] Aldridge was married to a Badtjala woman and had close association with the Badtjala people for much of his life. He was a

European with an unparalleled knowledge of the customs and habits of the Badtjala people as well as being privy to information from several generations. His rejection of the notions of human sacrifice and cannibalism supports the contention that the so-called fears of the castaways were in fact just part of the assumption that all 'savages' sacrificed captives and consumed their flesh. Within the Curtis narrative the castaways operated within a paradigm where savages were cannibals; indeed, the two terms coexist in nineteenth-century discussions of indigenous people.

Even within the subtext of the Curtis narrative the captives' fear was clearly unfounded, as the Aborigines never evidenced any intention to consume them. It is possible to reinterpret the actions of the indigenes and recognize instances of generosity in the supplying of food, water and shelter.[24] None the less, Curtis and the castaways preferred to see the Aborigines as animalistic 'barbarians' who were a 'quadruped brethren [to] the blood hounds'.[25] Cannibalism was therefore culturally prefigured, since European mainstream thought held the Aborigines in unquestioned proximity to an animal state.

Representations and colonialism

Australia's particular form of settler-colonialism was based on a logic of elimination. Aboriginal people needed to be removed in order to facilitate access to the land. The land was, after all, the primary motivation for settlement. Justifying the elimination of the natives could be achieved in a number of ways. Two of the most common justifications involved demonstrating the necessity of European intervention. Portraying the natives as either pernicious or pathetic ensures the soliciting of colonial intervention. The blacks were to be saved or sacrificed. Despite the fear that associating with the natives on their terms could result in degradation, associating with the natives on colonial terms was expected to be a more positive experience. The potential for the salvation of the black man was postulated in a *de facto* form. *Stirling Castle* crewman Corrallis, described as a man of colour who had been trained as a servant to the Europeans, personified the hope for retraining the black races. Mrs Fraser reminded the reader that redemption of the black savage through association with Europeans was possible when she noted that 'a sympathizing heart may be encased by a sable skin'.[26]

The Curtis text, through its descriptions of savagery, the insinuation of cannibalism, the abject cruelty shown to the civilized Mrs Fraser and the wretched childlike Robina, emphasized the importance of and articulated the necessity for European colonial confrontation. It is important to note that in this context I am not suggesting that the narratives in the Curtis text, nor the reports offered by Mrs Fraser, John Graham or John Baxter, were intentionally falsified to support the colonial enterprise. Intentionality is not my concern. Rather, I am suggesting that the *Stirling Castle* narratives were constructed within a specific context which supported and nurtured the colonial project. Furthermore, Curtis notes at the beginning of his book that praise was to be offered to those who might 'attempt to enlighten the minds of, and deliver from everlasting suffering the sons and daughters of ignorance and cruelty'.[27]

This justified colonization would be, to use Mary Louise Pratt's term, an anti-conquest. According to Pratt, anti-conquest is nourished by notions of reciprocity.[28] She argues that reciprocity is the ideology which underwrites capitalistic expansion. In exchange for land the settler-colonial experience brings civilization, education and ultimately enlightenment to the natives. In a similar vein, Said remarked that:

> Neither imperialism nor colonialism is a simple act of accumulation and acquisition. Both are supported and perhaps even impelled by impressive ideological formations that include notions that certain territories and people require and beseech domination, as well as various forms of knowledge affiliated with domination: the vocabulary of classic nineteenth-century imperial culture is plentiful with such words and concepts as 'inferior' or 'subject people', 'subordinate peoples', 'dependency', 'expansion', and 'authority'.[29]

Within nineteenth-century *Stirling Castle* narratives domination is implored through the textual representational styles and techniques I have outlined above.

Elsewhere I have shown that, in general, Australian settler-colonial representations minimized and abstracted spatial variation.[30] I term this the homogeneity paradigm which purports that all Australian Aboriginal peoples were the same. Differences in the form of distinct tribal or cultural groups were denied and a naturalistic, symmetrical vision of continental Aboriginal culture was proposed. As culturally distinctive and geographically distant groups were homogenized, the Aborigines came to be depicted as a feature of the landscape closely related to the fauna. Spatial homogenization and the development of a continental specificity were possible because the Aborigines were perceived to be a non-cultural entity. As I noted earlier, Curtis compared the natives to dogs; in another instance he links the Fraser Islanders with monkeys:

> many of both sexes, when young are far from ugly; nay, some of them are tolerably handsome, but the old women are absolute frights, and

appear only to want an additional member to render them analogous
with the long-tailed fraternity.[31]

According to Curtis the Badtjala were brothers to the long-tailed apes.

The Curtis text was constructed within the framework of the settler-
colonial enterprise. As such the Curtis text was also locked into the
homogeneity paradigm. Detailed discussions of the habits and customs
of the Badtjala appear in Chapter 9 of this text. This chapter is lifted
almost verbatim from Cunningham's *Two Years in New South
Wales*.[32] This plagiarism is curious: at one point Curtis quotes from
the same Cunningham text, acknowledging that he is familiar with
Cunningham's work. Yet Curtis presents the information as if it is
intended to be read as a factual account of the lifeways of the
Badtjala.[33] The interchange of material from the Port Jackson area as
an ethnographic account of the Badtjala indicates that Curtis was
operating within and reiterating the homogeneity paradigm. He, like
most nineteenth-century authors, assumed that all Aboriginal people
were the same. Is this the extension of the homogeneity paradigm?

First contact representations

First contact descriptions of Aboriginal people were offered by
explorers, colonists, missionaries and government officials. These have
frequently been used by anthropologists and historians as a source of
'ethnographic information'. The intellectual focus of this time was
characterized by an interest in the pursuits and mode of production of
the indigenes; social structure and mechanisms for social organization;
indigenous languages; indigenous belief systems and, most importantly,
whether or not the Aborigines had one or many gods. Observers often
concerned themselves with the Aborigines' intellectual powers and
whether there was any hope for 'civilising and Christianising' them.[34]
The Curtis version of the *Stirling Castle* narrative also provides us with
detailed observations which we can compare to other first contact
stories. For my purposes, such a comparison is not intended to identify
errors or correct misinformation; rather, such a comparison highlights
the general intellectual framework within which these first contact
observers were operating.

Perhaps the most influential of all first contact stories was provided by
first fleeter David Collins, who kept a detailed journal for the first years
of the colony from 1788 to 1790.[35] Like Cunningham, Collins' subjects
were the tribes of the Port Jackson region. Collins' text adhered to
portrayals of the romanticism of the childhood of mankind, portrayals
which also depicted these people as godless savages.[36] Any indigenous
religious life that had been observed by Collins, or for that matter the

castaways in Curtis' text, clearly did not register as sacred. Instead, both texts supported the notion that the focus of Aboriginal life was economic, and that the general nature and character of the indigenes could be judged within the categories of 'theft', stealth and barbarity. This is a common technique replicated in many Australian first contact stories. These positions confirmed the author's assumption that the Aborigines represented the infancy of the human race. They exemplified the ancestors of all civilized mankind. Within John Curtis' version of the *Stirling Castle* saga the Aborigines were presumed to be 'the very zero of civilization'.[37] The Aborigines as 'living fossil man' were fictionalized as 'the image of ourselves as we appeared many ages before'.[38] This intellectual hegemony promoted the Europeans as the legitimate heirs to the Australian landscape. The Aborigines as imaginary ancestors were legitimated as primitive man and members of a dying race. Such imaginings ensured that the Europeans wrote of themselves as legitimate heirs, civilized successors and concerned patriarchs.

Conclusion

I have sought to examine the subtext associated with the representations of Aboriginal people in the nineteenth-century *Stirling Castle* narratives. I have primarily relied on the John Curtis text, which I have argued conforms to the representational specifics that I have elsewhere identified for nineteenth-century first contact stories. The genre of the first contact story depends on the promulgation of the homogeneity paradigm, the use of diametrical imagery for descriptions of the Aborigines and an underlying theme of silence. Aboriginal people are marginalized by historical representations which were constructed within the framework of the colonial enterprise. European–colonial discourse addresses the Aborigines as subjects of study concomitantly with them being written of as subjects of the colonial-settler state. As I noted at the beginning of this chapter, we edge no closer to understanding the Badtjala through close readings of the *Stirling Castle* narratives. The Badtjala as they appear in these stories do not exist. These fictionalized constructions reconcile the observers' expectations with their actual observations. In the 1870s, Archibald Meston conferred with several of the senior Badtjala elders and on the basis of their 'very different' version of the story. He noted that Mrs Fraser

> must have either had a serious quarrel with truth or else her head was badly affected by her experiences … Certainly she gave a wildly improbable tale in Brisbane, accusing the blacks of deeds quite foreign to their known character, and quite unheard of before or since … [such tales] were evolved from her own imagination.[39]

Regardless of the validity of the descriptions offered in the Eliza Fraser narratives, it is possible to delve into the mechanics and structure of nineteenth-century first contact constructions of the Aborigines. These constructions leave us with little doubt that, in Michel Foucault's terms, the Europeans in writing of the Other were indeed writing of themselves. They wrote of an Australia populated with malicious violent savages whose salvation would be exchanged for access to the land.

Notes

1 Eliza Fraser is said to have exclaimed: 'The stories which we have read in our childhood, and the representations of savage life we have seen in theatres in our riper years, are mere trifles and faint representations, when compared with the facts of which I and my unfortunate companions were eye-witnesses.' J. Curtis, *The Shipwreck of the Stirling Castle* (London: George Virtue, 1838), 157.

2 T. Hobbes, *Leviathan* (1651; Baltimore: Penguin, 1968); J.J. Rousseau, *The Social Contract* (1755; New York: Dutton, 1938); Rousseau, *First and Second Discourses* (1762; New York: St Martins, 1964); F.M. Voltaire, *Essai sur les Moeurs et L'esprit des Nations* (Paris: Chez Werdet et Lequien Fils, 1745); Marquis de Condorcet, *Esquisse D'un Tableau Historique des Progres de L'esprit Humain* (1795; Paris: Masson, 1822).

3 M. Foucault, *The Order of Things: An Archaeology of the Human Sciences* (London: Tavistock, 1970).

4 cf. G.W. Stocking (ed.), *Observers and Observed: Essays on Ethnographic Fieldwork* (Madison: University of Wisconsin Press, 1983); M. Torgovnik, *Gone Primitive: Savage Intellects, Modern Lives* (Chicago: University of Chicago Press, 1990), 38; H. Kucklick, *The Savage Within: The Social History of British Anthropology, 1885–1945* (Cambridge: Cambridge University Press, 1991).

5 Curtis, iv.

6 Ibid., iv.

7 Lt. Col. D. Collins, *An Account of the English Colony of New South Wales*, ed. B. Fletcher, facsimile edition (1798–1802; London: A.W. Reed, 1975), 406.

8 P. Carter, *The Sound In-Between: Voice, Space and Performance* (Strawberry Hills, NSW: New South Wales University Press, 1992).

9 Curtis, 146.

10 Ibid., 52.

11 Ibid., 41.

12 Ibid., 60.

13 Carter, 25.

14 Curtis, 142.

15 Ibid., 160–1.

16 R. Evans and J. Walker, ' "These strangers, where are they going?" Aboriginal–European Relations in the Fraser Island and Wide Bay Region

1770–1905', *University of Queensland, Anthropology Museum, Occasional Papers in Anthropology* 8 (1977), 76.

17 E. Said, *Orientalism* (New York: Pantheon, 1978).

18 Curtis, 78.

19 Ibid., 68.

20 Ibid., vi.

21 G. Obeyesekere, *The Apotheosis of Captain Cook: European Mythmaking in the Pacific* (Princeton: Princeton University Press, 1992), 635.

22 Curtis, 41.

23 Harry Aldridge, letter in A.W. Howitt, The Ngarigo File, Howitt Papers, State Library of Victoria, Box 8.

24 Curtis, 61.

25 Ibid., 57.

26 Ibid., 160. The idea that the dichotomous relationship between civilization and savagery (or between the self and the Other) could be represented by a continuum of form has been postulated by numerous authors of which the most significant have been P. Abrams, *The Origins of British Sociology 1834–1914* (Chicago: University of Chicago Press, 1968); P. Abrams, *Historical Sociology* (New York: Cornell University Press, 1982); J. Burrow, *Evolution and Society* (Cambridge: Cambridge University Press, 1966); Foucault, *The Order of Things*; R. Laudan, Review of Paolo Rossi's *The Dark Abyss of Time: The History of the Earth and the History of Nations from Hooke to Vico, Philosophy of Science* 52 (1985); A. Pagden, *The Fall of Natural Man: The American Indian and the Origins of Comparative Ethnology* (New York: Cambridge University Press, 1982), and *Europeans' Encounter with the New World* (New Haven: Yale University Press, 1993).

27 Curtis, vi.

28 M.L. Pratt, *Imperial Eyes: Travel Writing and Transculturation* (New York: Routledge, 1992), 84.

29 Said, 123.

30 L. Russell, '(Re)Presented Pasts: Historical and Contemporary Constructions of Australian Aboriginalities', unpublished PhD thesis, The University of Melbourne, 1995.

31 Curtis, 115.

32 P. Cunningham, *Two Years in New South Wales* (London: Henry Colburn, 1828).

33 Curtis, 67.

34 A.P. Elkin, 'Anthropology in Australia: Chapter One', *Mankind* 5.6 (1958), 226–7.

35 Collins.

36 Ibid., 454.

37 Curtis, 114.

38 H. Basedow, *The Australian Aborigines* (Adelaide: F.W. Preece and Sons, 1929), 59; compare with Basedow, 'Burial Customs in the Northern Flinders Ranges', *Man* 13 (1913), 49.

39 Quoted in Evans and Walker, 44.

Chapter 5

'Our fair narrator' down-under: Mrs Fraser's body and the preservation of the Empire[1]

Rod Macneil

As far as decorous titillation is concerned, it would be difficult to imagine a book more satisfying to nineteenth-century readers than John Curtis' text, *The Shipwreck of the Stirling Castle*, published in London in 1838. Curtis describes in polite detail the desolation and gradual demise of the *Stirling Castle* crew and its single passenger, Mrs Eliza Fraser, following its grounding off the coast of central Queensland in May 1836. Having abandoned the wreck, the twenty survivors drifted in two boats for over four weeks, living on meagre supplies and, when these ran out, on shellfish scavenged from exposed reefs, before finally landing on the north-east coast of Great Sandy Island. In many ways, Curtis' account seems driven by the essence of romantic melodrama–peril on the high seas, an exotic tropical wilderness, and a beautiful young woman captured by the tribe of wild savages who had murdered her husband.

Similarly, if faced with the task of selecting a single narrative to allegorize the colonial experience in the New World, we would again be well served by Curtis' text, and its account of the rude exposure of European refinement to the crudity of an empirically virginal Australia. The story of the *Stirling Castle* is that of a confrontation between the colonizing West – led by the Captain and Mrs Fraser – and its absolute antithesis, the uncolonized tribes of the New World, represented here by the Aboriginal peoples of central Queensland. As the narrative unfolds, it describes its protagonists within a series of polarities that clearly delineate the boundaries of 'civilized' and 'uncivilized'. The fate of the heroine becomes symbolically that of the Empire: the threats made upon her life – and, more importantly, upon her virtue – by the

Aboriginal people mirror the colonial subject's resistance to colonization, and the replication and imposition of Western civilization at the colonial site. Mrs Fraser's survival represents not only the triumph, but also the prevalence of the authority and ideology of the West, implying the rightness of colonization as justified by its dissemination of an evidently superior morality. In this chapter I intend to trace the ebb and flow of Mrs Fraser's battle for 'civility', through the visual representations of both her and the Aboriginal peoples of Fraser Island, in John Curtis' account of the misadventure of the *Stirling Castle* crew and the 'horrible barbarity of the cannibals' that was inflicted upon them.[2]

By presenting the protagonists of the *Stirling Castle* narrative as ideologues within a series of polarities – white/black, clothed/naked, Christian/heathen and so on – each becomes an inverse statement of its Other, and therefore at the same time as their identities are mutually exclusive, they also become mutually dependent. To put this more simply in terms central to the Eliza Fraser story, the Aboriginal people can be identified as 'uncivilized' because they are represented as being everything that the Captain, his wife and the crew of the *Stirling Castle* are not – physically, intellectually, culturally and morally. Equally important is the inverse – that the Captain and Mrs Fraser (and, in degrees varying according to rank, the rest of the crew) epitomize the refinement of Western civilization in an environment that is its Other, where those elements fundamental to a civilized state appear either to be contradicted or absent altogether.

Having become stranded at the periphery of a continent barely acquainted with Europeans, the crew of the *Stirling Castle* battle not only for their physical survival, but also for the survival of their identity. In this contest the struggle is for the preservation of difference, for those tangible signs of cultural divergence that signify not merely their physical but also their moral difference from their (uncivilized) Aboriginal captors. In this most unsympathetic and contrary of environments, their struggle is to maintain those social and cultural tenets fundamental to their self-identification as European/civilized. Where there is nothing about their surroundings that can affirm this identity, their sense of self must instead depend entirely upon those cultural signifiers salvaged from the wreck of the *Stirling Castle*, and those they are able to muster from within themselves. As a consequence, the *Stirling Castle* crew foster their cultural identity via a process of negation, where a sense of cultural difference is heightened as a means of creating distance between themselves and the Aboriginal people. In the wilds of central Queensland these cultural signifiers are completely abstracted from their cultural source; decontextualized as they are, they are robbed of all other meaning, aside from the fact – for Captain Fraser and his party – that they simply exist.

In a sense, the experiences of the *Stirling Castle* crew on Fraser Island represent a microcosm of which the colonial project is the conglomerate, and in which colonialism's success can be gauged by the fidelity with which its identity is replicated and re-enacted at the colonial site. The struggle to sustain the signifiers of that identity – even when these signifiers are contextually meaningless – reveals their resonance, not so much as parts of a cultural ideology but as symbols of personal identity.

Probably the most important and most tangible of these signifiers were clothes. These at least, unlike most other provisions salvaged from the ship, were not in short supply. Most of the sailors had escaped the wreck with two outfits, one worn over the other, and despite the confusion and danger of the evacuation of the *Stirling Castle*, Mrs Fraser had none the less managed to save three trunks of her clothes along with her husband's sea chest.[3] Clothes, or lack of them, and the exposure and concealment of the European body, emerge as a central theme in the text and illustrations of John Curtis' narrative. The dichotomy of being clothed and going naked was fundamental to a 'civilized' identity: to be robbed of their clothes lessened the distinction between the *Stirling Castle* survivors and their captors, forcing them to confront the applicability of a social prohibition against nudity that was inherent, and almost sacrosanct, within European culture.[4] The exposure of the body diminished discernible cultural difference, creating a compromise of identity that significantly reduced the higher moral ground from which the Aboriginal people could be observed. Essentially, being naked made Europeans less civilized.

In John Curtis' account of the wreck of the *Stirling Castle*, and the ordeals suffered by her crew and passenger in the custody of the Aboriginal peoples of Fraser Island, the battle for identity is focused upon the experiences of Mrs Fraser. After all, it is her story, ahead of those of the other seven survivors, that Curtis recounts, and which has subsequently been told and retold in various forms. It is primarily because she was a woman that Mrs Fraser's story became more remarkable: the hardships she endured, although extraordinary, might well have been considered the lot of a sailor travelling in the unknown Antipodes. But for a respectable, middle-class mother of three to find herself stranded among savages in the rainforests and mangrove swamps of eastern Australia was an adventure considerably more rare, and thus all the more intriguing. The hardships of the climate and the treatment administered by the Aboriginal people became all the more harsh when suffered by a woman. Curtis makes the most of the unusual juxtaposition of genteel femininity and high adventure as he first describes the floundering of the *Stirling Castle* upon the reef:

the elements above seemed to have confederated together with those beneath, to strike alarm and dismay into the minds of the benighted and shipwrecked captain and his desponding and exhausted crew; and were imagination to be expended to its utmost bounds, it could form no adequate idea what must have been the sensations of one person on board the wreck, – a woman, a doating [*sic*] and affectionate wife.[5]

Much of the poignancy of the story of the *Stirling Castle* therefore lies in the meeting of opposites, in the midst of which Mrs Fraser represents the epitome of British civilization. In the extremes of the Antipodes she becomes envoy for Britannia herself, and her story is that of the moral victory of the Old World over the baseness of the New.

Curtis makes it clear that Mrs Fraser was an exemplary female citizen. He goes on to describe her as

one, who being influenced by conjugal fidelity, and anxiety for the health and welfare of her husband, had left her country, children and friends, to console him in the hour of sickness and exhaustion, from a consciousness, that while performing the duties which the law of connubiality enjoins, she had no reason to dread the terrors of the mighty sea.[6]

The extent of Mrs Fraser's conjugal heroism was such that it warranted illustration in Curtis' *The Shipwreck of the Stirling Castle*. The engraving, titled 'Mrs Fraser on the Rock' (Figure 5.1),[7] describes Mrs Fraser's search for fresh water for her husband, after the boats had set down on a small island five days after leaving the wreck.[8] In this illustration Mrs Fraser is depicted fully clothed, having even retained her shoes (which seems a probability considering that they had been adrift for only a short while, and had not at that stage made any contact with Aboriginal people). The island is perhaps not as small as the setting Curtis describes, and appears a little more Italianate than we might expect of a location just below the Tropic of Capricorn, but these are the forgivable excesses of the illustrator and, more than anything else, most likely represent his concessions to the contemporary aesthetics of the landscape. Curtis continues:

Walking along the beach, beside cliffs which the lashing of the sea had rendered almost perpendicular, she saw a shelf about fourteen feet high, from the edge of which dribbled fresh water. How was a weak and delicate female to reach this?[9]

The illustration, however, suggests that Mrs Fraser was less weak and delicate than might be expected. Curtis himself considers elsewhere that perhaps 'the hardships and exposures she had undergone ... in some measure divested her of the timidity and scrupulousness which

Figure 5.1   Engraving, 'Mrs Fraser on the Rock'. Collection: John Oxley Library, Brisbane

are ever the characteristics of well-educated and delicate females'.[10]
She is depicted in the pursuit of water, perched upon a small uneven
ledge half-way up the cliff face, and watched by a figure, presumably
her husband, who reclines in a boat pulled up to the shore below her.
Beyond them other members of the crew can be seen searching for
food and water further up the beach. Such is the intensity of Mrs
Fraser's search that she appears to have inadvertently turned her head
an impossible 100 degrees, peering over her right shoulder in order to
examine the cliff face above her. Whatever her exertions, Mrs Fraser
was both successful and resourceful, returning to the Captain with a
rag torn from her garments and soaked with fresh water for him to
drink. This was not the first time that the Captain's frailty had been
foremost in her mind; on leaving the ship, Mrs Fraser was sure to
include among their meagre provisions 'a box of jellies and jams,
which were of much use to her husband in his then declining state of
health'.[11]

In this contest of civilization and identity, the hopes of the Empire
appear to rest with Mrs Fraser as a model citizen and the embodiment
of feminine virtue. More specifically, the narrative centres upon a
contest over Mrs Fraser's body, where her physical and spiritual well-
being become symbolic of the prevalence of the West in the colonial
encounter. With both text and images, Curtis illustrates the frailty of
cultural identity when dislocated from its 'natural' environment. In this
instance it is Mrs Fraser who is charged with upholding the ideal of the
West, and upon whom its rituals are enacted, symbolized by the
exposure and concealment of her body, her struggle to maintain
difference, and her tenacious preservation of those traits which signify
her superiority over the savage, who is unclothed and uncivilized.

From Curtis alone it is difficult to ascertain the circumstances
surrounding the undressing of Mrs Fraser. In *The Shipwreck of the
Stirling Castle* Curtis provides two accounts of the wreck and ensuing
events (that of the second mate John Baxter, and of Mrs Fraser), each
of which differ in their account and chronology of the encounters of the
Stirling Castle crew with the Aboriginal people on Fraser Island.
Baxter's account is perhaps the more modest. When set upon by the
Aboriginal people, he states that it was only Doyle, Baxter, Brown,
Corralis and Captain Fraser who were 'left in a state of complete
nudity', while Mrs Fraser 'was allowed to retain an article of
underdress'.[12] Mrs Fraser's narrative as recounted by Curtis is quite
different: when denuded she was travelling with only her husband and
Chief Officer Charles Brown, and that they were 'divested ... of every
article of apparel, and the sex of Mrs Fraser did not exempt her from
this revolting exposure, as little it shielded her from the weight of their
waddies'.[13] It would appear that delicacy and a strong sense of decorum

prevented Baxter from suggesting that Mrs Fraser had been left naked in the company of men other than her husband.

Michael Alexander, in his investigation of the Eliza Fraser story, *Mrs Fraser on the Fatal Shore* (1971), states that once stripped by the Aboriginal men, Mrs Fraser 'made a modest effort to string around her loins a wreath of the mauve-coloured sea-grape that trailed everywhere across the sandhills, secreting her wedding ring and earrings among the tendrils'.[14] There is no mention of this in either account presented by Curtis; when later discovered by the Aboriginal women, Curtis writes only that Mrs Fraser 'had her arms laid across her bosom, to shield her person as much as possible from the fierce oblique rays of the setting sun, which had a very powerful effect, of course, upon a delicate female so recently denuded of her clothing'.[15] It is, however, described in some detail by the convict John Graham in his account of Mrs Fraser's rescue, as presented to Captain Foster Fyans, Commandant of the Moreton Bay prison settlement.[16] Graham states that Mrs Fraser was not entirely naked when he found her, but that she still wore remnants of European costume:

> On her head was a Southwester, the smell of the paint kept the Blacks from taking it. Around her loins were part of the legs and waistband of a pair of Trousers, which covered her thighs, wound round with Vines twenty fold as well for delicacy as the preservation of her marriage and Ear rings which she concealed under the Vines.[17]

Basic though it was, by providing herself with the rudiments of dress Mrs Fraser assured her own civility, and created a point of distinction between herself and the (naked) Aboriginal people. Graham ascribed her vines an even greater significance, suggesting that Mrs Fraser had been entwined in greenery by her husband, presumably as a gesture towards the preservation of both her modesty and chastity. When she finally met with Captain Otter's rescue party, Graham states that 'for the first time them vines were pull'd off which the hands of her Dear and much lamented Husband had put on'.[18]

Modesty was also foremost when it came to portraying the naked Mrs Fraser. Curtis' text was apparently uninformed by Graham's account, and thus in two illustrations in *The Shipwreck of the Stirling Castle*, Mrs Fraser appears entirely without clothes. The first of these is titled 'The Murder of Capt. Fraser',[19] and depicts his death as described by Mrs Fraser, who was an eyewitness. In the illustration (Figure 5.2), as in the narrative, the Captain has been speared through the back. Curtis writes that

> the deadly weapon struck him near the shoulder blade, and passing through his body, come out at his breast! ... The captain fell

Figure 5.2 Illustration, 'The Murder of Capt. Fraser'. Collection: John Oxley Library, Brisbane

immediately, and blood then flowed in copious streams from his mouth, nose, and ears, and before the current produced suffocation, he faintly articulated, 'Oh Eliza, I am gone!'.[20]

In this illustration the artist has been saved the quandary of how to properly and accurately depict Mrs Fraser without revealing her nakedness by his adherence to the narrative, in which she describes herself hiding behind a 'huge tree', only emerging after the Captain had been speared.[21] That is how we see her in this engraving, partly concealed, with her hand raised to her breast as she looks towards the Aboriginal man who has just thrown his spear. At the time of her husband's death, Mrs Fraser had been living with the Aboriginal people for upwards of five weeks.[22] This illustration, however, fails to include detail of the alterations to her appearance that had happened during this time, and instead she appears very much within the model of ideal womanhood that Curtis describes earlier. Her hair is still coiffed and her skin still white, despite her own descriptions of being 'stuccoed' in sand and mud after first being taken into the custody of the Aboriginal women.[23] She later described herself to Curtis as having been 'coloured, and her head bedizened with feathers and other ornaments, after the manner of the natives'.[24] And yet in this image the partial transformation of Mrs Fraser's appearance has been omitted, and instead the visible signifiers of her cultural identity remain unobscured, her 'civility' intact. Her identity is further enhanced by the presence of her husband, with whom, even in this culturally discordant environment, she fulfils a conjugal role within parameters determined by the values of the 'civilized' world, and affirmed by the wedding ring that, according to Graham, she kept hidden in the vines about her waist. Having been robbed of her husband, Mrs Fraser is denied yet another signifier of her identity, the role of wife, in an environment where the consequent role of widowhood is culturally unrecognized.[25]

In this illustration there is a marked contrast between the emaciated and spindly white body of the Captain and the muscular, well-proportioned and considerably taller figures of the Aboriginal men. Stylistically, they are easily compared to the engravings by Chambers, after Sydney Parkinson's (*c.* 1745–1771) frequently cited drawings of Australian Aboriginal men as the 'noble savage' of Western aesthetic and ideological fantasy.[26] Curtis devotes an entire chapter to 'a succinct account of the tribes which form the aboriginal population [sic] of the new world', drawn 'from the most authentic sources'.[27] He provides the following description of Aboriginal men:

whether on the northern and tropical, or southern and temperate shores of Australia, [they] possess the thick prominent lips, sunken eyes, high cheek bones, and calveless legs of the African, differing, however, in the hair, which (except in Van Diemen's Land, and the equally cold coast of Australia, where the heads of the natives are woolly) is long and coarse. The nose, though large, is not so flat as the Africanders', indeed it is sometimes of a Roman form, and the forehead is high, narrow, and at the crown formed somewhat after the manner of the roof of a house. Generally speaking they are of the middle height, but some of them are of lofty stature; the women are smaller than the men, but well made, as indeed is most generally the case with the male sex: the hands and feet are comparatively small, the shoulders finely rounded, but the abdomen frequently protuberant, and the arms long.[28]

The Aboriginal people depicted in this illustration represent an aestheticized equivalent of the phrenological and morphological analysis that Curtis provides. From this image alone there is little doubt that the Aboriginal men are different – distinctly 'not European' – and yet that difference is not represented as 'real', but instead is derived from the European fantasy of a South Seas Arcadia. Despite the fact that they are depicted in the act of murdering Captain Fraser, there is little about the appearance of these Aboriginal men that suggests depravity. That they are 'savage' and 'wild' is signified by their nudity, their weapons, and the decorated hair of the figures on the far right. And, almost paradoxically, it is signified by their refined physiques, which are as balanced and ideal as the lifestyle which the West imagined 'noble savages' to lead. Although it is highly probable that the illustrator had never seen an Aboriginal person, that in itself would not have prevented him from using his imagination to create a far more savage 'savage', such as is seen in an 1838 broadsheet illustration of the wreck of the *Stirling Castle*.[29] Despite the apparent immorality of the Aboriginal men in Curtis' illustration, they are none the less represented within an aesthetic discourse that depends not upon the literal representation of its subject, but upon a Western idealization of its colonial Other.

The final illustration in Curtis is of Mrs Fraser making her escape with the convict John Graham, with the assistance of Gormondy, an Aboriginal man with whom Graham was already acquainted and amicable (Figure 5.3). Although Curtis writes that 'on meeting with the Aboriginal people, Graham was soon divested ... of his clothing',[30] in this image he has managed to retain his trousers. This leads us to two interesting observations: first, the truism that depicting the nakedness of white men was considered inappropriate for publication in the early nineteenth century; and second, in light of this, the dilemma that must have faced the illustrator when he depicted Captain Fraser – white, naked and exposed. While it was possible to overlook mention of Graham's nakedness (when Baxter first saw Graham he described him

Figure 5.3 Mrs Fraser making her escape with John Graham. Collection: John Oxley Library, Brisbane

as having 'nothing on his person but a pair of canvas trousers'),[31] the narrative provided little opportunity for Captain Fraser's modesty. In contrast to both Graham and Fraser, Gormondy is black and therefore his nakedness is inherent to his uncivilized state and requires no apology.

Of most interest in this illustration is the figure of Mrs Fraser. Although she is naked and positioned facing towards the spectator, decorum is preserved by the fortuitous upward curve of the prow of the canoe, which leaves only her bare breasts exposed. Apart from her nakedness, the assault upon Mrs Fraser's civility is most evident in the colour of her skin. She contrasts both the blackness of Gormondy and the whiteness of Graham, and instead appears as a combination of both. As such she appears partially metamorphosed – no longer identifiably white, but not yet black either. The inference is that Graham has arrived in the nick of time – any later and the metamorphosis might have been complete, or progressed so far as to be irreversible. Already the weakening of Mrs Fraser's resistance and the consequent chipping away at the signifiers of her Western identity are evidenced by her complete nakedness and muddied hair. The narrative makes it clear that this cosmetic change, along with others such as the colouring of her skin with animal fats and dyes, was forced upon her by members of the tribe.[32] Curtis describes her appearance to Captain Otter:

> her swarthy shrivelled skin presented a figure truly grotesque to the British soldiers, who ... could hardly suppress their smiles. ... The quantity of gum which had been applied to her long hair, together with the fibres of bark, grass, feathers, &c. which were inserted in it, caused her head to appear the size of a band-box.[33]

Captain Otter described Mrs Fraser in similar, and surprisingly candid, terms, in a letter to his cousin, which Curtis includes as a footnote:[34]

> You never saw such an object. Although only thirty-eight years of age, she looked like an old woman of seventy, perfectly black, and dreadfully crippled from the sufferings she had undergone.[35]

Readers are reassured that Mrs Fraser's metamorphosis to Aboriginal identity was cosmetic and only transitional by the portrait at the front of Curtis' text. Here her skin is once again white and her hair restored. Symbolically, Curtis describes her 'coloured' identity as being no more than a facade: in trying to remove the pigment, he writes that both Mrs Fraser and Baxter 'subjected themselves so frequently to ablutions, that at length their skin began to crack, and it gradually peeled off, so that ... [they] shed their coats'.[36]

As an icon of the civilized West, Mrs Fraser's restoration to the colonial domain could only endorse the Empire whose morality she had fought so hard to sustain. Mrs Fraser had not only survived, but emerged from the wilderness with her cultural identity intact – physically decrepit but morally victorious. Coupled with her instinct for physical survival had been her instinct to preserve her cultural integrity, to continue to uphold those values that made her Other to her captors, and which assured her civility in an environment that appeared its absolute antithesis. In illustration, Mrs Fraser remains partly concealed, unlike her husband whose exposure and death might symbolize a weakness of spirit, and his lack of conviction in the prevalence of empirical ideals. Naked or wrapped in creepers, Mrs Fraser's body endorses the colonial project, by upholding the values of an omnipotent West in a realm unaffected by its morality.

Notes

1 It is important to preface this chapter with the explanation that its analysis centres upon the text and illustrations of John Curtis' 1838 publication *The Shipwreck of the Stirling Castle*. Accordingly, the references to Aboriginal people made in this chapter are figures of this particular nineteenth-century discourse of racial identity and relations, and terms such as 'savages' and 'natives' are reproduced here as they appear in the primary text.

2 J. Curtis, *The Shipwreck of the Stirling Castle* (London: George Virtue, 1838), title page.

3 Ibid., 24.

4 For a discussion of the historical association between nakedness and immorality in Western thought see Kenneth R. Dutton, *The Perfectible Body: The Western Ideal of Physical Development* (London: Cassell, 1995), ch. 2, 'The Body Re-born', 53–88, and ch. 3, 'The Visible Body', 89–118.

5 Curtis, 21.

6 Ibid., 21.

7 This is the title that appears in the 'Directions to the Binder for Placing the Plates', on page viii of Curtis. In Michael Alexander's book *Mrs Fraser on the Fatal Shore* (London: Michael Joseph, 1971) this image is reproduced on page 35, with the title 'Mrs Fraser in search of water'.

8 Ibid., 32.

9 Curtis, 133.

10 Ibid., 132.

11 Ibid., 128.

12 Ibid., 60.

13 Ibid., 140.

14 Alexander, 48.

15 Curtis, 143.

16 John Graham's report, reference no. Archives Office, New South Wales 4/232/5.5. There is a transcript published in B. Dwyer and N. Buchanan, *The Rescue of Eliza Fraser* (Noosa: Noosa Graphica, 1986), 28–32.
17 Dwyer and Buchanan, 31.
18 Ibid., 32.
19 Curtis, facing page 147. This illustration is reprinted in Alexander, 57, with the title 'The Spearing of Captain Fraser'.
20 Ibid., 147.
21 Ibid., 146.
22 Alexander, 55.
23 Curtis, 143.
24 Ibid., 164.
25 K. Schaffer, *In the Wake of First Contact: The Eliza Fraser Stories* (Cambridge: Cambridge University Press, 1995).
26 T. Chambers after S. Parkinson, 'Two of the Natives of New Holland advancing into combat', from Parkinson's *Journal of a Voyage to the South Seas*, 1773.
27 Curtis, 103–17.
28 Ibid., 104.
29 From the broadsheet *Wreck of the Stirling Castle* (London: J. Catnach, 1838).
30 Curtis, 162.
31 Ibid., 83.
32 In a letter to his cousin, reprinted in Curtis, Captain Otter describes Mrs Fraser's darkened appearance: 'besides her exposure to the sun and wind, the natives, in order to bring her as near as possible to their own complexion, had rubbed her every day with charcoal and fat' (ibid., 187).
33 Ibid., 165–6.
34 Ibid., 179–88.
35 Ibid., 186.
36 Ibid., 166.

PART 2

Modern Representations

Chapter 6

'We are like Eliza': twentieth-century Australian responses to the Eliza Fraser saga

Kay Schaffer

The title of this chapter comes from a conversation I had in 1991 with the Australian documentary filmmaker Gillian Coote about the making of her television documentary *Island of Lies*. What she told me reminded me that every generation of Australians since the mid-century has witnessed the emergence of a new persona for the legendary Eliza Fraser. One is tempted to say if she didn't exist we would have had to invent her. Why have Australians clung so long and fast to this woman and the legends which attend her? How is it that this woman returns, but always in a different guise, to haunt the national memory about every twenty years? What ambivalent fears and desires does her memory (or that created for us by others on her behalf) evoke today?[1]

In 1991 Gillian Coote directed a film which focused on the lies told by white Australians concerning the country's brutal colonial past. She wanted to screen the film on television during National Aborigines Week. It was to be a catharsis for the descendants of white Australian settler families whom she interviewed. As they told their stories they peeled back the layers of lies and evasions about the past in order to expose 'the truth', particularly in relation to white massacres of Aborigines in the nineteenth century. For Gillian Coote, Eliza Fraser represented all those white Australians, past and present, who knew about the frontier violence but chose to hide or deny it. The film was to be therapeutic – a cleansing. 'Eliza lied about her knowledge of Aboriginal culture,' she told me. 'People who lie or evade knowledge are punished. We are like Eliza.'

Coote's Eliza reflects something of the politics of racial reconciliation which has been on the national agenda since 1988 when the then Prime Minister, Bob Hawke, promised a Treaty of Reconciliation between white and Aboriginal Australians. But Coote was not the first to seize upon the figure of this nineteenth-century woman to represent present-day political and cultural concerns. Since 1947 a number of other famous white Australian artists have built up a fund of cultural capital in their imaginary reconstructions of Mrs Fraser. Their revisionings, like that of Coote but for different reasons, also excoriate the woman for her inadequacies in an attempt to cleanse 'us' of our collective guilt. Most notable among them, from the perspective of 'high' modernist art and culture, has been the 'Mrs Fraser' series of paintings by Sidney Nolan (1947–77) and the highly acclaimed 1976 novel *A Fringe of Leaves* by Patrick White. At the other end of the aesthetic spectrum there was the embarrassing (to the new guard intellectuals of the 1970s) but highly popular (among the mass theatre-going public) film spoof of British colonial authority created by Tim Burstall and David Williamson in their film *Eliza Fraser* (1976) the script of which was also released as a popular novel by Kenneth Cook. When Coote's version went on air in 1991 it took a new moral and ethical stance for the mythical Eliza. But it was no more 'true' than Nolan's evil seductress and betrayer, White's transcendental Everyman character or Burstall's *femme fatale* of the screen played by the lusciously beautiful Susannah York. It seems that in the 1950s, 1970s and 1990s the legendary Elizas have had an uncanny ability to tease out a number of guilty secrets about Australia and its sense (or lack) of identity.

The Australian adaptations of the story from Nolan's paintings to the novels and film of the 1970s retain the nineteenth-century preoccupation with the captivity and rescue of a white woman in an alien environment amongst members of an alien race. In these twentieth-century versions, however, her life is threatened more by sexual peril than by native savagery and cannibalism. Within the texts of the 1970s which might reflect a new phase in the Australian nationalist tradition (in its 'high' modernist as well as 'mass' populist variants) Mrs. Fraser is represented through the genre of romance, not as a victim of Empire but as the seducer and betrayer of her convict rescuer, David Bracefell. They focus variously on her salvation from 'a fate worse than death', the consequent romance between the 'lady' and the convict, and her final betrayal of his trust. These are elements of a larger narrative inscribed within Australian nationalism.

The 1970s renditions speak to a new audience of Australians, flushed by the victory of the Australian Labor Party under Gough Whitlam, who want to imagine a new, more independent, relationship with Great Britain. Bracefell comes to represent the Australian underdog, the little Aussie battler, and Mrs Fraser his hostile and haughty British nemesis.

The retellings of the story in the 1970s establish a Western and specifically Australian masculine authority for the narrative, one in which political and racial dimensions of the event are displaced through the figure of woman caught within a romantic fantasy, woman as spectacle.

Sidney Nolan's paintings

The importance of a modern reading of visual cues has been spurred by Sidney Nolan's stunning and provocative paintings in his 'Mrs. Fraser' series. Nolan took up the theme of Eliza Fraser in at least four different periods of his artistic career (1947–48, 1957–58, 1962–64, 1971–77), producing upwards of fifty paintings, thirty of which were exhibited in his retrospective exhibition at the Whitechapel Gallery in London in 1956. The exhibition, although not fully a 'retrospective', introduced him (and, through him, Australian art) to a European audience. Towards the end of his life Nolan related that the first series of paintings, in which he brought together Mrs. Fraser and the convict, was connected to his emotional state at the time of painting, a state which resulted from having been 'betrayed' by 'a bewitching, daemonic, and extraordinary woman'. The haunting 'Mrs. Fraser' painting (Figure 7.1), which depicts the naked woman in a bestial pose on all fours against the backdrop of the hostile bush as she is spied upon by her convict rescuer, belongs to this series. The next series of thirty sombre, melancholic and somewhat surreal paintings depicts Mrs. Fraser and Bracefell as lonely lovers in a rainforest landscape, a fallen Eden. The third series returns to the theme of Adam and Eve in a richly coloured, dreamlike paradise. One of the paintings from Nolan's third series, 'Mrs. Fraser and Convict' was painted at Nolan's instigation for the dust-jacket first edition Cape and Penguin editions of Patrick White's novel, *A Fringe of Leaves*. The fourth period in which Nolan took up the Eliza Fraser story occurred during the decade of the 1970s. At this time he reworked the materials in conjunction with the publication of a particularly vicious volume of poems, accompanied by rainforest colour plates and drawings, *Paradise Garden* (1971), and two series of paintings: 'Ern Malley' (1972) and the 'Baptism' (1977). These paintings recast themes from Nolan's earlier 'Mrs. Fraser' and 'Ned Kelly' paintings. Along with the poems they make specific reference to his unresolved relationship with the traitoress Sunday Reed dating back to 1947. Over time, Nolan confided, Mrs. Fraser became for him 'a byword for endurance strangely matched with treachery'.[2] It appears that Nolan had a preoccupation with the Eliza Fraser story from his earliest period as an artist in the 1940s until his death in 1992. Through Nolan, Mrs. Fraser as the English lady turned seductress and betrayer enters the Australian legend.

In a manner typical of expressive currents within modernist criticism, art critics refer to the 'Mrs. Fraser' series of paintings as figures grown from Nolan's personal life and the circumstances which led to his separation from his patrons John and Sunday Reed at Heide with whom he had lived in a *ménage à trois* for nearly a decade in the 1940s. Read in terms of the modern artist as a tortured genius, Nolan's evocation of Mrs. Fraser's betrayal of Bracefell parallels a betrayal in Nolan's own life. While living at Heide with the Reeds during the 1940s Nolan fell in love with Sunday Reed and hoped that she would leave her husband and marry him. When she refused Nolan was devastated. He escaped to Fraser Island where he heard the local legend of Mrs Fraser's captivity and rescue by David Bracefell, the escaped convict and legendary lover, and transformed it into a personal statement of his own lost love and woman's betrayal.

But there is more to this story – both in terms of Nolan's own life and his ability to transpose mythic elements from a Western, Christian legacy into a mythology of Australian nationhood. Nolan lived through the decade of the 1940s as a deserter from the army. During this phase of his life he also began the 'Ned Kelly' series of paintings and imagined himself, like Kelly, as an outlaw within Australian society. The ways in which Nolan positioned himself within self defined as well as culturally defined working-class and Irish/ethnic traditions within Australian culture, allowed him to slide easily into a mythologization of himself as a larrikin figure, an outlaw, identifying with the heroes of his paintings: the Irish larrikin outlaw Ned Kelly, the ill-fated explorer Robert O'Hara Burke, the Gallipoli soldier, and the convict David Bracefell. These paintings have had strong resonances for his appreciative audiences both within Australia and overseas. They contribute to his reputation for creating a specifically modernist and Australian myth of nation.

In addition, Mrs Fraser and Bracefell, as representatives of mythologized Australian history, represent an enduring but imagined political and aesthetic relationship between Australia and England. Here the Australian (white) native son, represented by Nolan through Bracefell, is the innocent party, naive and untainted by the 'civilized' ways and aesthetic traditions of Europe represented by Mrs Fraser. He struggles against her in an alien environment in order to wrest a separate identity from an English parent culture – which betrays him.

The fantasy of woman as traitor also has resonances with the Adam and Eve myth of Christianity – and the Edenic myth is one Nolan also borrowed for his series. That symbolic woman, who is ambivalently loved and loathed, has been intimately connected with Nolan's work, his fantasies of Mrs Fraser/Sunday Reed and by extension, the Australian landscape, and the mythology of Australia within a modernist tradition. The woman/land by whom he felt betrayed gave rise not only to his myth of Eliza Fraser as betrayer, but also to an enduring mythology of the feminine/landscape within an Australian imaginary. In Nolan's paintings can be found both the most sublime and the most debased representations of Australia and the specular body of woman.

In terms of modern art and art criticism, the ways in which the artist transforms the trials and traumas of his life are of interest because they become, through his creative and liberating role, exemplary models for the rest of society: his insights become our redemption; as prophet and seer, he speaks for us. This was, at least, the modernist context for Nolan's work although, more recently, postmodern critique has shattered this particular set of beliefs, revealing the politically grounded nature of its 'neutral' perspective and deconstructing its universal disguise.

The trials and traumas of Sidney Nolan (and those of the nation and the critics who speak on his behalf) transform a personal disappointment, a frustration, into an essential betrayal which is then projected on to the figure of woman. The manner in which the artist and his critics come to terms with this theme allows us to examine the male psyche as it connects to the wider discourses of psychoanalysis, Christianity and Australian nationhood. They provide insights into the ways fantasies concerning man's inadequacies are projected on to woman and become embedded in a national imaginary.

Patrick White's novel, *A Fringe of Leaves*

Patrick White's fascination with the Eliza Fraser story parallels the trajectory of his relationship with Sidney Nolan. The writer allowed the tale to germinate in his imagination for almost as long a time as Nolan painted the subject. White first met Nolan in Fort Lauderdale, Florida, in 1958, at a time when Nolan was finishing his second series of Mrs Fraser paintings and just after he had visited the Florida Everglades, an area he found surprisingly similar in appearance to the swamps of Fraser Island. Although White's heritage was as English and patrician as Nolan's was Irish and working class, this first meeting of the two Australian artists-in-exile sparked an enduring friendship. David Marr, Patrick White's biographer, reports that during this first intense meeting Nolan told White the story of the shipwreck of the *Stirling Castle* off the coast of Fraser Island.[3] The novel would not be finished for another seventeen years.

During this time White had been awarded the Nobel Prize for

Literature (1973), which was accepted in Stockholm by Sidney Nolan on his behalf. In awarding the prize the judges claimed that Patrick White had 'introduced a new continent to literature'.[4] In 1975 White was named 'Australian of the Year' (1975), an honour he detested. His reputation both in Australia and abroad had peaked. He had also maintained his abiding friendship with Sidney Nolan, which, however, came to an abrupt end with Cynthia Nolan's death a few weeks after the publication of *A Fringe of Leaves* (1976). Marr concludes that 'the patron of this friendship, from first meeting to final wreckage, was Eliza Fraser'.[5] Once again one is reminded that the mythical Eliza has many ghosts.

A Fringe of Leaves is not, nor does it purport to be, an historical reconstruction of the *Stirling Castle* episode, although critics often refer to parallels between the historical event and its fictional representation. White himself saw the novel as a reflection on his personal and the nation's collective identity. He writes in his autobiographical memoir, *Flaws in the Glass*, that critics 'sense in its images and narrative the reasons why we have become what we are'.[6] His examination of the past event provides an insight into what he and others in the 1970s perceived as a present dilemma. The novel, in its treatment of the relationship between England and colonial Australia, the convicts and their masters, and the gap between white and Aboriginal Australia, offers a critique of what White perceived to be the deep malaise of social, moral and spiritual emptiness in twentieth-century Australian society stemming from its English inheritance and the brutalities of the convict system. Ellen Roxburgh, as protagonist in the fictionalized Eliza Fraser role, bridges the gaps between nations, classes and races. Her perspective, or rather White's construction of her perspective, makes her a spokesperson for his existential vision and his cultural critique.

White's telling of the tale pits nature against civilization, the instinctual self against the social self, the woman, Mrs. Roxburgh's Aboriginal captors and her convict rescuer against a stultifying colonial white society, the bush against the city.[7] Ellen's quest becomes 'our' quest in the novel, one which takes her from an instinctual childhood in the mythical Cornish landscape of her youth; through a sterile marriage to Austin Roxburgh, a sickly, pompous, effete gentleman of the English middle class; to a journey with him to Van Dieman's Land to visit his brother, Garnet, an English settler with a shady past with whom she discovers her sexual awakening. Her guilty departure from Hobart is followed by a brief visit to Sydney before sailing for home to England with her husband. The voyage results in the shipwreck, and Ellen gives birth to a stillborn infant at sea, an event from which she recovers with great fortitude. She arrives on 'the fringe of Paradise', only to be enslaved by her Aboriginal captors on Fraser Island, who treat her with an indifference which she experiences as cruelty. The 'captivity' culminates in an act of cannibalism in which Ellen participates and which she views as sacramental, leading her back to the dark, instinctual side of her nature. It ends in the midst of wild and frenzied dancing at a corroboree, during which time Ellen Roxburgh is 'carried away' by Jack Chance, a runaway convict who had been transported to the colony for killing his mistress and who had escaped the penal settlement, preferring a life with the natives to its sadistic regime. He escorts her back to Moreton Bay, during which time the couple share a transformative, passionate sojourn in which they were 'equally exalted and equally condemned'.[8] Although she had promised fidelity to him, she leaves him on the edge of the settlement, crawling back to civilization with 'a knowledge of life beyond words' but troubled by self-disgust, fear and guilt at the greed, passion and sensuality found within the depths of her being. At the end of the novel Ellen meets a London merchant, Mr. Jervons, whom she is likely to marry and with whom she will ultimately return to 'an ordered universe'.[9]

The novel has been read as a critique of what White called 'the Great Australian Emptiness', the immense physical, psychic and cultural void which was his experience of Australia and Australians. He expands on this belief in his essay, 'The Prodigal Son'. Here, White reflects on his feelings in 1959 after his return to Australia from America (where he met Nolan) and Europe. He writes:

> Returning sentimentally to a country I had left in my youth, what had I really found? Was there anything to prevent me packing my bag and leaving ... like so many other artists? Bitterly I had to admit, no. In all directions stretched the Great Australian Emptiness, in which the mind is the least of possessions, in which the rich man is the important man, in which the schoolmaster and the journalist rule what intellectual roost there is, in which beautiful youths and girls stare at life though blind blue eyes, in which human teeth fall like autumn leaves, the buttocks of cars grow hourly glassier, food means steak and cake, muscles prevail, and the march of material ugliness does not raise a quiver from the average nerves. It was the exaltation of the 'average' that made me panic most, and in this frame of mind, in spite of myself, I began to conceive another novel.[10]

White wrote only two novels with historical antecedents, *Voss* and *A Fringe of Leaves*. In both he renders a complex, psychological study of the individual struggling against the constraints of a colonial Australian past which also reveal, for White, something of the present social, moral and spiritual malaise. In *A Fringe of Leaves* he turns a critical gaze on nineteenth-century English authority, morals and manners as they reflect the present imperfect Australian human community. Like

Nolan, he imagines Australia as a fallen garden, with Ellen Roxburgh and Jack Chance taking up their respective roles in the Adam and Eve myth as sinners seeking redemption. Within these terms, Ellen can be fashioned as an Australian heroine. She can also slide into a persona for the mythical Patrick White imagined as Australia's Prodigal Son, or as the outcast from an artificial society who leaves, is transformed by his experience and returns exalted as a prophet with a new vision. In the novel, Ellen, the outcast by circumstance, with Jack, the outcast by necessity, form a bond through their romance. Like Jack Chance, Ellen suffers intense privations in a harsh landscape through which she achieves some ultimate truth.

This rendition, like the other versions of the 1970s, mythologizes the woman and places her in service to a larger cause – be it Christianity, colonialism, patriarchy, Australian nationalism, modernist humanism or the prurient interests of a modern film-viewing public. The figure of the instinctual woman, tied to nature and a pre-social primitive existence, also represents primal fantasy for man, a yearning for cosmic oneness beyond cultural divisions, often conveyed through the figure of woman as man's access to the essential. Patrick White, like André Brink in his South African novel *An Instant in the Wind*, attempts to allow the woman to speak for both colonizers and colonized peoples, white 'barbarians' and their civilized convicts/slaves, locating a redemptive possibility for society as a whole through the woman's experiences and cultural transgressions. This vision gives her fictional existence a metaphorical power. But it may be at the expense of actual women – and indigenous peoples – whose existence is appropriated into his grand modernist vision.

White, like Sidney Nolan and André Brink, is positioned as the modern intellectual who has 'the redemptive task of caring for the nation's soul, and of saving the nation from the terrible nothingness taking over the world'.[11] White may have imagined Australia as a great emptiness, lacking spiritual, moral or aesthetic depth. But many Australians demur, seeing the country not as culture caught in a meaningless void, but rather as one full of diverse, contradictory and significant meanings. His is a story of cultural decay, the search for a lost soul of the nation. It keeps the problem of national identity on the agenda – but in terms of the search for one identity which denies internal contradictions as well as racial, class and gendered differences. The novel is yet another staging of the retarding story of fall and redemption in which women and Aboriginal people are implicated, their concerns appropriated, their identities absorbed into a new version of an old and increasingly vulnerable white man's mythology.

Eliza Fraser: the film

Tim Burstall and David Williamson's film version of the Eliza Fraser story, *Eliza Fraser (1976),* which screened during the same year that *A Fringe of Leaves* was published, departs radically from the high moral seriousness of a Nolan or a White. An appreciative public turned out to see the film in large numbers, but the critics hated it. It was this film, with its attendant media publicity and mass audience appeal, which had the power to supplant other knowledges and to largely become the public perception of the event.

The diversity of reactions provoked by the film at the time give evidence to what was becoming a more fluid, culturally diverse Australia. In general, reviewers were hostile, as is evidenced by the headlines for their reviews: 'Eliza Goes to Pieces', 'Eliza's on the Rocks', 'Eliza Hits a Reef', 'Eliza Do Little' and 'Eliza Purple' – the last heading a damning reference to Tim Burstall's embarrassing (to the emerging radical establishment) 'beds and buttocks', Ocker sex-romp film *Alvin Purple* (1973) and its popular sequels. Geraldine Pascall, a major film reviewer for *The Australian*, the nation's leading national newspaper, reviewed *Eliza Fraser* as a 'bland, unexciting, pointless, limp, tasteless, clichéd, banal and boring' production.[12] There was a scandal, which had less to do with reports of a romance between the director and the lead actress which were leaked to the Press at the time, than with the profligate spending of public funds on what was deemed to be a vile and vulgar dramatization.

Critics writing in the serious press raised questions of to what degree the film told the 'truth' – the truth of Australia's history as well as Mrs Fraser's 'true' story. In addition, film critics associated with the politics of the Left berated the film, its director and scriptwriter, mainly on aesthetic grounds. They were embarrassed by its 'unabashed celebration' of an Ocker way of life. Even the tabloids were scathing. The public, however, supported the film, making it one of the most popular of the year. These diverse reactions sparked further nationalist questions in relation to who can or will speak for 'Australia'. Given the advance publicity, critics expected to see a 'great' Australian film, one which would respectfully and seriously represent Australia's colonial past. Mass culture's pleasures, anxieties and desires – the more pervasive elements of this film event in terms of popular culture – were subjected to less critical analysis.

Burstall, it seems, understood his audiences. In response to the hostile criticism he told the press: 'They didn't want to see their history portrayed on screen as basically bullshit, even though they know it is really the case.'[13] Burstall's comment reminds us that history itself is an object of public scrutiny. Mass audience enjoyment of the film's irreverent approach to history may be, in part, a product of history's perceived inaccessibility; its pretences of respectability; its reputation, in some quarters at least, as being 'basically bullshit'. So, despite the dismay of some sections of the Australian public, the film raised important issues for Australia in the 1970s: of Australian national identity in opposition to a British heritage; of fears of sexual deviance (particularly male homosexuality and woman's sexual excess); and of a repressed history of white brutalities and atrocities rather than those ascribed to the Aborigines. It did so, however, in a way which parodied history, turned tragedy into comedy, and epic into adventure melodrama.

Despite the film's (ironic) full title, *The Faithful Narrative of the Capture, Sufferings and Miraculous Escape of Eliza Fraser*, this is not a film about Eliza Fraser but about a particular articulation of Australian nationalism. Like many other films produced in the early years of New Australian Cinema, *Eliza Fraser* measured an emergent national identity against an inglorious British past. The hero of this piece is the convict David Bracefell who, along with an enamoured Eliza, stands out against the British colonial administrators, his gaolers at Moreton Bay. Bracefell and Graham are introduced together as they enter the grey walls of the prison settlement, shackled in leg-irons, to await inspection by Foster Fyans, the sadistic Commandant. Fyans singles them out for 'special favours': a gratuitous flogging followed by onerous commissions in his service. Graham will act as an informant; Bracefell as a bedwarmer to the 'conscientious and exacting' head of command. In the early sequences of the film, then, the spectator's interest is aroused by the convicts' dilemma (sadistic, colonial rule), the possibility of mateship (a defence against authority) coupled with the spectre of homosexuality (here perhaps a projection of Ocker male insecurity on to Fyans, and by implication, the sodomizing British) which set the plot in motion. Bracefell, with a broad Aussie accent, acts the 'good mate', supporting Graham through his flogging ordeal and inviting the audience's approval for and identification with him as a larrikin hero. The churlish Graham, with his Cockney snarl, fails to reciprocate the comradely gesture. Atypically, in terms of the myth of Australian nationalism, the film offers a spoof of mateship. Its sympathies may be Australian, but they derive their comic effects with regard to a number of national insecurities: about political power, homosexuality, excessive female sexuality, race relations, class struggle and authoritarianism, to name a few.

Eliza (Susannah York) acts as a foil for the men and a delightful spectacle for the audience. She functions as an alluring object of sexual exchange. Always a spectacular body, a site of visual pleasure, she moves the plot along. Together with Bracefell, she foils the

Commandant – and contains the threat of homosexuality. Early in the piece we view her in the bedroom as she moves the audience through a typical comic romp of mistaken identities, managing to entertain, while at the same time keep hidden from each other, three amorous suitors and managing to unite four disparate men around herself: the brutal Commandant Foster Fyans, the boorish Captain Fraser, the exploitative ladies' man Rory McBryde and the innocent convict David Bracefell – who manages to gull them all.

All is not sweetness and light in this film. It has a dark side – one which involves the viewer in an encounter between shipwreck victims and an inhospitable bush, white and Aboriginal culture, and the murderous instincts of desperate white men. At times the comedy hovers close to critical social commentary, particularly in its satire on the sadism of the colonial administration and its subversion of dominant British colonial attitudes towards both the convicts and Aboriginal culture. The first encounters of the Frasers with their Aboriginal hosts calls attention to the latter theme. Captain Fraser responds to first contact with the natives with stereotypic fears of savagery; his fears stand in marked contrast to Mrs Fraser's bemused interest. Their encounters with a small band of cautious but curious islanders (announced by the Captain's words, 'Cannibals, I knew it!') provide comic relief. The islanders chatter, examine and disrobe their specimens, kicking the Captain up the bum for their irreverent amusement and his poor judgement of the situation. 'I'm a British sea-captain' he exclaims, 'I'm damned if I'll be ordered around by a savage!'

These comic scenes are juxtaposed against more sinister ones in which the mutinous seamen fight the hostile landscape, hunger and their own cannibalistic impulses. Their separate ordeal tests Captain Fyan's farewell warning to the Frasers: 'Nothing out there but hell swamps of heat, pestilence, reptiles and murderous savages.' They 'draw lots', taking action to reduce their number dramatically, thus enacting the macabre scene of white cannibalism which was suggested by Michael Alexander in his populist history, *Mrs Fraser on the Fatal Shore*.[14] Somewhat incongruously, these scenes are juxtaposed with the Captain and Mrs Fraser's encounters with 'the natives', as they are groomed for their respective roles at a corroboree.

Although the film neither romanticizes nor ridicules the Aborigines, it does present them as childlike creatures of the senses; that is, through enduring European perspectives of the Noble Savage, here put to comic effect. Viewers largely perceive the islanders through other European characters in the film. If they sometimes appear dignified, strong, assertive and humorous, at other times they are presented as primitive, menacing creatures of the senses, unable to rise above their momentary impulses and base desires. Through these contradictory representations, the film offers a critique of colonial attitudes and fears and also a re-enactment of them.

Both Eliza and Bracefell cheerfully adapt to traditional Aboriginal society, Eliza temperamentally and Bracefell through his acquisition of bush survival skills. The sympathetic identification of the pair with Aboriginal culture works in several directions. They provide for the audience a critique of colonial and racist stereotypes; at the same time their affiliation places women, the lower orders and the 'natives' together within a symbolic relationship of affinity – as Others. Thus the film both challenges and affirms categories of difference.

Overall, the film reinforces an assertive 1970s style of Ockerism. Although in a satiric mode, it adheres to the pattern of the heroic (white) Australian native son battling against the British and the bush. The English upper-class authorities are represented as sadistic, conniving and sexually aberrant; the naval merchants as boorish, exploitative and/or deceiving; the working class as violent, depraved and duplicitous. All, except for Bracefell and Eliza, are incompetent in Australia's harsh and testing environment. The film betrays history, but that was its intention. It also reifies myth.

As Kenneth Cook's novelistic version of the film asks, 'If you can't know the truth about history, what can you know the truth about?'[15] The film may be a send-up of history, but at the same time it repeats, albeit often with a sharp irony, many themes which structure Australian historiography: the relationships between Australia and England, convicts and their masters, the working class and middle class, Aborigines and Europeans, women and men. It challenges but also reinforces (white, male and middle-class) Australian mythologies of race, class and gender transplanted into the present. The representation of Eliza as a figure of sexual excess may signal a crisis in Australian nationalism. Our fascination with *her* enables us to disavow any guilty identification with the savagery, the cannibalism, the sadism, the authoritarianism, the fear of homosexuality and the exploitative race relations present in Australian cultural life, which the film, on another level, challenges.

Gillian Coote's *Island of Lies*

This brings us back to our starting point and the words of film-maker Gillian Coote that 'We are like Eliza'. Each of the versions of the Eliza Fraser saga presents us with projections, repressions or fears about national identity held by aspects of the dominant white culture. These fears shift over time and are expressed and received differently by different segments of the population. Coote's film of the 1990s gives evidence of significant changes in attitudes and beliefs about what it means to be an Australian which came about in the context of the 1988 Bicentennial and its aftermath.

The bicentennial year signalled a renegotiation of power relationships and notions of national identity between Aboriginal and non-Aboriginal Australians, signalled by the Prime Minister's promise to pursue a Treaty of Reconciliation with Aboriginal peoples, a promise which depends upon the efforts of the descendants of both settler and indigenous cultures to respond to each other ethically and morally, beyond the white Australian models of identity and difference. Another marker of significant change in race relations is the 1992 Mabo Native Land Title decision of the High Court, which overturned the doctrine of *terra nullius* which held that Australia had been empty, unowned and unoccupied prior to the arrival of the white colonizers. The decision has significance for a variety of reasons, not the least of which is that it acknowledges the validity of indigenous knowledges, oral traditions, kinship structures and ongoing relationships with the land.

The bicentennial year also prompted a new awareness of Australia's relationship to its northern neighbours. The Prime Minister insisted that Australia was geographically an Asian-Pacific nation and needed to identify culturally in these terms. From the outset it was clear that the motivations for a geopolitical redefinition were more economic than geographic or cultural. With the increasing economic dominance of Japan within the Australian Stock Exchange, the emergence of profitable new markets and trade links for Australia in South-East Asia, and the growing importance of Australia as a tourist destination for Asian travellers, Australia could no longer afford to maintain a 'Yellow Peril' mentality in relation to its northern neighbours. Business symposia, trade delegations, research collaboration, cultural exchanges and overseas student initiatives flourished, designed both to increase understanding and diminish irrational fears of 'Asia' within Australia and to presage a greater economic presence in the Asian-Pacific region.

Thus the fragile boundaries of identity were contested within both national and international arenas – and the mythical 'Eliza Fraser' story entered these circuits of meaning. She re-emerges in Coote's documentary film as a repository for white Australian guilt about its past relationship to black Australians. But the film also engages in an uneasy relationship with Australia's northern neighbours – the nation's newest 'Others'. These ways of presenting the Eliza Fraser story re-invent the categories of 'Aborigine' and 'Asian' in relation to white Australian culture. The most recent images are informed by, even as they transform, those of the past.

Coote frames the documentary with reference to the tradition of the Japanese Noh play, a model suggested to her by her friend Alan Marett, who had produced the Noh play 'Eliza' a year earlier and toured it in New South Wales and Japan. (The production itself was a sign of the closer economic and cultural ties between Australia and her northern neighbours which were being exhorted by the Prime Minister.) In *Island of Lies* Coote revisits Fraser Island, metaphorically positioning herself as the ghost of Mrs Fraser, and speaks with Aboriginal descendants and early white settlers to examine the 'lies' which underwrite a white history of settlement. The film-maker as traveller enters upon a quest for truth and transformation. Early in the film the narrator provides questions which will guide the traveller on her quest: 'Will she encounter the ghosts of [white Australian] history? What secrets lie buried in the land? Who has the courage to break the silence? And will we be liberated by these encounters?' As Coote travels up the New South Wales coast towards Fraser Island, she stops at three massacre sites and interviews descendants from both Aboriginal and white settler families about their knowledge of the past.

Coote employs a range of primary source materials used as 'natural evidence' to call forth a counter-memory of white settlement. These include visual and oral references to abandoned Aboriginal middens, hinges from fence posts used by settlers to trap Aborigines prior to slaughter, the remains of skeletal bones buried in places with names like Slaughterhouse Creek, documentary film and oral histories of abusive practices towards Aborigines from the mission stations, anthropological maps containing the names and locations of Aboriginal territories obliterated by white surveyors' maps and replaced by crass, commercial development.

Although the film unsettles notions of a unified (white) national identity, it also evokes some deep (and not always counter-hegemonic) emotional responses. The ways in which the film chastises the crass materialism of contemporary Australian culture and appropriates aspects of Aboriginal and Japanese culture to reconcile contemporary Australians to their violent frontier past deserve close analysis. As Coote drives north along the coastal road, the camera pans across a landscape which shows the signs of a 'progressive' history of white settlement – logging camps and lumber yards, electrical transmitters and power plants, as well as patches of farmland. After passing a McDonald's restaurant, Coote remarks that the land, no longer sacred, is now 'just another commodity available to the highest bidder'. Viewers are invited to ponder this remark as they watch a number of pointed visuals. The ancient land and its sacred origins have been overtaken by the debased remnants of modern capitalism.

Soon the spectre of new forms of Japanese economic exploitation of Australian resources replaces the previous marks of white settler greed and American enterprise and exploitation. These include billboard advertisements, storefront hoardings and real estate displays of prime land and expensive homes directed at Japanese tourists as well as pointed camera shots of pagoda-style, neon-lit, Chinese take-away shops and Asian film posters. At one point viewers are shown a directional map in Japanese which includes an arrow and the English phrase 'YOU ARE HERE' in the corner. Who is the YOU in these (un)familiar Australian settings? In another, a Japanese couple pass a real estate sign filled with Japanese writing with the English phrase 'We'll look after you' printed boldly at the bottom of the board. This is followed by a shot of a real estate display window featuring photographs of houses for sale in the price range of $200,000 to $700,000, with descriptions in Japanese, in case the Australian viewer wondered what was being promoted on the curb-side chalkboard.

At another point in the film, when Coote is interviewing Len Payne about the Myall Creek massacre of Aborigines by white settlers, the camera lingers on another site of Japanese terror. This time it is an imposing advertisement for a Charles Bronson film, *Kinjite*, meaning 'prohibited' or 'forbidden' in Japanese, and translated as 'Forbidden Subjects' in English. The poster features a dangerously alluring, orientalist representation of an Asian/Japanese nude woman lying prone across its lower border. Bronson stands above her, poised for action and clutching a revolver. Red Japanese writing appears beside the two figures and runs the length of the poster's right side, announcing the film's Japanese title. The oversized billboard film advertisement features on the side wall of an historical museum at Myall Creek to which Len had taken Gillian. The museum had refused to display the fence posts and hinges Len had found on his property, shameful artefacts of the white massacre of 1838. But its walls give evidence of other, less suppressed, external threats to national identity. While Coote interviews Len about the past, the camera frames the talking heads then pans back from close-up to mid-perspective to allow the bold red lettering of a sign to come into focus. The sign reads 'Now Open'. Does it refer to the museum – or the country? There are a number of 'forbidden subjects' which trouble this film. Some are well explored; others seem to do their work through visual cues which are best left unstated.

Island of Lies also includes 'authentic' first-person accounts by white and Aboriginal speakers. They are mainly those of an Aboriginal woman, Ethel Richards, and a white man, Rollo Petrie, both descendants of Fraser Island families. As the film progresses the two become emblems of a hope for a national reconciliation. Ethel and Rollo repeat to Coote their own memories and knowledge of oral histories of their regions which have been silenced by settlers' fears, the aftermath of a bloody history of white settlement. They stand in the place of the ghost of Eliza Fraser and the cultural destruction she/white settlement set in motion. The place of the Noh pilgrim priest is occupied by Coote the film-maker, who, like him, finds 'no starting place, no places of pilgrimage' to trace an Aboriginal pre-contact history behind the facade of a Captain Cook monument or the place name, referred to ironically as her point of departure: 'Kurnell: Birthplace of a Nation'. The white people whom she encounters during her travels represent the present-day emanations of ghosts, like Eliza Fraser, for whom 'the front of falsehoods fails'. The first-person accounts lend an aura of authenticity to the film which gives it its oppositional power.

These oral recollections provide the viewer with incontrovertible evidence of a shameful past. At the same time, the local informants are woven into the symbolic texture of the film so that they become constituted as figures in a Christian morality play, as seekers of enlightenment with reference to Noh traditions but also as black and white Australians united against a new, common menace of Asian, and specifically Japanese, foreigners. The film ends in a symbolic ceremony of reconciliation between Aboriginal and non-Aboriginal inhabitants. But this focus on national unity requires an Other to establish its identity. National identity cannot exist without difference. In the film the threat of difference (which threatens the boundaries of 'Australian' identity) is deflected on to the Japanese, the enemy of the nation in the form of foreign investment and tourism.

Conclusion

These various narratives have supplemented and come to stand in the place of the shipwreck of the *Stirling Castle* and Eliza Fraser's survival. The 'real' Eliza Fraser cannot be rescued from these narratives, although they attract their readers/viewers with their guises of history. Furthermore, history, or academic knowledge, cannot be separated from mass or popular knowledge. Both forms of knowledge circulate together and reinforce each other within different domains of cultural life. In these domains, 'Eliza Fraser' becomes a locus for new ideological representations of Australian nationalism. The 1970s versions, inflected by Sidney Nolan's paintings which made a legend of the Eliza Fraser story, reiterate several recurring themes: in each of them the interest is centred on Mrs. Fraser and not on the other survivors; in each her sexuality is central. The indigenous people provide an exotic context for a romance between the lost woman and her underdog rescuer-hero. In terms of the dynamics of fear/desire, each of the texts eroticizes the woman and fetishizes her body as a site of excess. Each turns the story into a romance which enables the legend to rescue the convict as the underdog anti-hero of Australian nationalism. The 1970s versions of the Eliza Fraser story also romanticize the 'primitive'; the Fraser Island Aboriginal people are demonized in some accounts and made mystical bearers of a new world order in others. All promote the continued circulation of ideas about otherness within white, Western and masculine, neo-colonial contexts.

Coote's film turns the story to political ends. It disrupts the codes of cultural meaning previously received and accepted and prepares the ground for a new version of Australian history, one which acknowledges the hidden history of Aboriginal genocide and cultural dislocation brought about by white settlement. In attempting a form of racial reconciliation for the nation, however, it links indigenous and non-indigenous Australians to a common culture of universal humankind; at the same time it manages to identify racial, class, ethnic and gendered differences which mark the internal and external, national and international boundaries of the nation. Here, Asia, and specifically Japan becomes the threatening Other at the border.

So Eliza Fraser lives on. But her stories tell us more about our own preoccupations with identity and difference than they could ever say about the woman whose historical trace has sustained a multitude of imaginings.

Notes

1 Much of the discussion is derived from my previously published book *In the Wake of First Contact: The Eliza Fraser Stories* (Cambridge: Cambridge University Press, 1995).

2 H. Brown, 'Nolan's Journey to Paradise', *Weekend Australian Magazine*, 21–22 October 1989, 24.

3 D. Marr, *Patrick White: A Life* (Milson's Point, NSW: Random House, 1991), 377–8.

4 Ibid., 541.

5 Ibid., 378.

6 P. White, *Flaws in the Glass* (London: Jonathan Cape, 1981), 104.

7 P. White, *A Fringe of Leaves* (Harmondsworth: Penguin, 1976).

8 Ibid., 279.

9 Ibid., 366.

10 P. White, 'The Prodigal Son', in *Patrick White Speaks* (Sydney: Primavera Press, 1989), quoted in Marr, 277.

11 A point made by A. Lattas, 'Primitivism', original paper, an abridged version of which appears as 'Primitivism, Nationalism and Individualism in Australian Popular Culture' in *Power, Knowledge and Aborigines*, eds B. Atwood and J. Arnold (Melbourne: La Trobe University Press, 1993), 51ff.

12 The adjectives are culled from the article and do not appear in this exact sequence. G. Pascall, 'Eliza's on the Rocks', *The Australian*, 18 December 1976. The newly formed Australian Film Commission had invested $250,000 in the film, money which was never recovered by box-office receipts.

13 T. O'Regan, 'Cinema Oz: The Ocker Films', in *The Australian Screen*, eds T. O'Regan and A. Moran. (Ringwood, Victoria: Penguin, 1989), 97.

14 M. Alexander, *Mrs Fraser on the Fatal Shore* (London: Michael Joseph, 1971).

15 K. Cook, *Eliza Fraser*. Based on the original screenplay by David Williamson (Melbourne: Sun Books, 1976), 1.

Chapter 7

Home ground and foreign territory: the works of Fiona Foley and Sidney Nolan

Jude Adams

In *The Art of Australia* first published in 1966, Robert Hughes confidently claimed that 'neither myth nor history is a vital part of Australian awareness yet' (Hughes, 1966, 250). Perhaps this was applicable to the period Hughes was writing about; however such a statement could hardly be supported today when contesting myths of nation, place and identity abound. Neither, of course, did the importance of history or myth elude artists such as Tom Roberts, Arthur Streeton and Sidney Nolan – artists who have all been credited with creating a 'national art'. Contemporary artists have also recognized the importance and power of myth and history, but their interest lies more with dismantling rather than commemorating myth.

Specific incidents in Australia's history have proven to be particularly susceptible to the mythologizing impetus. The experience of Gallipoli, tales of bushranging and the failed journeys of inland explorers, while having their origins in factual incidents, have since attained the status of myth or legend. Fiona Foley and Sidney Nolan are two artists whose work is linked by their interest in one such incident – the shipwreck of the *Stirling Castle* on Fraser Island and the ensuing legend of Eliza Fraser's survival.

Sidney Nolan's interest in the Eliza Fraser story spans a period of 30 years. Nolan, often considered to be Australia's most significant modern artist, developed the theme of Eliza Fraser during four different stages of his artistic career. Altogether he produced more than 50 paintings between 1947 and 1977 that related to the Eliza Fraser incident.

While the paintings vary in style and treatment, Nolan's interpretation of the story always remained the same: a narrative of treachery and betrayal. At one level, Eliza Fraser's betrayal of the convict Bracefell can be read as the betrayal by British imperialism of its colonial/convict son. On a more personal level, the story of Eliza Fraser and Bracefell can be read as an allegory for Nolan's relationship with his patron and lover Sunday Reed, and his belief that she betrayed him.

The Eliza Fraser theme has also been explored by Fiona Foley, a descendant of the Badtjala people of Fraser Island (Thoorgine). Foley has stated that all her work, whether it be her striking pastel and gouache interpretations of landscape or those which make more direct reference to the Eliza Fraser story, are in one way or another concerned with Fraser Island.

Fiona Foley attended European-based art schools and has worked regularly with Aboriginal communities. She has travelled widely as well as exhibiting both nationally and internationally. Foley was a founding member of Boomalli, an Aboriginal art co-operative in Sydney and has been actively engaged in promoting Aboriginal art. Her work, which deals with the issues of colonialism, personal language and the attachment to place, has received critical acclaim. Three exhibitions/ installations relate specifically to the Eliza Fraser episode and to the effects of colonization on the Badtjala people. They are 'By Land and Sea, I Leave Ephemeral Spirit' (1991), 'Lost Badtjala, Severed Hair' (1991) and 'Givid Woman and Mrs Fraser' (1992).

The work of both Sidney Nolan and Fiona Foley can be seen to inhabit structures of opposition. Foley's work is located within the discourse of post-colonialism/postmodernism, whereas Nolan's work is inextricably tied to modernism and neo-colonialism. His work is concerned with narrative and expression; its meaning universalized. In contrast, Foley's work is minimal, abstract and quotational. Nolan's own fantasies are projected on to an essentialized Australian landscape, while Foley's landscape is located and specific (all her work being in one way or another about Fraser Island); her story is political.

Nolan speaks from 'outside' the story, as author/narrator, framing the narrative in terms of his own identification with the 'betrayed' convict Bracefell: his is the controlling gaze. Foley can be seen to speak from 'inside' the story, from the position of the silenced, marginalized 'Other', the Aboriginal presence displaced by colonialism and the dominance of the Fraser/Bracefell narrative. Unlike Nolan, Foley does not need to borrow identification, for she has been directly affected by the *Stirling Castle* incident and by colonial dispossession, which, as Kay Schaffer notes *In The Wake of First Contact* (1995), 'stirs her memory, inflects on her life history and motivates her art practice' (Schaffer, 1995, 279).

The work of Sidney Nolan and Fiona Foley would thus appear to be defined by their differences rather than by any similarities. Certainly, if the usual criteria for categorizing and evaluating art – signature, style, period, creative intent, etc. – are employed, there appears to be little commonality beyond the tenuous link of theme. Yet if these works are positioned not as objects but as texts, we may find that beyond relations of opposition, Nolan's and Foley's work share correspondences and coincidences that, when read in relationship to one another, extend our understanding of the work of both artists.

To read a work as a text is to decode it as a language; to see meaning as made in the relationship between the reader and the text. Foley's and Nolan's works, if considered as discrete bounded objects of modernism, occupy different times and spaces. But in the field of intertextuality they inhabit the same space where 'codes, visual conventions, half-formed memories, dismembered remnants of previous images all collide' (Carter, 1990, 131). Within the traditional discourse of art history, the artist is the central figure whose biography provides the narrative structure, and whose signature confers authority, value and meaning. The artist hovers over the art object, endowing it with expression, creativity and originality. Hence this structure or system for categorizing and evaluating art impels us always to return to the artist and to artistic intent. In contrast, a textual reading of a work requires that the artist be no longer privileged as (sole) source of meaning and truth. Instead, the focus is on the artworks themselves – on examining the codes and conventions operating within a work, investigating relationships between works, and exploring encounters between art and its spectators.

In discussing the Eliza Fraser works of Nolan and Foley, my intention is therefore to place them within an intertextual field that draws on a variety of written and visual texts.[1] To read the works of the artists Sidney Nolan and Fiona Foley in conjunction with each other is not to deny difference or establish a false unity. The aim is not to 'read into', as if delving beneath the surface to extract some hitherto unknown 'truth' or essence, but rather to read across, in order to establish links of theme and meaning (a practice not generally endorsed by traditional art histories). Reading across is also to skim the surface like a map – tracking back and forth, drawing imaginary lines from one point to another – in order to see how new meanings might be generated by the 'reading together' of the work of Foley and Nolan.

This chapter will not attempt to summarize the story of the shipwreck of the *Stirling Castle* and Eliza Fraser's captivity, survival and eventual rescue; this has been undertaken elsewhere in this anthology. Likewise, it is assumed that the reader has some knowledge of the biographical details of Nolan's life, in particular the connection between his personal relationships and his interpretation of events. As such, this will be referred to but not explained.

I will begin by listing the elements I see as familiar to the work of both artists (including referring, where relevant, to works other than those specifically dealing with Eliza Fraser or Fraser Island). I will follow this by reading selected works in terms of 'sets of relationships' and will conclude by focusing on the representation of Eliza by both artists. For the sake of exposition, I will limit my discussion to specific examples, rather than attempting to refer to all of Nolan's or Foley's works that allude to Fraser Island or to the Eliza Fraser incident.

The elements that are common to the work of both artists include the following:

- the significance of landscape
- the representation of space and distance
- the horizontal division of the picture plane
- the use of the untutored or naive image
- the iconic use of the head/image (in the case of Nolan, Ned Kelly's armour head; similarly, Fiona Foley's use of Eliza Fraser's head).

Landscape as either (traditionally) an essentialized 'Australian' landscape or, as more recently, the landscape of a specific place is the dominant, all-pervasive theme in Australian art. Both Nolan and Foley have commented on the importance of landscape to their work but their different relationship to the land is suggested by the different way they represent it.

Landscape and place

For Nolan, although he stated that landscape 'was the most real aspect of life because of the smell and light and everything else' (Barber cited in Clark, 1987, 71) it is in fact secondary to his interest in narrativity, to finding stories to put *in front* of landscapes (Clark, 1988, 212).

> I feel the desire to paint the landscape ... *involves a wish to hear more of the stories* which take place within the landscape.
> (Nolan cited in Clark, 1987, 71; my emphasis)

Nolan's approach to the landscape perpetuates the drama of the individual and the land – man's 'heroic futile struggle' to make his mark on the vastness of the Australian landscape. This is seen in his explorer series and the Ned Kelly paintings where the landscape is presented as a benign, sometimes lyrical backdrop to the unfolding tragicomedy. (Nolan himself indicated his awareness of this 'staging of landscape' when he claimed that he wanted his panoramic summer landscapes 'to be as close as opera backdrops' (Lynn, 1985, 97.)

Alternatively, landscape is represented in Nolan's work as a sublime 'other' – empty, unknowable, ultimately fearful. Works such as the Central Australian landscapes (1949–50) present the land as the object of wonder and awe, 'immense, unique invested with meaning' (Morris, 1988, 139).

Both of Nolan's approaches (the landscape as backdrop and landscape as sublime) are common to the colonial way of seeing, with its emphasis on spectacle and a viewer-centred perspective.

In contrast, Foley's landscapes reject the view of the land as object of the gaze, instead representing the land as a space to be traversed, to be experienced, rather than to be gazed upon. For example, works such as *Moon Fish* (1988) and *Fresh Water Salt Water* (1992) show the tracking of movement and the marking of specific places, rather than the picturing of place. Foley's descriptions of her method of working indicate this sense of journeying or moving across a space. As the following quote, in regard to the series 'Men's Business' (1988) implies, the artist's approach is to emphasize the passage of time and movement:

> I was looking at the ceremony in the afternoon, at night and early dawn and it felt to me that the drawings had captured the whole evening without having to be representational ... but I could do it in an abstract way looking at the land from an aerial perspective, and capturing the evening, night and dawn.
>
> (Isaacs, 1990, 11)

Paul Carter, in his book *The Road to Botany Bay* (1987), has referred to the making and naming of place as creating a spatial history, a bringing into existence of a place by the act of representing it. Therefore, it would seem that Foley is engaged in a similar task – in an understanding of the land, not by seeing it or visualizing it, but by knowing it 'associatively'. This 'writing of the landscape' is also a way of constructing oneself as well as constructing place, and this is perhaps more clearly indicated in Foley's installations and her photograph *Native Blood* (1994), in which she aligns her own contemporary image with the Badtjalas' 'history of loss'; the loss of land, culture and ancestry (Foley, 1992, 15).

Thus Foley's view of landscape is not that of the outsider gazing at an elsewhere (Morris, 1988, 139) but rather that of the insider writing herself/her history. Foley does not present us with a 'recognizable' image of Fraser Island – there is no picture postcard view or expressive interpretation. Our desire to 'see', to know Fraser Island/Thoorgine is not acknowledged or satisfied. Instead we are given Foley's construction of place as a set of personal, communal and cultural symbols. Foley's work is thus concerned with creating 'memory places' rather than with producing traditional iconic representations of landscape as ordered and possessed panoramas.

Nolan's representation of landscape as backdrop or spectacle contributes to the mythologizing process (in that it seeks to essentialize a particular point of view) and fixes the position of the spectator (aligned with that of the artist). In contrast, Foley's work demands new ways of reading, requiring the viewer to enter into a relationship with the work, in order to construct meanings from the signs and symbols that refer to the history of Fraser Island and to the artist's relationship to place. Meanings in Foley's work therefore remain open and fluid. Schaffer suggests that Foley's work establishes a network of relationships that infer rather than fix meaning. For example, the rat trap, which is one of Foley's recurring motifs, can be read in a variety of ways:

> In one [work] it takes the ambiguous form of a black rectangle placed in the foreground of the painting on the sand. The black rectangle can be read as a stick of dynamite, a blackened votive candle, or even an iconic reference to other Australian artists' motifs: the black rectangle as an inverted reference to Nolan's Ned Kelly head or the dark rectangle in the paintings of Imants Tillers, in which it signifies an indeterminability of meaning.
>
> (Schaffer, 1995, 250)

This emphasis on the fluidity of meaning in Foley's work could be understood as positioning her unproblematically within the discourse of postmodernism. But to do so would be to deny cultural difference, for the concept of meaning, as multiple and dependent on relationship or context, is (also) part of traditional Aboriginal culture. Tim Johnson refers quite explicitly to the difficulty of 'tying down meaning' in Aboriginal art, in his catalogue essay 'Paying the Rent' for the exhibition 'Stories of Australian Art', held in London in 1988.

> For example, concentric circles in a painting could be sites in an overview of the landscape as in a map, but they could also be one site at different times in a narrative or different episodes hierarchically placed according to their meaning in the story.
>
> (Johnson, 1996, 227)

With the first series of the Eliza Fraser paintings, Nolan depicts Fraser Island as a sunny paradise. Simple expanses of blue and pale yellow echo the blue/gold of the Heidelberg School and the lyrical/banal backgrounds of Nolan's Ned Kelly series. Most of the images are devoid of human presence – instead they present a pristine wilderness which sets the scene for the ensuing story of Eliza Fraser's captivity, survival and betrayal of the convict Bracefell. Juxtaposing the two

Nolan paintings *Lake Wabby* (1947) and *Mrs Fraser* (1947) (Figure 7.1) demonstrates the function of landscape-as-background, no longer specific but universalized to stand for an Australian paradise. *Lake Wabby*, an empty expanse of pristine sand framed on each side by tropical scrub and bordered by blue sky and a strip of blue sea, constructs a place in the foreground which anticipates the spectacle of Mrs Fraser's entry, 'an image of humanity at its lowest ebb' into the space of the viewer's gaze (Clark, 1987, 91).

Nolan's second Eliza Fraser series presents a darker landscape of browns, blues and olive greens, interspersed with some images of bright, watery wildernesses. The magnificent but mysterious jungle vegetation harks back to the tropical forests of the nineteenth-century 'sublime'. Even the tiny figures of Bracefell and Eliza Fraser conform to the conventions of the genre which represent nature as awe-inspiring, and human existence as insignificant. No longer a picturesque backdrop, nature refuses to keep its distance and looms claustro-phobically close, revealing 'the protagonists as figures in a fairy tale, tiny like birds or butterflies caught in the branches of trees against an enveloping forest darkness' (MacInnes, 1961, 150).

Landscape, as object of the gaze, is displayed for the viewer's pleasure, like the body as object of desire. However, landscape as 'sublime' (in this instance languorous, steamy, fecund) evokes terror as well as desire. This swampy region where figures merge and emerge from their environment can be identified as belonging to the realm of 'the pre-oedipal imaginary mother of dyadic bliss and abjection' (Schaffer, 1995, 153). Similarly, in Schaffer's reference to Nolan's linking of woman/land/Aboriginality, her account of how these elements 'come together to signify both a mysterious/alluring and an alienating/fearful feminine realm beyond language' (Schaffer, 1995, 153), provides an apt description of the images of Eliza and Bracefell in the lyrical/monstrous rainforest.

Nolan's third series of the Eliza Fraser works sees a return to the sunnier images of the first series. The figures of Bracefell and Eliza Fraser are given more substantial human form but at the same time depicted as if they are part of the landscape – like sand-castle figures that blend into the colours of sand and sky. Landscape is no longer backdrop, nor awesome sublime; instead its function is to naturalize, to subsume the specificity of the Bracefell and Eliza Fraser story within the universal Christian myth of Eve's betrayal and the expulsion from the garden of Eden (Schaffer, 1995, 152). Nolan, in depicting the mythology of Eliza Fraser, inserts his own narrative (of woman as desirable, demonic and betrayer) into the story and Eliza becomes Eve in an Australian paradise lost. The function of the landscape is to reinforce the narrative of which Bracefell/Nolan/man is the centre. Thus in

Figure 7.1 Sidney Nolan (Australia 1917–1992) *Mrs Fraser* 1947. Ripolin enamel on hardboard 66.2 × 107cm (26 × 42 ^{1}/$_8$). Reproduced by permission, from the Collection of the Queensland Art Gallery, Brisbane. Purchased 1995 with a special allocation from the Queensland Government. Celebrating the Queensland Art Gallery's Centenary 1895–1995

Nolan's works, the role of landscape is that of 'lending support' to a particular interpretation of the story.

In contrast, Foley's landscape does not exist to serve the prior function of narrative, but is brought into existence by the 'space of movement [hers] and historical action' (Carter, 1989, 182). Foley's work, like much of Nolan's, signifies a sparseness; but instead of a preoccupation with the distance between the spectator and the object seen, Foley's work with its stark figuration connotes spiritual and emotional distance between people, beliefs and ideas. The juxtaposition of elements within the works establishes relations of distance or proximity, thereby directing particular readings. For example, in *Mrs Fraser Heads For Trouble III* (1990), the placing of Eliza's head near the rat trap suggests the following possible interpretations:

> When Foley allows Mrs Fraser's head to be caught in the trap, she registers a new and sinister reading of the story. ... The 'trap' can also be read, colloquially, as one's foul mouth, as in the cockney expression 'shut your trap', perhaps a reference to the story of Aboriginal captivity attributed to Mrs Fraser and reiterated repeatedly by white Australians.
>
> (Schaffer, 1995, 252–4)

Yet when Eliza's head is isolated, upside-down in the bottom corner of the visual field, it could indicate a sense of alienation, or more prosaically her distance from all that was familiar and known. Again, she can be seen as literally 'cut off' from others. In *Eliza Heads For Trouble I* (1990) (Figure 7.2) the diagonal linking of Eliza's head in the lower left-hand corner with the placement of the moon in the upper right-hand corner could imply that Eliza/white colonial woman had lost touch with a 'natural' or feminine self.[2]

In Foley's work, motifs, symbols and sometimes biomorphic forms are placed on plain coloured grounds.

> Organized around the horizon line which divides the surface into geometric landscape planes, [the works] have a stark abstraction which is balanced by an equally spartan figuration.
>
> (Saurin, 1991, 12)

The relationship of one sign or form to another is never made explicit. Yet given the importance of arrangement and planning to Aboriginal ceremonial life, and Foley's recognition of and respect for these traditions (Isaacs, 1990, 11), it is highly likely that the location of images in Foley's work is both considered and significant in terms of Aboriginal culture.

In Foley's work, the space of landscape, rather than framed or staged, is both map-like and flag-like. (The division of the rectangular horizontal field into two equal parts echoes the format of the

Figure 7.2   Fiona Foley *Eliza Heads For Trouble I* 1990. Oil on canvas 37 × 30cm (14½ × 120. Courtesy of the Roslyn Oxley9 Gallery, Sydney

Aboriginal flag.) As a map the land requires reading, not visualizing. Movement or journeying through the land is indicated by tracks or implied lines which link diagonally from one corner to the other, or from one motif/symbol to another, suggesting an itinerary of events. As a flag (sign of ownership and occupation), Foley's landscape evokes a Thoorgine that is both past and present, reminding the viewer that the effects of colonialism are ongoing.

Meaning is therefore made from the movement and events that take place within the landscape, not from what is staged in front of it. Foley comments, 'My drawings are event-orientated, it may be a place where I've been or something that has taken place' (Isaacs, 1989, 42).

Thus it is in this way that Foley's art refers to indigenous culture. Not in the sense that it pictures a traditional Aboriginal lifestyle, illustrates traditional stories, or repeats traditional designs, but in the way that it is based on movement within and across the landscape – on crossing the country, deciphering trails, tracking the moon's journey across the night sky (Isaacs, 1990, 11). Equally, the traditional activities of collecting and gathering are also fundamental to her work. Walking along the beaches of Fraser Island and collecting shells, bones and pieces of driftwood is part of her work process.

> Such walks are conducive to the gathering of myriad objects, each worn
> by its passage through the ocean, each endowed with its own narrative.
>   (Thomas, 1993)

The 'reading together' of works relies on the evocation of relations of similarity or difference between works. These relationships are brought into play by the reader/spectator, independent of authorial/artistic intent. There is, however, one work of Fiona Foley's that does seem to insist on a closer dialogue between the artists' works, and may perhaps indicate a deliberate strategy undertaken by Foley to refer to the work of Nolan.

Fraser Island Lost in Space (1990) (Figure 7.3) is a witty comment on the distanced perspectival view of the European-based tradition of landscape painting. Framed within two painterly rectangular blue frames is a bright blue and gold image of a beach/desert scene. *Lost in Space* (Lost in a world of Renaissance Perspective? Lost in European traditions? Lost in a space that was colonized?) calls attention to these landscape conventions, and more specifically to the dominant conventions of Australian landscape painting (established by Tom Roberts, Sidney Nolan, Fred Williams), by its ironic reference to the 'blue/gold' tradition of the Heidelberg School of nationalist art. Additionally the work seems to engage specifically with Nolan, by quoting his 'picture within a picture' strategy, whereby a representation of Ned Kelly within the landscape is included in the painting *Constable*

Fitzpatrick and Kate Kelly (1946). With this work, Nolan comes close to parodying himself with his 'Nolan inside a Nolan'. So is Foley playfully quoting herself – with a 'Foley' on the dark blue ground, reminiscent of her more abstract representations of landscape? There are further possible references to Nolan in this work, for the dark blue field could be a close-up view of the Ned Kelly helmet, and we could be looking at the landscape through the eye slit in the mask – as in fact occurs in a number of Nolan's Ned Kelly works.

In the exhibition 'By Land and Sea I Leave Ephemeral Spirit' (1991), Foley's inclusion of 'landscape vignettes' in some of her more abstract works can be read as a strategy to reference distance; to play with 'the suggestion of near and far, in terms of (a) landscape within a landscape' (Saurin, 1991, 12). Considered in these terms, the function of Foley's 'vignettes' is similar to that of Nolan's Ned Kelly mask, which has been interpreted as a device 'to emphasise distance but (also) draw the background forward' (Lynn, 1985, 9).

Spatial relations

As noted above, a sense of distance and the significance of spatial arrangements are characteristics of Foley's work. Likewise distance is also a feature of Nolan's work, particularly in his Ned Kelly and explorer series, and his outback and central Australia paintings. But distance in Nolan's works is used to enhance human activity, to provide a setting or a frame for human drama, rather than the representation of space or distance that is negotiated, or that provides its own drama.

Aerial perspective has been employed by both artists, but to different ends. For example, Nolan's view of the McDonald Ranges produces an endless timeless sameness, whereas Foley's use of aerial perspective, akin to traditional Western Desert painting, relies on signs and symbols to indicate the passage of time and the mapping of events. The latter approach suggests the view from *within* the landscape, not the framed, distanced view of the e(x)ternal spectator.

Both artists produce works that are characterized by a deceptive simplicity (given further emphasis by a sense of empty space or flatness) as well as a spatial symmetry. With Nolan's Ned Kelly works, such as *Ned Kelly* (1946) (Figure 7.4), *Bush Picnic* (1946) and *The Encounter* (1946), there is a simple horizontal division of the flat surface into blue sky/yellow earth. Flatness signifies modernity, while the blue/yellow planes can also be read as a reference to the blue/gold of the Heidelberg School. Foley's work also repeats both the division of her surfaces into flat geometric planes as well as the blue/gold theme, as in *Eliza Heads For Trouble I*. This work, however, is not a light, lyrical evocation of a sunny Heidelberg, but rather a thick, heavy rendering of yellow ochre

Figure 7.3   Fiona Foley *Fraser Island Lost in Space* 1990. Acrylic, pastel, oil crayon, aquarelle, ink and wax on paper 57 × 76.5 cm (22½ × 30). Courtesy of the Roslyn Oxley9 Gallery, Sydney.

and dark blue, intensified by the black figures that are overlaid or emerge from that space of the night sky. As quotation it is less ironic and playful than it is disturbing and confronting. Alternatively, the link with the Heidelberg School via Nolan can be read as indicating the hybridity of the post-colonial subject who can lay claim to both traditions, to the myth of nation as well as to Aboriginal culture.

The 'artless' image

Both Foley and Nolan draw on the 'naive' or untutored image in their work. Nolan's work relies on a simple or childlike treatment of the figure, combined with an emphasis on frontal composition. He readily acknowledged his interest in the tradition of unsophisticated imagery, particularly the influence of the French naive artist Henri (le douanier) Rousseau on his Ned Kelly paintings of 1946/1947.[3]

Foley's works are bold, minimalist and often compositionally 'crude'. Like Nolan's her figures or symbols are economical and simplified. Foley's iconic representation of Mrs Fraser is based on a drawing of her commissioned by John Curtis for his book *The Shipwreck of the Stirling Castle* (1838). Foley's 'copy' is artless, like a schoolgirl's sketch in an exercise book, yet as a symbol it is powerful in its starkness.

The iconic head

The aim of naive works is to seek an emotional rather than an intellectual engagement with the viewer, to privilege memory and narrativity over artifice and sophistication. Narrativity and memory are also important in the work of both Foley and Nolan. Nolan has acknowledged the impact of poring over firsthand accounts of the Kelly gang and of Ned Kelly's trial, and has stated that these reports reinforced his interest in this theme. The accounts of the trial 'faithfully reported the language of the day from the judicial to the vernacular' (Lynn, 1985, 8). Moreover, as Lynn notes, 'it was the immediacy and the vividness of these reports that moved Nolan' (Lynn, 1985, 8). An indication of the importance to Nolan of these texts is that he included passages from them to accompany individual paintings from his first Ned Kelly series.

Foley's desire to investigate her origins, reclaiming a history that has been lost, also involves a piecing together of information from a variety of sources including official, historical and familial accounts. Foley has commented upon the importance of oral histories to her own family and kinship structures, and in particular the influence of her great-uncle Wilf Reeves, who was an oral story-teller and whose stories and myths were recorded and published.

Figure 7.4 Sidney Nolan (Australia 1917–1992) *Ned Kelly* 1946. Enamel on composition board 90.4 × 121.2cm (35³/₄ × 47⁷/₈). Reproduced by permission of the National Gallery of Australia, Canberra. Gift of Sunday Reed 1977

Nolan also acknowledged the importance of oral traditions in his own family background. As a child, the young Nolan would listen to tales about Ned Kelly, told to him by his grandfather who had been a sergeant in the Victorian police force during the era of the Kelly gang.

Historical sources, in particular oral accounts, would therefore seem to be important to both artists. In the case of Nolan, drawing on historical records appears to have directly influenced his adoption of the naive approach, for as the following quote demonstrates, he believed that painting shared a closer relationship with the oral tradition than did writing.

> [W]hen you take an oral tradition and write it down there is always a degradation. When you take an old tradition and paint it there is less of a loss. Painting is simply a more immediate language than writing.
>
> (Lynn, 1985, 8)

We may therefore conclude that both artists recognized the power of the naive image to convey immediacy, emotion and authenticity and may well have considered it to be the visual equivalent of the personal narrative and/or oral traditions.[4]

Ned Kelly's helmet and Eliza Fraser's head both function somewhere between the iconic and the symbolic. Nolan's black square of modernity, with a post-box slit that is sometimes for eyes to peer through and sometimes for framing the landscape, is instantly recognizable as Ned Kelly. Equally the helmet functions as a sign of alienation, signifying the outsider or the anti-hero. The Ned Kelly head is also a device to reference distance in order to establish a contrast with the landscape, defining it as either idyllic or banal.

Foley's Eliza Fraser head is also more than just a recognizable sign. Detached from a body and from its surroundings, it also implies alienation and exists in an uneasy relationship with the other elements in the work.

The Ned Kelly head generally occupies the foreground or middle ground signifying action, whereas the Eliza Fraser head is placed seemingly randomly on a flat plane. Closer inspection however suggests that her location is neither random nor without meaning. In *Eliza Heads For Trouble I*, Eliza's head is placed awkwardly in the lower section of the pictorial field, positioned like an upside-down postage stamp, suggesting that contrary to popular opinion of the time, it was British sovereignty and 'European sensibility' – not the Antipodean world – that was inverted and out of kilter.

In *Eliza Heads For Trouble I* and *II* her head appears to tumble like a decapitated statue, but the action appears frozen, adding a touch of comedy or unreality to possibly macabre or disturbing implications.[5] A further element of comedy is provided by Foley's use of the vaudeville-like, generic title 'Eliza Heads For Trouble!' Does such whimsicality imply, that we should read Eliza Fraser humorously or as a figure of fun?

To mock or satirize figures of authority is to attempt to divest them of their power and status. Therefore depicting Mrs Fraser as a silly woman 'heading for trouble' is not to trivialize the tragic consequences of colonial rule for Aboriginal people, but rather could be seen as a strategy to disempower and to decentre the authoritive white version of the story, which casts Bracefell and Eliza Fraser as the main characters and dignifies Eliza Fraser's role by presenting her as either 'suffering victim' or 'betrayer'.

There is also a similarity of placement between Foley's Eliza Fraser head (as, for instance, in *Thoorgine Country III* and *Eliza Heads For Trouble I*) and Nolan's *Death of Captain Fraser* (1948). In the latter work the speared Captain is bent over in the right-hand bottom corner of the picture; the lightness of his face against dark clothing suggests a separation of head and body. The features of Captain Fraser's face, presented in profile, are also not dissimilar to those of Eliza's as represented in Foley's work.

In its apparent referencing of Nolan's work, Foley could be aligning Eliza Fraser, not with the drama of Bracefell and betrayal, but with her husband Captain Fraser and the project of colonization. It is, after all, a white European perspective that privileges the reading of the shipwreck and subsequent events as a story of love/rescue/betrayal. For the Aboriginal people of Thoorgine, the event is read from a radically different historical space; not as a story of individuals, or of survival and settlement, but rather a narrative of cultural dispossession.

Shifting the Eliza Fraser story to the margins clears a space for a reclaiming of Fraser Island by the Badtjala people, who emerge in *Eliza Heads For Trouble I* and *Eliza's Shipwreck* (1991) from the shadows or from the horizon line to occupy the centre space.

Common to all Nolan's depictions of Eliza Fraser is his representation of her as 'other'. In the first instance, otherness is signified by her status as not-human, as animal-like, as ghostly apparition and as a 'natural' rather than human presence. Second, otherness is indicated by her association with Aboriginality. Finally however, it is her nakedness, in contrast to the mainly clothed convict, that most insistently identifies her as other/body/woman. (Although Bracefell is also represented as naked, when depicted with Fraser his body is inscribed with the marks of his convict stripes, signifying his position within culture not nature.)

In contrast to Nolan's image, Fiona Foley's depiction of Eliza Fraser is Eliza as 'head' not body, 'clothed' not naked, and as 'a white woman' not WOMAN.

Eliza Fraser's head, like the head on a postage stamp, could be read as a signifier of British colonial rule (Head of State). Her head, neatly encased in its bonnet, could also signify Victorian propriety. She is clearly *not* represented as debased or dehumanized in the way Nolan represents her in his first image. All the same, she's 'heading for trouble'! For the Eliza head, a decapitated and inverted head, could imply that colonialism is being 'turned on its head' – that decorum is giving way to disorder. Positioning the head in the lower part of the picture plane, falling towards the corner or lying to one side, also suggests a spatial (and hence social) disordering and gives rise to many questions. (Is it that Eliza Fraser's presence remains ubiquitous, all-pervasive, stamped across the landscape, or is it that the British colonial presence was, and remains, an alienated and estranged presence in this land?)

The association of the Eliza head with rat traps 'registers a new and sinister reading of the story' and most certainly implicates Eliza Fraser in racial and colonial exploitation (Schaffer, 1995, 252). But most significantly, Foley's Eliza Fraser is not an expressive figure symbolizing the artist's feelings and ideas; instead she is a recycled image, a representation cut adrift from any notion of identification with the 'real'.

Nolan interprets Eliza Fraser through the lens of his own personal drama, identifying with the character of Bracefell and reworking the story in terms of his own narrative. This perspective is then framed within the larger story of the expulsion from the Garden of Eden; thus Eliza/Eve's betrayal is seen as an example of 'woman as man's betrayer'. Nolan sought to find stories that encapsulated an 'authentic Australian experience'. As a modernist, he saw myths as socially cohesive. Today myth does not get such a good press, for it is clear that it privileges one story, one way of telling it and one hero. Nolan's 'authentic Australian' narratives accommodate only one speaking position, that of the white male. All 'others' (women/black/non-Australian) are pushed to the margins; silenced, to be spoken for but not to speak.

Foley's interest in myth is to deconstruct it, to set meaning adrift rather than to fix it. There are no ready-made, received meanings we can take from Fiona Foley's works about Eliza Fraser/Fraser Island/Thoorgine, but there are questions we can ask. Foley does not speak for Eliza Fraser; we gain no knowledge of 'her' from the circulation of that bland countenance. Neither does she essentialize Eliza Fraser, but she does politicize her. Foley registers her as a sign, a marker, an event, an incident, a history. Thus the politics of representation prompts us to ask: Who positions Eliza Fraser as the central theme of this story of shipwreck, survival and dispossession? Who gains from its narration? Who is silenced by it? Whose story isn't told?

Notes

1 Griselda Pollock has referred to this as an 'archival' approach with its emphasis on complex interrelations between texts, images, events and individuals (Pollock, 1993, 39).

2 Foley has acknowledged 'elements of femaleness' in her work, such as references to fertility, 'to flowers, leaves in the shapes of hearts, sea pods, hair, fish, the moon and the sea' (Isaacs, 1990, 12).

3 Ned Kelly is Australia's most famous bushranger. He was hung in 1880 at the age of 25 and has since acquired the status of a folk hero. Ned Kelly attracted attention not only because of his exploits, but because he was perceived as a romantic rebel who had himself suffered injustice. Nolan identified closely with Kelly: Nolan's background was working-class Irish, as was Kelly's, he had family living in 'Kelly country' in north-eastern Victoria, and he considered himself to be, like Kelly, a rebel and an outsider.

Sidney Nolan produced his first Ned Kelly paintings in 1946/47 followed by a second series in 1954/55. This however, did not exhaust Nolan's interest in the theme, for Ned Kelly continued to figure regularly in Nolan's works until his death in 1992.

Perhaps, however, the most significant factor of the Ned Kelly paintings has been Nolan's transformation of Kelly's iron helmet – part of his home-made armour – into one of the most enduring and powerful icons of Australian art.

4 A recent reference by Foley to the artist Ian Abdullah could be interpreted as an acknowledgement of the link between oral history and the naive image in Aboriginal art. Ian Abdullah uses words and text to record his memories of growing up on the Murray River near Adelaide. His works combine the immediacy and emotional engagement of the naive artist with bold, simplified compositional elements. Foley indicates that his work, like hers, demonstrates the strong links that urban artists (or artists perceived by European standards as 'non-traditional') still have to their own country (Foley, 1991, 108).

5 There is a noticeable resemblance here to Nolan's strategy of 'frozen movement' as depicted in *The Death of Constable Scanlon* (1946), a 'comic gravity-defying figure' (Clark, 1988, 212) and in *The Slip* (1947). Nolan has also used a 'decapitated' head image in works such as *Gippsland Incident* (1945), *Soldier* (1964) and *Rimbaud* (1938/39). Furthermore, the placement of the figure/head within the picture plane predisposes it to particular readings. Nolan himself has indicated that in placing a figure on the margins of a work the intention was to mock silliness or pretension (Lynn, 1985, 44).

Chapter 8

No woman is an island: the Eliza Fraser variations

Jim Davidson

Legends come, and legends go. The Victorians, confronting the primal fear of shipwreck, placed the emphasis on rescue, and found heroines in both England and Australia to symbolize and project this particular concern. Initial English interest in Mrs Fraser centred on the terrors to which she had been exposed.

Serious Australian interest in the story was slow to develop, and could become possible only when a number of jointly shared British-imperial assumptions became questioned. With the exception of Sidney Nolan, whose pronounced interest in myth-making led him to the subject in 1947, it was to be another fourteen years before other Australian creative artists took up the subject.

Why has the story now become so important to us, after having lain dormant for so long? Like all myths, it contains primal elements which are capable of yielding a multiplicity of meanings: for a time the variant story of Mrs Fraser's rescue by the escaped convict Bracefell took flight, highlighting the element of betrayal – and indeed in this form was relocated in South Africa in André Brink's novel *An Instant in the Wind*.

But today other elements are of greater interest: it is less Mrs Fraser's rescue that is emphasized than her adaptation to the new land. While the Badtjala artist Fiona Foley rightly sees her as the precursor of white invasion, for whites she is increasingly becoming a symbol not only of adaptation to the ecology of this country but also to its indigenous culture. The story of Mrs Fraser can be recast as a reconciliation myth.

Further readings will continue – although, interestingly enough, a clear feminist one does not yet appear to have been given. Even so, the day may come when Mrs Fraser has less to say to us: new symbolic figures will arise to discharge new anxieties. The shipwrecked Victorian lady may come to be forgotten as surely as her contemporaries, the heroine-rescuers

* * *

One of the unlamented losses of the current period, eclipsed by the unassailable advantages of faster and greater mobility, is our sense of the sea as the locus of travel, of connectedness and of mystery. Yet all of these things were at the centre of consciousness in the imperial age – perhaps even earlier, if historians of tourism are to be believed, for it was the very wildness of the waves that first drew people to the littoral as a kind of instinctive protest against the tamed landscape of the Enlightenment.[1]

Whatever the case, control of the sea lanes was inseparable from maintaining a colonial empire. Thus it was that Britannia, about a century and a half after she came into common use as a symbol of Britain, took up position on the seashore. Indeed, on any seashore: the first coat of arms of the colony of South Australia depicted her landed, and then immediately accepting a spear handed over in all eagerness by a waiting Aborigine. More usually, as on the coinage of Victorian England, Britannia sat firmly with her shield and spear guarding added bales of produce, a nearing ship headed seemingly straight for them. A distant lighthouse on Britannia's other side would ensure that this would be done in safety. Imperialism required a smooth extraction; no shipwrecks. And so, after the initial pathos of such shipwrecks as did occur, survivors tended to be forgotten. Such disasters were the car accidents – the necessary risks – of their day.

Instead, Victorian lore immortalized the bravery of the daughter of a Northumberland lighthouse keeper, Grace Darling, and her colonial emulant Grace Bussell in Western Australia. Both were remembered in popular and in educated consciousness almost down to the last P&O regular passenger services. The way they had gone out to sea again and again to rescue floundering passengers was recalled with gratitude, and they were held up, like many people who become mythologized, as exemplary figures.[2] Implicitly, Grace Bussell was being celebrated as much as anything for the personal contribution she had been prepared to make to help sustain the lifeline of imperial communications.

The masculinist bias of Australian settlement – first through the convicts and again through the diggers – meant that, even within the context of societies shaped by patriarchal values, women would have a considerably more secondary role here than their sisters in North America, New Zealand or South Africa. The virtues which came to be elaborated in the Australian legend – toughness, laconic speech, resourcefulness, perhaps even egalitarianism – were decidedly male virtues; and although bush values could be transferred to women, the abiding recollection of Henry Lawson's short story 'The Drover's Wife' is of the woman's endurance, her capacity to put up with it all. Australian heroes then were going to be male heroes, as this accorded with the developmentalism very much in vogue until the 1960s.

Indeed, the Mrs Fraser figure nineteenth-century Australians were most aware of was one who had little basis in fact at all. Rather, her value was precisely that of being, perhaps, a chimera. In a number of places in Australia, as had happened in a similar fashion on the American frontier, there were persistent rumours of a white woman, the survivor of a shipwreck, being held captive by the blacks. The most famous case was that of the White Woman in Gippsland, the subject of a recent novel by Liam Davison.[3] A number of people, the first of them no less than the explorer and settler Angus Macmillan, claimed to have sighted her, and at least two major expeditions were sent out in the 1840s to rescue her. One went so far as to litter the bush with linen handkerchiefs, appealing to her in English and her imputedly native Gaelic; but there was no response. A contemporary estimated that at least 50 blacks were killed in the search. In the end nothing more tangible was located than the figurehead of a ship, around which Aborigines conducted corroborees. This was not, however, enough to end the story: the rumours continued.[4]

Why? Established dominance is relatively serene; British cemeteries in India fully partook of the as yet unenunciated doctrine that the graves they contained made those places 'forever England'. But dominance being asserted is as neurotic as dominance in decline: the Americans, it will be remembered, insisted on burying their Vietnam war dead at home. And then – in an appropriate parallel with the White Woman of Gippsland – there persisted the long pursuit of chimerical MIAs (soldiers missing in action), fuelled by rumours not so dissimilar. In nineteenth-century Australia, women and children represented the Achilles' heel of colonialism: hostages to fortune, to the success of the whole enterprise. The idealized woman of Victorian times presented the sharpest contrast to the so-called savagery colonial menfolk were intent on subduing. So the elusive White Woman was always presented as a captive (never as somebody rescued), subject to a fate worse than death – doubly inflaming to men who were themselves often far from the comfort of wives and girlfriends.

Hence the probability of such a woman being found was really a secondary element in the equation; she had most value as a will-o'-the-wisp, something desired but always elusive. Meanwhile, in the pursuit of her, the new land would become subdued. And if – just let us suppose – she really had existed, then eventually her fate could be borne with equanimity. Hers would then become the sacrifice of

Iphigenia at Aulis – the necessary price to be paid for the advancement of the whole enterprise, whether the return of the Greek fleet or the onrush of colonization.

The case of Eliza Fraser is somewhat different. She was not, like the White Woman of Gippsland, pure archetype; and the initial publication of her story was designed to confirm contemporary assumptions rather than seeking to modify or upset them. In this, as we know, she was a willing participant, even if much of the embroidery of the tale originated with her second husband, Captain Greene.[5] Eliza was perfectly happy to be pitied as a victim of circumstance, so long as she could cash in on it. And who could blame her?

The emphasis here, of course, was on her retrieval: the past-ness of the various ordeals she had undergone. Australia, or more correctly the yet unnamed Queensland, was simply the Fatal Shore: a dangerous exotic abstraction rather than a particular place. In a sense, then, she is enacting the other Iphigenia legend, Iphigenia in Tauris – the girl carried off by a goddess to the edge of the world, there to live with a kind of special status among barbarians, until rescued by agents of the imperial power. In both cases, the tale becomes in part a testament of the supremacy (if not the universality) of imperial values. Mrs Fraser's experiences on the Fatal Shore are an elaboration of the implications of their absence, and become a call for their effective imposition.

For a long time Mrs Fraser's return to England was seen to complete the narrative, particularly as Aboriginal people were, amongst other things, seen to exist without a history. While Australia was politically and imaginatively sited within the British Empire, there was no extra dynamic in the story to explore. Indeed, when Sidney Nolan became drawn to the subject on first going to Fraser Island in 1947, he was well in advance of historians and, generally speaking, writers. Interestingly, it was an Englishman, Michael Alexander, who wrote the first modern account, *Mrs Fraser on the Fatal Shore*, published in London in 1971; the relevant volume of the *Australian Dictionary of Biography*, published in 1966, passed her over. This was not because she was simply a shipwrecked sheila, a Girl Friday to Robinson Crusoe, but rather because the nationalist project at that time – before the 1967 referendum – had not yet embraced the need to comprehend Aboriginal culture. *Australian Civilization*,[6] as Peter Coleman's distinguished 1962 symposium was styled, was still innately Anglocentric: cultural cringe in the rawest form may not have been much in evidence, but it still persisted in the ideal of adventurous emulation. Intellectual Australia was still more concerned with realizing the possibilities inherent in being a New World variant of an Old World culture rather than setting up a free market of multiculturalism.

The 1960s nevertheless saw a boom in Australian history, and with it an increasing sense that the linearities of an imperial context left out much. Mrs Fraser began to draw some interest precisely because she was an aberration; soon creative possibilities were seen, and not only by White and Sculthorpe, in the fact that she had lived among the Aborigines for so long. The actual five-week period Eliza spent with Badtjala people seemed to expand, enlarged by the prism of its suggestive power.

While the *terra nullius* mentality was sovereign, any time Mrs Fraser spent in Aboriginal Queensland was itself in effect a nullity. The old equation was a very rigid one, with white woman and superiority (mocked by vulnerability) on the one hand, matched by 'primitive', temporarily ascendant blacks on the other. But once Aboriginal life began to be considered and scrutinized, with a new attempt made to understand some basic values and assumptions, the old certainties bound up in that equation began to be disturbed.

We can now accept, for example, that the arrival of these strangers presented a problem for the Aboriginal community. The sudden appearance of extra mouths to feed prompted their allocation to different members of the band; a good case can be made, not for 'slavery', but for Aboriginal hospitality.

Beyond that, it is worth noting that the presence of strangers has been problematic for all sorts of cultures. While Greek city-states sometimes chose a 'foreign' Greek to lead them, the inhabitants of Tauris (the present Crimea) habitually sacrificed anyone unfortunate enough to be shipwrecked on their shores. In India a middle road was sometimes taken: an eligible stranger might be called upon to deflower a bride, but he would then have to clear out, on pain of death.[7]

So the otherness of Mrs Fraser among the Aborigines need not, in itself, be perceived as the problem it always had been. Once their existence was first recognized and then viewed positively, the whole story became softer-edged. The Fraser stranger could then become a precursor, in effect engaging in a reconnoitre of what was, and remains, valuable on the other side.

Initially the story could be said to be a straight imperial one, of captivity and rescue; but since its rebirth in the mid-twentieth century, Eliza Fraser has been reconstituted around quite different elements. Captivity has been downplayed, as have her sufferings; instead, it is her capacity for survival that has been stressed, and increasingly her adaptation to a new human environment. Again, it is not simple rescue that became emphasized so much as her deliverance as she is conducted through the wilds by an escaped convict. One version of the story, as we shall see, makes much of the bargain struck between them: safe conduct in exchange for free pardon.

Patrick White's novel *A Fringe of Leaves* (1976) follows Michael Alexander's 1971 account quite closely in detail, but the tone is, of course, very different.[8] In one sense the novel is a little old-fashioned for the time it was written: Ellen Roxburgh – the Eliza Fraser figure – adapts to Aboriginal life, but the Aborigines themselves are notably undifferentiated – none of them is even named – while they are most remarkable for their chattering communality. The rainforest environment envelops them as much as it does Ellen. In all it is a distinctly greenie approach: an echo, perhaps, of White's boyhood rambles in the Blue Mountains of New South Wales.[9] The land dominates, even to there being no wildlife; White's interest in the Aborigines seems to be purely as exemplars, as people at home in this environment. If Ellen becomes like them it is purely in order to survive, not because she now perceives the world more from their point of view, or feels that she ought to. Indeed, Ellen's tasting of human flesh awakens her more to her own nature than it does to theirs.

An element built into the story, and a real mark of its mythologization, is the appearance of the convict figure, Bracefell (Jack Chance in White's novel). The official rescue expedition, from which the convict Graham made his final sortie to rescue Mrs Fraser, simply disappears. Bracefell has been built up because the story, to function better as a myth, needs a counterbalancing presence. He is not only a man to the woman Eliza, but an escaped convict, someone who chose the wilderness rather than someone of social standing who finds herself stranded in it. If they become lovers, if they trust each other, then the deliverance bargain has added force; the greater the betrayal then (and perhaps, too, its necessity) if Ellen turns her back on the Bracefell figure just as surely as Orpheus turned round to face Eurydice.

One of the more curious variants of the legend – and one most instructive about its parameters – is the novel *An Instant in the Wind* (published in Afrikaans in 1975, in English in 1976; see pp. 129-30 this volume) by the South African writer, André Brink. In an interview conducted in 1982, Brink told me that it was seeing the Nolan paintings in a Thames & Hudson book which first attracted him to the story.[10] Initially he thought of setting it not only in Africa but also in the present; the Eliza figure would be guided to civilization by a black terrorist after a plane crash in Angola.[11] But Brink soon moved away from this idea, for his purpose was to emphasize deliverance, and the bargain struck – for the bargain, the social contract in this novel written in apartheid South Africa, is not between free woman and escaped convict, but between black and white.

For all the difficulties inherent in a close relationship between a white woman and a black man in a racist society, Brink's purpose is to show that it is both possible and desirable, whatever the social difficulties and the outcome. Adam is betrayed, but that betrayal runs so strongly against the current of his relationship with Elisabeth, and his fatal compulsion to endorse it by having it recognized at the Cape, that one feels the deep injustice and total arbitrariness of such a social order. The bargain is a relatively slight element in *A Fringe of Leaves*; in the sadly named *An Instant in the Wind*[12] (a moment of reconciliation) it is of the essence.

Brink, incidentally, deliberately did not turn Eliza Fraser into an English-speaking 1820s settler, even though he knows a great deal about that considerable migration having lived for a long time in Grahamstown, the town closely associated with it. On the surface this would have provided a fair translation of the events following the wreck of the *Stirling Castle* in 1836. But the story would have lacked resonance, because since then the English have had difficulty indigenizing themselves in South Africa. For this reason, too, he chose to pass over the wreck of the *Grosvenor* in 1782, with the subsequent rumours of white females surviving to become the wives of Mpondo and Xhosa chieftains.[13] Instead, Brink chose to transfer the story to the Cape in the eighteenth century – the cradle of white South Africa, complete with a relatively empty hinterland to enable him to make his principal characters even more allegorical.

Eliza Fraser has thus leapt continents and across artforms. We have considered the conditions which have led to the retelling of the story, but why has it become important to us after lying dormant for so long? One answer perhaps lies in the way recent formulations of the legend have gone. Alan Marrett's piece of music theatre[14] de-emphasized deliverance altogether: this Eliza Fraser adopted Aboriginal ways, becoming at one with the people as well as the land. The forms of Noh drama were used, effectively echoing corroborees.

The fact that Eliza is a woman is significant on a number of levels. 'Men', as Marina Warner observes in *Monuments and Maidens*, are individual, 'they appear in command of their own characters and their own identity'. A monument centred on a man invites the question, Who is he? But Britannia, or the figure of Justice, or the various women who used to adorn the tops of insurance buildings, are simply seen in that one-dimensional form. Women, Warner continues, are not even always denoted by the allegorical representation of the female form: 'the female form does not refer to particular women, does not describe women as a group, and often does not even presume to evoke their natures'.[15] Had it been Captain Fraser who survived, rather than his wife, the particularities of the story would have remained more firmly in place – as they have with another (male) figure even more mythologized than Eliza, Ned Kelly. Indeed, 'white blackfellows' (as they have been dubbed in one popular account)[16] were usually able to find a place of influence in their adopted tribe – and by the end of the nineteenth-century contemporary folklore recognized this: an Irish-American adventurer on the island of Yap was dubbed 'His Majesty O'Keefe'.

Instead, the femaleness of Eliza gives her a *tabula rasa* quality, along the lines Warner suggests. But there is this difference: not being a monument, but instead someone who underwent a rare experience, the female nature of Eliza also now becomes a positive factor. Instead of the male heroic pioneering values, necessary in earlier stages of Australia's history, the Eliza of today proposes a second set more appropriate for an Australia in a later phase of its development. Instead of the old linear values, ultimately connected with a lifeline back to London, these are circular, or at least concentric, more female perhaps than male: adaptation (within parameters laid down by others), endurance, watching and waiting, intuiting, being prepared to meld with the land. These kinds of values are perhaps the key not only to coming to terms with the country, but also to coming to terms with the region. Prescient in her unpeeling, the twentieth-century Eliza becomes archetypal, someone we must follow.

For Aboriginal people, as Fiona Foley's paintings remind us, Eliza Fraser has most force as a precursor of invasion; but for the rest of us she functions as the embodiment of a reconciliation myth. After all, we cannot go back to Britain, despite Germaine Greer's urgings (though even Greer, apparently, has kept her Australian passport); rather, we have to make the best sense – humane, intelligent sense – of our collective life on this continent.

Here the Fraser myth as it is developing is important for three reasons. First, it involves acceptance of the land (together with a greater ease in it). As a corollary of that it encourages, second, an acceptance by whites of the Aboriginal people (and hopefully the reverse). These in turn entail not repatriation for us but reparation for them. In short, Australia is in need of a reconciliation myth as much as South Africa (more, now), and Eliza Fraser seems best placed to provide it.

Women take much of the cultural initiative today, and Eliza suits the spirit of the age. Certainly John Batman does not: a white Anglo male who shot Aborigines could not be honoured on the occasion of Victoria's sesquicentenary in 1984–85. And so, having been the centrepiece of the centenary poster in 1934,[17] he was now virtually passed over. Even William Buckley, the wild white man who lived with the Aborigines around Port Phillip for 30 years, is now less in people's consciousness than he was a generation ago – despite the radio play and verse novel of Barry Hill,[18] to say nothing of Buckley's own impressive survivalism. It seems that the male is too individualized, the centre of a story, his story, rather than becoming, as can a woman, the progenitor of a myth. Her relative lack of definition is more ripe with possibility.

Particularly, one would have thought, for a feminist reading: Eliza standing alone could be viewed as a useful symbol of women's strength and capacity for independence. Somewhat surprisingly there has been no notable statement along these lines to date.

Eliza Fraser is a long way now from the haughty upper-class Englishwoman she probably was, though her capacity to drink salt-water and her experience of the tropics thanks to a girlhood spent in Sri Lanka meant that she was somewhat physically exceptional[19] – or already the site of mythologization – right from the beginning. She has been through a number of metamorphoses since, and we may yet see more.

One clue here is provided by the way Liam Davison has dealt with the Gippsland variant in his novel *The White Woman*. Here, indeed, the fact that the woman appears to have been a chimera allows him considerable licence in retelling the story. His narrator, an old man, does actually see a woman. He is struck by her heavy-footedness, by the possibility that he might be looking on a man in drag, 'playing out some perverse role he'd imagined for himself to sate whatever urges the years of isolation had forged inside him'. But no, this is not so. Instead this 'almost stumbling' figure in a dress carrying a book turns out to be Aboriginal, 'hideously daubed with white paint'.[20] The 1990s absorption in gender bending and role-play thus finds expression in this text, and does so more easily than it might, say, in another contemporary text based on Mrs Fraser. The Gippsland White Woman, being chimerical, is not a *tabula rasa*; even better, she can be made to order. For this reason she, and figures like her, could end up displacing Eliza.

It is just possible that in another hundred years Mrs Fraser may fade away, from both public and educated consciousness, in much the same way as has happened to the two Graces, Darling and Bussell. Myths can be evanescent as well as protean: one need only think of the way a hotel in Melbourne, the Grace Darling, is now more commonly spoken of as the Grey Starling. The shift in the break between the two words is certainly humorous; but it is kept in place by the fact that practically no one now knows who Grace Darling was any more.

Notes

This chapter is essentially supplementary to my earlier account, 'Beyond the Fatal Shore: The Mythologisation of Mrs Fraser', *Meanjin* 49.3 (1990), 449–61. A more extended discussion of particular works appears there.

1 A. Corbin, *The Lure of the Sea* (London: Penguin, 1995), 60–2.

2 Grace Darling rescued four men and a woman from the wreck of the *Forfarshire* off the English coast in 1838; Grace Bussell rode into the sea with an Aboriginal stockman to rescue survivors from the *Georgette* in 1975.

3 L. Davison, *The White Woman* (St Lucia: University of Queensland Press, 1994).

4 D. Watson, *Caledonia Australis: Scottish Highlanders on the Frontier of Australia* (Sydney: Collins, 1984), 161–3, 172–6; see also K. Darian-Smith, 'The White Woman of Gippsland: A Frontier Myth', in *Captured Lives: Australian Captivity Narratives*, ed. K. Darian-Smith, R. Poignant and K. Schaffer (London: Sir Robert Menzies Centre for Australian Studies, 1993), 14–34.

5 K. Schaffer, *In the Wake of First Contact: The Eliza Fraser Stories* (Oakleigh: Cambridge University Press, 1995), 45.

6 P. Coleman, *Australian Civilization* (Melbourne: F.W. Cheshire, 1962).

7 E. Leed, *The Mind of the Traveler: From Gilgamesh to Global Tourism* (New York: Basic Books, 1991), 124.

8 P. White, *A Fringe of Leaves* (London: Jonathan Cape, 1976); M. Alexander, *Mrs Fraser on the Fatal Shore* (London: Michael Joseph, 1971).

9 P. White, *Flaws in the Glass* (London: Jonathan Cape, 1981), 16.

10 Probably K. Clark, C. MacInnes and B. Robertson, *Sidney Nolan* (London: Thames & Hudson, 1961).

11 J. Davidson, Interview with André Brink, *Overland* 94.5 (1984), 28.

12 A. Brink, *An Instant in the Wind* (London: Fontana, 1976).

13 M. van Wyk Smith, ' "What the waves were always saying": *Dombey and Son* and Textual Ripples on an African Shore', 28. I am grateful to Professor van Wyk Smith for making this manuscript available.

14 See Schaffer, 231–5.

15 M. Warner, *Monuments and Maidens* (London: Wiedenfeld & Nicolson, 1985), 12.

16 C. Barrett, *White Blackfellows* (Prahran: Hallcraft, 1948).

17 J. Arnold and J. Ross, *1934: A Year in the Life of Victoria* (Melbourne: State Library of Victoria, 1984), cover.

18 B. Hill, *Ghosting William Buckley* (Melbourne: Heinemann 1993). The author note to this verse novel mentions an unnamed radio play on the same subject.

19 Alexander, 18, 32.

20 Davison, 60–1.

Chapter 9

From Eliza to Elisabeth: André Brink's version of the Eliza Fraser story

Sue Kossew

Apart from the more recent interventions by female commentators and artists, such as Kay Schaffer with her anti-colonialist feminist rereading and Fiona Foley with her artistic Aboriginal rendering of the Eliza Fraser story,[1] this is very much a myth inscribed by masculinist and nationalist ideologies. These male-oriented accounts have two important common features, making the story not so much an enabling one (as A.J. Hassall describes it[2]) as a disabling one in terms of its representations of the woman and the indigenous other. The notable features in the masculinist accounts are: the white woman's fragility, weakness and purity in the face of the perceived heart of darkness, represented by the indigenous people; and the necessity for a white man to lead Mrs Fraser (or her avatars) back to her accustomed domestic role, from wilderness to civilization, a journey which is metonymic of the progressive nature of nation itself and of the legitimizing narrative of historical discourse.

South African novelist André Brink's version of this story, in his novel *An Instant in the Wind*, published in 1976, the same year as Patrick White's *A Fringe of Leaves*, transfers the originary event to eighteenth-century colonial South Africa. Brink uses the relationship between the colonial woman, Elisabeth Larsson (the Eliza Fraser figure) and a runaway 'coloured' slave, Adam Mantoor, to explore the colonial encounter, in particular that between white woman and black man. Adam's name itself suggests a link with the Adamastor myth, the 'white man's creation myth of Africa', which focuses on the black man/white woman relationship.[3] This relationship has represented the ultimate

'Thou shalt not' for apartheid South Africa with its emphasis on racial purity: the possibility of a sexual relationship between white woman and black man. By writing about such a relationship in the mid-1970s, as a dissident Afrikaner writing against this potent Afrikaner taboo, Brink was engaging in deliberate interrogation of the propaganda of revulsion disseminated by the South African Nationalist government as character-istic of any contact between white woman and black man. By setting the novel in the early days of the Cape Colony, Brink also demonstrates the failure of this potential relationship in 1970s South Africa with its legislated political, social and sexual apartheid. Thus the betrayal which is at the heart of the Eliza Fraser story, is, in Brink's novel, also a betrayal by the apartheid system of a potentiality for a positive interaction between settler woman and indigenous 'other'. By envisaging the possibility of a relationship of equality, albeit a temporary one, Brink is resisting one of the basic tenets of apartheid. At the same time, though, his text can be read as remaining caught within the masculinist discourse which figures the woman's body as the site of desire and transgression, and which could thus be read as providing another version of the white man's creation myth of nation.

Brink's South African version of the Eliza Fraser story differs from its Australian counterpart in significant ways: his Elisabeth is not captured but lost, to be rescued by a Hottentot male slave (not a white convict) who agrees to return her to the Cape (signifying not so much civilization as repressive colonial authority) from which he has had to escape, having been imprisoned on Robben Island[4] for defying his master. Thus *both* woman and indigenous other are metaphorically shipwrecked, which complicates the way the novel can be viewed as what Australian critic A.J. Hassall has described as a foundational myth for nation. Whereas in twentieth-century Australian versions of the story, the convict hero is figured as 'nation builder' by saving the white woman from the vicissitudes of the unknown and the Aboriginal people are written out or written off, as Kay Schaffer has pointed out,[5] Brink's version seeks to re-establish the possibilities in an apartheid South Africa for an idyllic relationship between settler woman and indigenous man, both of whom share, in their own ways, a kind of enslavement. Brink himself has explained his exploration of the relationship between a black man and a white woman, previously used by him in his novel *Looking on Darkness*, within the context of the eighteenth century as 'an attempt to probe the origins of the racial tensions of today'.[6] Thus the return of white woman and runaway 'black' slave to the Cape represents not so much a return to a haven of civilization, but rather the inevitable recapture of each of the escapees into their own particular kind of enslavement, one as a woman in a patriarchal society, the other to the death sentence as an escaped slave.

Each of them returns, as well, to the inevitability of their respective social and colonial roles – she as 'madam' and he as 'boy'. However, by figuring a different kind of relationship between these two that has been possible outside society's borders, in the great leveller of the wilderness, Brink is challenging the very strictures of these roles which developed from eighteenth-century slavery into twentieth-century apartheid. Yet this in itself can be viewed as problematic, as an 'opting out', in its romanticizing and historicizing of the relationship between white woman and black man.

Despite its convincing historical detail, Brink's novel is an historical fabrication, derived from Sidney Nolan's paintings of Mrs Fraser. Brink has described the derivative nature of the work in this way:

> I was fascinated by the story of her [Eliza Fraser's] shipwreck and her trek across the desert of Australia ... exactly the same story used by Patrick White in *A Fringe of Leaves*. And the interesting thing was that these two books – my *Instant in the Wind* and his *A Fringe of Leaves* – were published within the same week in London, although I have the perverse satisfaction that my Afrikaans edition came out a year before! When I first came across that story I thought I'd like to transpose it to South Africa today ... but because at that stage I had been reading so extensively in old Cape history for a completely different purpose, it occurred to me that there was such fascinating material in the narratives and the travelogues of the foreigners who visited the Cape in the eighteenth century especially, that it gave me a wonderful opportunity for using some of this material and transposing the Australian to the Cape of that time.[7]

History has a paradoxical function within Brink's text: it both determines personal fates and yet at the same time disempowers the personal by means of its supposedly objective discourse. The personal histories of each of the protagonists are emphasized at the beginning of the novel, so Adam Mantoor, the slave, is shown to be the descendant of a slave from Madagascar significantly named Afrika, who murdered his master and was executed in 1702; while Elisabeth is of Dutch Huguenot heritage, who, though born in the colony, is constantly told by her Dutch-born mother of its shortcomings and lack of civilization. So personal history could be seen as determining social and political roles. Yet the first section of the novel begins with the question, 'Who were they?' and outlines the 'documentary' evidence the narrator has 'found' concerning Elisabeth and Adam. Brink has commented that this transposition from Australian history to Cape colony was achieved 'with so much verisimilitude that many readers have tried to look up the documentation in the Cape Archives'.[8] To Brink's narrator, though, this documentary evidence is incomplete: it is the *re*creation of history that is important in an effort to understand the woman who wrote the 'Memoir' and 'Journals' referred to in the beginning, and to come to understand her words. As the narrator writes: 'But history as such is unimportant. What is important is that phrase, *This no one can take away from us.* ... Or those other words, *Such a long journey.*'[9] As the narrator goes on to say:

> It is to this end that the crust of history must be scraped off. Not simply to retell it but to utterly expose it and to set it in motion again. To travel through that long landscape and back, back to the high mountain above the town.... Back through that wild and empty land – *who are you? who am I?* – without knowing what to expect, when all the instruments have been destroyed by the wind and all the journals abandoned to the wind, when nothing else remains but to continue. It is not a question of imagination, but of faith.
>
> (p. 15)

The implication here is that the journey is one for writer and reader as well as for the two main characters, and the questions of identity ('who are you? who am I?') span the time divide between the historical account and the present. In other words, the travelling is not only a journey back in time to find out who these historical characters were and what they thought and felt but will somehow, at the same time, provide a key to the present identity crisis faced by the writer and reader (presumably representatives of present-day South Africans) who are also implicated in the 'you' and 'I' of the questions. The fact that it requires more faith than imagination raises the question, 'Whose faith?' Is it that of the reader who must accept the narrator's version of history or is it the faith of his two main characters? 'When nothing else remains but to continue' could be a description of Elisabeth's and Adam's journey, or the reading process itself, or the thrust of history. The wind in the extract quoted above (and throughout the novel, as the title suggests) seems to take on a metaphorical quality (the winds of time?) by destroying or blowing away the props of civilization or the ways history has been 'measured', leaving only the essentials behind in the form of the account which follows. Reading itself thus becomes an act of faith, not only in terms of accepting Brink's account but also in abandoning previous judgements ('without knowing what to expect').

Brink's text signals the close connection between language and the colonizing process. It is interesting to note that *An Instant in the Wind*, written just after *Looking on Darkness* which Brink was forced (by the banning of the Afrikaans version) to 'change' into English, was written in both English and Afrikaans simultaneously. Brink has written of this process of composition:

> Since the novel deals, essentially, with two modes of experiencing Africa (expressed in terms of a journey undertaken, in 1750, by a white woman and a black man from the wilderness of the Cape hinterland back to civilization), it was interesting to see how far the planning of the book could be influenced by thinking in English when dealing with the white character and in Afrikaans when imagining the black slave ... It was remarkable to see to what extent the two languages spontaneously associated themselves with the two spheres of experience represented by the main characters.[10]

The irony of this is, of course, that although Afrikaans is the language used by 'Cape Coloureds', it is still perceived by many blacks as the language of the oppressor. There is a great deal of unintended irony in Brink's linking of Adam and the Afrikaner in this way, reinforced by his somewhat puzzling statement that 'he [Adam] is the Afrikaner after all'.[11] This passage also reveals something of Brink's perspectives in the novel: the way he uses the terms 'wilderness' and 'civilization' seems here to be without irony, and yet he does explore, in the novel, the shifting meanings of these two terms by emphasizing the skills in living that Adam, the slave, has in the 'wilderness' and the slavery that 'civilization' enforces on women.

The role reversal situation is also incorporated into the narrative, so that not only are the boundaries between mistress and slave overcome within their sexual relationship but the idea of knowledge is reversed too, so that the illiterate Adam Mantoor becomes the one who can 'read' the landscape and Elisabeth Larsson, for all her 'civilized' knowledge, is helpless. This ironic reversal of power is signalled from the beginning of their encounter with Elisabeth described as 'surrounded by the remains of her trek, the relics representing in this wilderness the achievements of her civilisation' (p. 17). The list of items which follows ends with a description of a map, useless as she is lost, on which some details have been inscribed in a 'narrow patch ... surrounded by white emptiness containing only a few tentative lines and dots, open and exposed, *terra incognita*, great and wide' (p. 17). That this unknown territory refers not just to the land itself but also to Elisabeth's own inner psyche is reinforced in her later connections between exploration and self: towards the end of the novel she refers to 'this incalculable thing – my self, this secret unexplored interior' (p. 249).

The map, symbol of European knowledge, control and ownership, is shown to be increasingly pointless. Elisabeth's husband, Erik Larsson, whom she has accompanied on this journey, is an explorer who is seeking to draw his own map of the interior, confidently cataloguing and naming species of plants and animals, and details of the landscape so that 'something of this vast continent ... will be my own' (p. 41). Larsson, however, gets lost and dies while in search of an uncatalogued bird, leaving only his incomplete map behind. It is Adam, the black slave, who is able to read the landscape itself and who senses the route they must take. The meaninglessness of the map is reinforced by Adam who asks Elisabeth, 'You think it makes any difference to the land out there?' She, however, still clings to this remnant of European control over the landscape, and is upset when the map she has so fiercely guarded is used by the Hottentots, the indigenous tribe who nurse her through her miscarriage, to make a fire. This more practical use for the map points up its acquired, rather than its inherent, power.

Both Larsson and Elisabeth are, in their own ways, forced to draw their own map.[12] In this way, the journey is used as a metaphor for both physical and spiritual exploration and the landscape takes on metaphorical significance, reflecting the wilderness of the unmapped interiors of self. When Elisabeth and Larsson are in the early stages of their marriage, for example, she asks him, 'Don't you think people are like landscapes too to be explored?' (p. 38) and silently begs: 'Here I am, explore me. Don't you see I am a prisoner here? [in the Cape]' (p. 40). The prison image is an important one, linking, as it does, Elisabeth's sense of enslavement in her role as a woman amidst the restrictions of Cape society with the slavery of Adam, who asserts, 'I was kept as a slave. I never *was* a slave' (p. 55). Elisabeth has long felt this kinship with the underdog. She says to her father: 'You think a slave is nothing but a woman!' and the narrator adds, 'Thinking: and a woman no more than a slave' (p. 26). Later, Elisabeth says of the woman's lot within the strictures of Cape society: 'Never to be able to do what you really want, because you're a woman; never to be allowed to become what you desire, because you're a woman. Like those dwarf-trees imported by the Governor' (p. 65). Like Adam, who has escaped from imprisonment on Robben Island, she refuses to be imprisoned by her status as a slave/woman – 'What is there in me which refuses to be possessed by another?' (p. 65) – and it is in the 'wilderness without end' where she is 'alone' that she can, with Adam, find her 'true' self away from the pressures of society's imposed marginality. Like the bush in Australian mythology, the wild interior of the Cape Province represents a space which is as yet uncolonized and which therefore offers a kind of freedom, however transitory, to escapees. It is interesting that it is in relation to this uncharted space that Brink mobilizes the shipwreck image of the Eliza Fraser story. To Larsson, this lack of control is threatening: 'The whole interior is like a sea of wind on which we toss and drift unsteadily' (p. 14). But the shipwreck image is also figured not so much as a loss of direction, but as a way of escaping the directedness imposed on the two protagonists by society. As Adam reflects when they draw nearer to civilization: 'One may drift timeless through the days, abandoned like seaweed to the tide, but in the end you're washed ashore' (p. 134).

In fact, Brink figures the wilderness not as a place bereft of civilized values, but a place where 'true' values can be rediscovered, as an Eden. As in the biblical Eden, the issue of clothing and shame becomes a metaphor for innocence and experience, though in this case in reverse, as both start off clothed.[13] Clothes become a recurring symbol not of 'civilized' European values but of imposed social attitudes, with Adam initially trying to look 'civilized', like a 'master' by wearing Larsson's clothes and then re-establishing his 'true' indigenous identity by stripping them off; with Elisabeth at first similarly covering her nakedness and then discovering the freedom of nudity, only to regain her sense of shame when contact with other people is imminent. In an obvious allusion to Eden, the narrator reports their responses when they both don clothes again in preparation for encountering other Europeans: 'The clothes had an effect of estrangement on them. They felt ashamed to look at each other, as if they had just discovered that they were naked' (p. 240). It is the clothing which masks their inner selves, emphasizing difference rather than commonality. Elisabeth compares the effect of clothing on her identity with that of the decay of flesh in the wilderness: 'A skeleton is what one should be allowed to be, clean and bare, bones. Discovering it in the veld you can't even tell whether it was man or woman. It's pure bone-being; human thing' (p. 66). The veld acts as a leveller beyond the petty divisions imposed by society, causing Elisabeth to rethink the system she has always accepted and to try to work out the relationship between mistress and slave in this new environment, as she asks Adam: 'What is place? Have you any place – or do you come and go like the wind?' (p. 66). This image ironically reverses their situations, so that, in the interior, it is Adam who is free as the wind and it is Elisabeth who is 'obeying like a dog, forced back into womanness' (p. 66). That this place might hold the key for her own freedom, though, is asserted by Elisabeth earlier: 'But this once I refuse to obey them, I shall break free. This once I'll trek into my own wilderness' (p. 65).

The 'two modes of experiencing Africa' (that is, settler versus indigenous) are expressed linguistically, too, by means of naming. The colonizer's arrogant imposition of names on to the landscape as well as on to the indigenous people is highlighted in the character of Larsson the explorer, Elisabeth's husband. His obsessive naming of species ('trees she doesn't know, shrubs she doesn't know, named by Erik Alexis Larsson, Latin names, meaningless to her ears' (p. 19)) is in contrast to the indigenous people's response, which is beyond naming. This is shown when Elisabeth asks Adam where he comes from and he merely gestures to the 'dusky world behind him'. Elisabeth at least, lacking Larsson's arrogant Eurocentrism, realizes her inability to find the words to inscribe the landscape (as J.M. Coetzee expresses it, 'a language ... in which to win it, speak it, represent it').[14] This is summed up in her response to Adam's gesture:

> How apt that you should merely motion, saying nothing: for this land has not yet been given a name, certainly not a Latin one; it does not yet exist. And it's yours, all right, you may have it. But what am I doing here? I must have come in search of something.
>
> (p. 20)

The notion of naming in relation to Adam himself becomes an important issue in the text, as he wishes Elisabeth to call him Aob, his Hottentot name, rather than the Europeanized Adam (which both incorporates him into the centre and functions metaphorically as expressing the pre-lapsarian, pre-colonial paradise momentarily established by Adam and Elisabeth).

The link between naming and the colonial process makes this an important issue in the text. Elisabeth herself unwittingly echoes the language of her explorer husband when she asserts to Adam that she is 'probably the first person ever to come here ... I'm making history!' (p. 84). Adam replies:

> 'You think you're taking history with you wherever you go ... I suppose history, to you, is what happens to the people of the Cape. ... But don't you think history can happen here, too, without you?'
>
> (p. 84)

Neither Adam nor Elisabeth, though, is able to escape from history nor from the roles within the colonial equation that history has imposed on them. The theme of betrayal is one that is common to the Australian versions and to this version, though Brink's emphasis is somewhat different. Whereas the Australian versions emphasize the woman's betrayal of the convict's trust (or, as Kay Schaffer points out, its opposite – the unrecorded but likely betrayal of Mrs Fraser by Bracefell's rape of her when they are within striking distance of 'civilization'[15]), the betrayal at the end of this novel is of *both* the woman and the slave. Betrayal has been foreshadowed from the beginning of the text, as the reader is told of the outcome before reading the events leading up to it. But there are many kinds of betrayal in the text: Adam is betrayed by Lewies, his white Afrikaner childhood friend (p. 29); Adam betrays the animals they befriend in the wilderness by killing them for food, for survival; and Elisabeth characterizes love itself as inevitably 'the beginning of violence and betrayal. Something in oneself or the other is killed or betrayed' (p. 101). It is significant that at the end of the novel, as Adam is imagined awaiting his fate, Elisabeth recalls his betrayal of these animals, concluding, 'One has to learn to live with betrayal' (p. 250). Once again the inevitability is stressed as Adam realizes that she will not return to him – 'He would not even consider an alternative any longer: it had been given from the beginning' (p. 250). But the personal betrayal is shown to be dependent on the wider political betrayals represented by the Cape itself. As the two draw nearer to the Cape, Adam doubts its meaning as 'home', asking 'Which Cape are we going to? ... Our Capes are different. Surely you know that' (p. 230). While Elisabeth is confident she will be able to arrange a pardon for Adam, he doubts that the Cape will accommodate a relationship between a white woman and a black man. As he says to Elisabeth: 'They'll never forgive you. ... If their white women start doing this sort of thing: it undermines everything in which they've got to believe if they want to remain the masters in the land' (p. 231). Yet neither of them has any choice but to return. Interestingly, Adam figures his return to civilization in the imagery of the shipwreck: 'Bred for the land – but banished from it. But I was washed ashore again like a piece of driftwood: I've come back' (p. 148).

The ending of the novel confirms Adam's fear of betrayal, as he waits for his fate, unstated at this point in the novel but previously outlined in the 'historical' records of the beginning when it coldly states: 'Finally, in March 1751, he was flogged (three rixdollars) and strangled (six rixdollars)' (p. 10), the money being the bonus paid to the men who administered punishment. By rereading this beginning, and contrasting its tone with that of the emotional ending, the narrator's aim of understanding the motivation behind the characters' words is apparently realized and the 'crust of history' which hides the real feelings and responses of those involved has indeed been 'scraped off'. Adam's words at the end of the novel – 'The land which happened inside us no one can take from us again, not even ourselves. But God, such a long journey ahead for you and me. Not a question of imagination, but of faith' (p. 250) – replicate those of Elisabeth in the final sentence of her 'Memoir' referred to at the beginning, '*This no one can take away from us, not even ourselves*' (p. 12) and the final entry in her journal: '*Such a long journey ahead for you and me. Oh God, oh God*' (p. 14). Significantly, Brink's book is dedicated to Breyten Breytenbach, the exiled *Sestiger* poet, and the message for him, too, is 'such a long journey ahead for you and me'. The past and present, the white woman and the black man, the dissident author in exile and the dissident author within South Africa are thus all linked in this journey image, the journey, which has not yet ended, through the 'landscape of truth' (p. 194).

The image of journeying and mapmaking is a central one for Brink which encapsulates for him the very nature of writing itself in a repressive society and provides an important insight into the way he sees his text as functioning. Significantly, his collection of critical essays is entitled *Mapmakers* and, in the essay of that name written in 1978, he quotes from the journal of a Danish explorer who seems to be the model for the cartographer Roloff in *An Instant in the Wind*, as he, like Roloff, was threatened with imprisonment by the Dutch East India Company, who governed the Cape, if he published his maps of the interior. He, however, continued to draw these maps in secret. Brink comments:

> The parallel is startlingly obvious. The strange territory explored and mapped for the first time; the assiduous cartographer offering his map to the world and threatened, to his dismay, with thirty years in chains should he disclose it; and the long lonely years afterwards, during which he continues to draw and redraw his map, refining it all the time in order to correspond more and more closely to the land he has explored. Here is the writer slaving away in his ceaseless attempt to draw the map of his vision of truth, risking his liberty in order to offer to the world a view of itself. And, opposing him, is a government prepared to go to any extremes in order to keep the truth locked away ... It would seem that the most he can hope for is the discovery of his map by someone else, some time in the distant future, possibly after his own death.[16]

This is a summary of Brink's own writerly credo, expressed metaphorically through the themes and method of *An Instant in the Wind*: the writer as truth-teller whatever the consequences of leading the reader through the 'landscape of truth' and redrawing the colonial 'map' of history in order to offer a closer representation of the landscape of the present, to offer 'to the world a view of itself'.

However, there are a number of problems with this romantic view of the writer's role. Ironically, the mapmaker image encapsulates both the positive image of the writer exploring new and uncharted territories of the human psyche, but also the more negative one, which the text itself has implied, of the colonizing activities of European domination and appropriation. It seems that the white male writer is stuck in this double bind, for as he attempts to 'understand' both woman and indigenous other, he himself becomes inevitably complicit in the process of othering and incorporating. This is particularly evident in Brink's assertion of the links between Adam, the indigenous slave, and dissident Afrikaners like himself and Breytenbach who are seeking to establish, through their rebellion against the authority of apartheid, their birthright in Africa.[17] Similarly, the linking of Elisabeth's sexuality with the recuperation of a relationship between settler and land and her status as object of desire and transgression for the black man – Adam describes her as 'the ultimate thou-shalt-not, the most untouchable of all, you, white, woman' (p. 22) – are problematic. Thus, despite the obviously oppositional intent of the writer, such eliding of difference and reiterating of the gendering of land as woman could be argued as creating just another version of the white man's myth, another expression of the colonizer's justification of nation. Read in this way, the novel can be seen in the light of Kay Schaffer's comment that: 'There is no "real" Eliza Fraser to discover in the annals of history [or of narratives] – only more and more layers of motivated discourse'.[18]

Notes

This chapter is adapted from part of a chapter in my book, *Pen and Power: A Post-colonial Reading of the Novels of J.M. Coetzee and André Brink* (Amsterdam and Atlanta: Rodopi, 1996), reprinted with kind permission of Rodopi Press.

1 K. Schaffer, *In the Wake of First Contact: The Eliza Fraser Stories* (Cambridge: Cambridge University Press, 1995), and Fiona Foley's paintings and installations which engage with representations of Eliza Fraser, such as the 'By Land and Sea I Leave Ephemeral Spirit' exhibition of 1991.

2 A.J. Hassall, 'The Making of a Colonial Myth: The Mrs Fraser Story in Patrick White's *A Fringe of Leaves* and André Brink's *An Instant in the Wind*', *Ariel* 18.3 (1987), 4.

3 For further discussion of this issue, see A.J. Hassall's 'The Lives of Adamastor' in R.L. Ross (ed.), *International Literature in English: Essays on the Major Writers* (New York and London: Garland, 1991), 184; S. Gray, *Southern African Literature: An Introduction* (Cape Town: David Philip, 1979), 15–37; and D. Driver's 'Women and Nature, Women as Objects of Exchange: Towards a Feminist Analysis of South African Literature', in M. Chapman, C. Gardner and E. Mphahlele (eds), *Perspectives on South African English Literature* (Johannesburg: Ad. Donker, 1992), 455–7. Brink's novel, *The First Life of Adamastor* (1993), shows his ongoing interest in this myth.

4 The island off Cape Town which was for many years a harsh political prison. Nelson Mandela was one of its most famous prisoners.

5 K. Schaffer, 'Captivity Narratives and the Idea of "Nation"', in *Captive Lives: Australian Captivity Narratives. Working Papers in Australian Studies*, Nos 85, 86, 87, ed. K. Darian-Smith, R. Poignant and K. Schaffer (London: Sir Robert Menzies Centre for Australian Studies, 1993), 12.

6 J.W. Ross, 'André Brink', in *Contemporary Authors* (Detroit: Gale, 1982), 55.

7 J. Davidson, Interview with André Brink, *Overland* 94.5 (1984), 28.

8 Ross, 55.

9 A. Brink, *An Instant in the Wind* (London: Fontana, 1976), 15. Further references will appear in the text.

10 A. Brink, *Mapmakers: Writing in a State of Siege* (London: Faber & Faber, 1983), 114.

11 This is referred to in K. Schaffer, *In The Wake of First Contact: The Eliza Fraser Stories* (Cambridge: Cambridge University Press, 1995), 196, where Brink's statement that 'he [Adam] is the Afrikaner after all' is quoted. The source is an article by Brink entitled 'A Bit of Wind Around at the Moment' which appeared in Afrikaans in *Rapport* 6.3 (1976), 24–5 (see Schaffer, *In The Wake of First Contact*, n. 29).

12 When Larsson seeks the advice of the German explorer Roloff, a Kurtz-like figure, whose map of his exploration was banned by the Governor of the Cape because 'the people here are afraid of their own country: they prefer not to know what it looks like' (p. 193), he is told to 'go and look for yourself. Draw your own map' (p. 193). This is, in effect, what Elisabeth is forced to do when Larsson loses his way.

13 Mrs Fraser's nakedness is, of course, also an important issue in both written and visual accounts of the story, often representing the degree of degradation to which she has been subjected, while at the same time exposing her body to the male gaze as an object of desire and pity.

14 J.M. Coetzee, *White Writing: On the Culture of Letters in South Africa* (New Haven and London: Yale University Press, 1988), 7.

15 Kay Schaffer asks: 'Was Bracefell betrayed by Mrs Fraser as he claimed? Did he rape her on the edge of civilisation?' (*In The Wake of First Contact*, 12).

16 A. Brink, *Mapmakers: Writing in a State of Siege* (1976; London: Faber & Faber, 1983), 167.

17 For further discussion of this issue, see S. Kossew, 'Re/presenting the Afrikaner: André Brink and the Politics of Representation', in *Africa Today*, ed. P. Alexander, R. Hutchinson and D. Schreuder (Canberra: Humanities Research Council, 1996), 221–32.

18 K. Schaffer, 'The Eliza Fraser Story and Constructions of Gender, Race and Class in Australian Culture', *Hecate* 17.1 (1991), 138.

Chapter 10

'Fears of primitive otherness': 'race' in Michael Ondaatje's *the man with seven toes*

Gerry Turcotte

Prologue

Michael Ondaatje's *the man with seven toes* is among the least-known works of the Canadian writer's canon, and certainly of the Eliza Fraser stories. Along with the Barbara Blackman libretto to 'Eliza Fraser Sings' (1977) and Gabriel Josipovici's 'Dreams of Mrs Fraser' (1989), *the man with seven toes* has been displaced by the more 'famous' accounts produced by writers such as André Brink and Patrick White and by the painter Sidney Nolan. And yet the poem is as resonant, as misleading, as offensive and as provocative as any of the better known versions, and it yields fascinating insights into the way myth-making (sexual, racial, national) is manipulated.

This chapter will take as its starting point a phrase borrowed from Kay Schaffer's *In the Wake of First Contact*.[1] Although she has argued that *the man with seven toes* is a type of dream-sequence, a struggle 'between the woman's conscious memory and unconscious state' which sees her represent 'for Man his mirror image, the terror of otherness, a repressed fear of disintegration into the undifferentiated body, the body of woman/nature', Schaffer notes that the poem is largely about 'Man's fears of primitive otherness'.[2] This study will focus primarily on the way this fear is articulated through the language of the poem to re-confirm existing stereotypes and hence reproduce a not uncommon variant of the Eliza Fraser story.

Essentially the poem speaks through occlusions – of gender and of nation – and this is particularly true of its representation of indigeneity.

At once horrifically present, the Aboriginal figures are also strangely absent, existing only through their violence, their rape, their mutilating gestures. Reduced to a series of tropes of primitivism, the indigenous figures are also entirely undifferentiated one from the other. It is this generalized, generic primitiveness which helps articulate the nightmare situation of the poem. Certainly it is the marker by which readers can measure the extent of the woman's suffering – her ineluctable slide away from civilization. It may even be true to suggest that the white convict's violence is understandable only in the context of the primitive barbarity signposted by indigeneity. His sub-human descent can only be spoken through the language of the primitive other. The racist construct which emerges in *the man with seven toes* is particularly surprising in the work of a writer who has otherwise challenged such representations and may explain his own reluctance to allow the poem to be reprinted. It remains an odd contribution to Ondaatje's *œuvre*, and one which invites stricter scrutiny.

Border towns and bibliophilic abominations

Michael Ondaatje has always slipped delicately across borders. He is unquestionably one of Canada's 'major' writers. His most recent book, *The English Patient*, won not merely the Booker Prize but also the Canadian Governor-General's Award for fiction in 1992, not the first time he has won this prize. He has spent much of his creative life contributing to a questioning of the very parameters of that nation. He has done this in a number of ways. One of these is rather commonplace (if you'll forgive the pun). Ondaatje migrated from Sri Lanka to England in 1954, and then to Canada in 1962. In this way Ondaatje joined the many writers who now call Canada home, but who also force a qualification of that label as a type of birthright.

Of course, this is not unusual, particularly for Canada. As David Staines has pointed out in *Beyond the Provinces*, four of the last five Governor-General's Award winners for fiction were either born elsewhere, or have set their books in other countries. Nino Ricci's *Lives of the Saints* is set in Valle del Solle, Rohinton Mistry's *Such a Long Journey* in Bombay, *The English Patient* in Tuscany, and Carol Shield's *The Stone Diaries* is not only set in the US, the Orkney Islands and Canada, but was written by a migrant from Illinois.[3] Again, to claim this as a sign of destabilization may seem far-fetched to many, but we should remember that such details, in Australia at least, resulted in Glenda Adams' *Dancing on Coral* winning the NSW Premier's Literary Prize but being denied the money, and Frank Moorhouse's *Grand Days* being disqualified from the Miles Franklin Award for not being set in Australia.[4] In the cases of Adams and Moorhouse the judgements concerned writers actually born in the country. As the question of nation and nationalism becomes increasingly fraught, so the definitions and particularities by which we defend the concept become increasingly petty. Ondaatje, at this level alone, has helped contest those fixities of nation, in a country which prides itself on its multicultural mosaic. Naturally he is not alone in this, as the above examples attest.

Ondaatje, of course, has also had a lasting impact on Canadian writing which should not be overshadowed by the foregoing and perhaps spurious discussion of birthplace. His work has pressed against restraints of all sorts, be they of nation, genre or expectation. Even the title *the man with seven toes*, set in lower case, both frustrates and enchants traditional expectations and publishing formalities, as does the volume itself. Indeed, one reviewer noted somewhat petulantly that

> A poet must insist that his poetry be read at blood-speed ... but to do so by changing the shape of a book to the shape of a child's picture book is doubtful practice. The librarians may have to file *the man with seven toes* sideways, without the title showing – a bibliophile's abomination.[5]

With *The Collected Works of Billy the Kid*, his justifiably famous poetry began to blur the lines between poetry and prose, between 'real' and fictional subjects for narrative, and between Canadian and American heroes. Billy the Kid, of course, was unquestionably an American anti-hero, but for some reason he had slipped across the border into Canada through Ondaatje's writing. Indeed, in one scene, Billy actually comments that he and his friend Charlie Bowdre 'criss-crossed the Canadian border. Ten miles north of it ten miles south. Our horses stepped from country to country.'[6] The movement is almost like stitching, where the ligature is myth. Had the Miles Franklin judges been Canadian they would no doubt have been torn about this figure, and this unsettling 'seme', just as they were over the Canadian prototype on whom Moorhouse based his novel. If the question were asked, why had Ondaatje turned to the USA for his source material, the answer would have to be, why should it matter?

In fact, it was not long before Ondaatje returned south of the border with *Coming Through Slaughter*, to trace the life of cornetist Buddy Bolden. In *Running in the Family* Ondaatje then travelled to 'Ceylon' to find his father, unaware that this may also have been Eliza Fraser's birthplace.[7] Perhaps he trod in her footsteps as he searched for his family – we can never know. But for a writer who plays off coincidences and manipulates their detail, this was one which he did not seem to anticipate and control.

It was not until *In the Skin of a Lion* that Ondaatje set a novel entirely in Canada. Perhaps to make up for this, he exiled some of those same characters to Italy with *The English Patient*. The point in these reflections is not merely to offer a brief summary of Ondaatje's works, but also to show how he has elided/eluded borders in every way – like a fugitive Billy the Kid or an Ambrose Small (from *In the Skin of a Lion*).

Losing *toes*

As I have argued elsewhere, Ondaatje's haunting and brutal poem, *the man with seven toes*, is based on a number of absences and errors.[8] He was certainly responsible for the former. In an interview on ABC radio, Ondaatje stated that *seven toes* was his 'first attempt at writing a long poem and it was obviously, for me, more of a mental landscape than a real one because I had never been to Australia (as one can probably tell by reading that poem)'.[9] Australia, then, is a major absence at the heart of this poem, and Mrs Fraser is another.

For Ondaatje, however, accuracy of detail was never his objective, a fact which can be deduced from his character's nameless state – she is referred to merely as Mrs X by one reviewer[10] – and by her elision in the title to the poem itself. *the man with seven toes*, in name and in substance, immortalizes, indeed celebrates, the convict rescuer and the suffering he has undergone in order to save the nameless woman.[11]

It is possible to argue further that the poem is not merely predicated on two central absences – Australia and Mrs Fraser – but also on erroneous information. Like so many before him, Ondaatje based his poem on 'some paintings by Sidney Nolan called, "The Convict and the Lady" or something like that, and this was a story about Bracefell and Mrs Fraser'. Before he went on to do 'a lot of research on the whole convict situation in Australia ... which I left out at the end', Ondaatje gathered what he knew from the gloss by Colin MacInnes which accompanied the Nolan paintings. It is important to note, as has Douglas Barbour, that 'Ondaatje works to undercut the obvious document' to produce 'a more stringent kind of re-writing, gleefully overturning its pre-text, putting it under erasure in order to write something new in its place'. Barbour concludes by suggesting that the MacInnes gloss 'is a palimpsest, where the erasure of the earliest, now hidden layer of the 'original version' of the story ensures a site for the invented one newly inscribed there'.[12] This, then, is what Ondaatje read, and veered away from to some degree:

> Mrs Fraser was a Scottish lady who was shipwrecked on what is now Fraser Island, off the Queensland Coast. She lived for 6 months among the aborigines, rapidly losing her clothes, until she was discovered by one Bracefell, a deserting convict who himself had hidden for 10 years

among the primitive Australians. The lady asked the criminal to restore her to civilization, which he agreed to do if she would promise to intercede for his free pardon from the Governor. The bargain was sealed, and the couple set off inland.

At first sight of European settlement, Mrs Fraser rounded on her benefactor and threatened to deliver him up to justice if he did not immediately decamp. Bracefell returned disillusioned to the hospitable bush, and Mrs Fraser's adventures aroused such admiring interest that on her return to Europe she was able to exhibit herself at 6d a showing in Hyde Park.[13]

Most critics will know how scurrilous this particular account is: for its sexism (an extraordinary sleight of hand which turns Mrs Fraser into a betraying Eve[14]), and for the canonization of Bracefell as convict rescuer over John Graham. If it seems ludicrous in these postmodern times to insist on accuracy of representation or on the verities of history, then it is downright foolhardy to attempt to impose such a conservative view on someone as challenging as Ondaatje, whose very writing practice contests over and over again the limits which prescribe subject matter, direction, linearity and plot. And yet it is not because a writer is innovative that he is exempt from scrutiny – even self scrutiny. Ondaatje, I believe, has recognized the poem's representational weaknesses. As he himself put it during the above-mentioned interview, *'the man with seven toes* is a book I don't really like very much any more ... it didn't work for me although it was published and you know I have sort of kept it hidden in the closet'.[15]

Despite his attempts to lose *seven toes*, it has surfaced time and again, as a poem called 'Peter' which resembles it greatly and preceded it, as Billy the Kid who may have emerged through Nolan's Ned Kelly paintings viewed at the same time as the Eliza paintings, and perhaps even as an echo in the title of a later collection of poems, *There's a Trick with a Knife that I'm Learning to Do*. It is certainly coincidence, but the convict's toes are cut by 'ideal knives' as he carries Mrs Fraser through a swamp.

'Primitive machines'

To what extent, in a fragmentary, expressionistic poem, where characters and voices speak in – or out of – turn, but where identity is often difficult to pin down, can the question of 'race' and representation be addressed? Sheila Watson, for one, describes Ondaatje's *seven toes* this way.

The world which he explores is a primitive world invaded by primitive machines. He begins with a train in a desolate part of the Australian continent and ends with a domesticated outpost of Victoria's empire – the Royal Hotel. In this world the absent-minded train hums like a low flying bird and stops for water like any beast; birds stagger doped with cocaine sucked from the bark of trees; the lady and the convict suck half flesh out of two pale green eggs; swamp-flesh with teeth as sharp as 'ideal knives' severs toes from the convict's feet which have been strengthened with wolf's blood and have out-witted bird-disguised men so primitive that their maps are 'encoded in the soles of their feet'.[16]

Watson recognizes that the indigenous people stand in for primitive machines, a metaphor which re/places indigenous peoples in a hybrid space, between human and machine, between man and beast, between civilized and uncivilized. Their (re)presentation, in other words, makes of them a missing link of sorts, inhabiting the border world of becoming and un-becoming. The poem's iconography, then, makes them bo(a)rders, which Mrs X crosses with difficulty.

Bo(a)rders, of course, are generally impermanent residents. They also occupy and represent a liminal space, since borders are an edge only inasmuch as some might choose to define them as a starting or an ending point. As Homi Bhabha has argued, for example, borders are in fact an in-between space which 'provide the terrain for elaborating strategies of selfhood – singular or communal – that initiate new signs of identity, and innovative sites of collaboration, and contestation, in the act of defining the idea of society itself'.[17] Borders, by extension, are the perpetual, the ever-existent state of becoming for all of us – social, political, sexual – a state which emphasizes that there is no condition of oneness, of 'purity'. Indeed, such terms elicit, now, and for many, a negative, rather than a positive response.

Purity, these days, reeks of 'ethnic cleansing' – a strangely obscene euphemism for the filth of genocide. On the other hand, 'contamination', 'hybridity', 'polyphony', can be positive terms (though not unproblematic), and strategies of resistance and theorization seek increasingly to re-inscribe epistemologies which would inflect these terms otherwise than in empowering, mutating, challenging and contestatory ways. Ondaatje's 'primitive machines' escape such efforts and unfortunately echo a discourse of science which depersonalizes indigeneity, and which re-situates the Aboriginal figure in the purlieu of savagery and primitiveness. Their border existence, then, is lived in a disempowered space, where they are divested of agency. As a people they are an indistinguishable mass, a homogenized group, easily outwitted by the menial convict figure, himself already a signifier of debasement and decay. In the imperial account, of course, it makes complete sense that the lowest of the 'human' order should still be significantly superior to the indigenous figure.

Object (vs.)/knowledge

It is probably not a bold thing to say that the penultimate moment of curiosity in the Eliza Fraser story is the instance of contact between Mrs Fraser and her Aboriginal 'captors'. This moment, of course, has already occurred long before she sets foot on land. It is already written. The fear of landing on shore expressed by the crew, the fear which reminds them to carry weapons or to avoid travelling alone, all of these are responses to already clearly established emblems of Aboriginality. As Schaffer has argued, the Aboriginal peoples have long since become 'an object of knowledge',[18] and are given no space to object to such knowledge.

One could go so far as to say that the crew has already been captured; they are already contained by the narratives of containment, so that the 'fact' of the Aboriginal presence is almost incidental. Indeed, their appearance is a confirmation of all that has been predicted and written about (in other captivity narratives, for example), in the same way that a stereotype always exists, foretells its own inevitability and hence confirms it.[19]

The 'border crossing' which takes place at the moment of contact, then, is exhilarating, but it is eternally one-sided, because it will always be expressed anthropologically. Whatever abuse, violence, antagonism or fear occurs will always be communicated and articulated via European discourse, and hence its conclusions will always be predetermined. This does not preclude debate and contestation, but it does make European discourse the pretext for discussion.

If the penultimate moment in the story is the point of contact, then its climax is the instance where intercourse between native and white slips from its nineteenth-century to its twentieth-century signifier: where word becomes act. Not surprisingly, this pornographic moment occurs in virtually every account of the Fraser saga. In *the man with seven toes* it is articulated within exactly the same space as those of the nineteenth- and twentieth-century retellings. The land is left metaphorically resonant by being significantly vague; the Aborigines are made infinitely 'palimpsestic' through a generic characterization of primitiveness, and Mrs Fraser is represented in familiar victimized fashion, her body the subject of extensive sexual scrutiny.

What emerges here, however, is a retreat to a sequence of stereotypes about blackness which has virtually always (mis)informed the tale, one which plays on the sexualized/fetishized black body as an agent of threat, insatiability and rapaciousness. The bodies – the primitive machines – of Ondaatje's text rehearse what feminist writer bell hooks has quite rightly called a 'story, invented by white men ... about the over-whelming desperate longing black men have to sexually violate the bodies of white women'.[20] As hooks goes on to argue,

The central character in this story is the black male rapist. Black men are constructed, as Michael Dyson puts it, as 'peripatetic phalluses with unrequited desire for their denied object – white women'. As the story goes this desire is not based on longing for sexual pleasure. It is a story of revenge, rape as the weapon by which black men, the dominated, reverse their circumstance, regain power over white men.[21]

Like the moment when Mrs Fraser, in one account, is forced to nurse a sickly Aboriginal child, the instance of rape here enacts a reversal of fortune, and literalizes a repeated white fear of savagery's ability to harm, or worse, enslave, 'enlightened' cultures. Mrs Fraser as nursemaid is an indignity, because it suggests the reversal of roles – the mistress made servant.[22] The rape similarly articulates the perversion of order and so serves to sanction punitive exercises intent on restoring control. Perhaps, at this point, it would be useful to turn more specifically to the poem itself, and to see how it negotiates such moments.

Eat your heart out

Written initially in the third person, the poem describes as an accident Mrs Fraser's arrival in the desert landscape. A train rolls to a stop and then departs before she can board again. 'the train shuddered, then wheeled away from her,/ she was too tired even to call./ though, come back, she murmured to herself.'[23] Then she sleeps, wakes, and wanders. There is nothing to be seen except a dog, which licks its penis 'as if some red flower in the desert./ she looked away but everything around her was empty'.[24] *Terra nullius*, perhaps.

The appearance of the Aboriginal figures does not occur until the third page of poetry, or page 11 in the book's oddly numbered sequences. It is fitting that their arrival should intimate the first rupture of point of view. The passage begins:

> entered the clearing and they turned
> faces scarred with decoration
> feathers, bones, paint from clay
> pasted, skewered to their skin.
> Fanatically thin,
> black ropes of muscle.
>
> one, whose right eye had disappeared
> brought food on a leaf.
> they stripped clothes off like a husk
> and watched my white
> tugged my breasts and lifted

> my long hair, their fingers
> writhing in my head
> and laughed,
>   then threw
> the red dress back at me.[25]

Mrs Fraser, as I have argued elsewhere, has not only been portrayed persistently as the Other, but she has also been cannibalized regularly by writers and critics.[26] In a sense this process of ingestion and regurgitation has produced a figure both enlarged and reduced. Certainly she has been reduced in numerous accounts until she has faded often entirely from the picture, whether it is her own handwritten account, shredded and dispersed until its influence is lost, or remade in the guise of another – as wanton woman, bad mother, and so forth.[27] In Ondaatje's poem, and in the above passage, Mrs Fraser is temporarily restored at the arrival of the *other* other (that is, she speaks, at last, in the first person). She finds her voice, as it were, even if only momentarily, at the appearance of the Aborigines.

Given the particular politicized emphasis which I am attempting here, I think it is significant she should find her voice at that moment when her sense of self is about to be horrifically obliterated, and that this moment should occur in the space which is so often elided – but always underscored, always present – in so many accounts. I mean, of course, the rape of Mrs Fraser. Indeed, where so many accounts skirt the issue (but titillate none the less through inference), Ondaatje dwells on it, and presents the details in almost carnivalesque terms:

> tongued me
> felt cold metal, put
> hot fingers in my mouth, pulled
> silver filings [*sic*] out,
> threaded, wore them like a charm
>
> tongued me
> spat love in my ear
> bit the lobe off,
> ate it, that a wedding band
> in his stomach growing there
>
> then him in me
> in my body
> like a like a
> drum a drum[28]

The passage focuses on the image of eating:

> stretched their arms
> coiled with their bodies
> chewed the tangle, tossed limbs away
> that one imagined
> grew from others,
>
> yelled out souls
> feasted their bodies
> and in the eating grew bellies fat[29]

The rape here is conjoined with festival and with cannibalism, linking the indigenes – unquestionably 'peripatetic phalluses' – with a perverted notion of barbarism.[30] This is followed by the most chaotic poetic language, which blurs the line between animal and native:

> goats, black goats, balls bushed in the centre
> cocks rising like birds flying to you   reeling on you
> and smiles smiles as they ruffle you open
> spill you down, jump and spill over you
> white leaping like fountains in
> your hair your head and mouth till it dries
> and tightens your face like a scar[31]

The text then goes on to describe the slaughter of foxes and goats and 'blood spraying out like dynamite' which the children run about trying to collect with their joyous, open mouths. The stanza resolves itself with a ceremony of dismemberment – 'the men rip flesh tearing, the muscles/nerves green and red still jumping/stringing them out, like you'. The sequence ends with the most shocking imagery of all. Once they have ripped the bodies open they

> put their heads in and
> catch quick quick   come on
> COME ON! the heart still beating
> shocked into death, and catch the heart still running
> in their hard quiet lips   and eat it alive
> alive still in their mouths throats still beating   Bang
> still! BANG in their stomachs[32]

A number of shifts have taken place here. Certainly, the primitive other is resoundingly illustrated in this brutal sequence. Just as early illustrators dressed Mrs Fraser's aggressors in whatever garb they thought appropriate to the scene so that distinct indigenous cultures were fused indiscriminately,[33] so too does Ondaatje resort to a catalogue of images which instantiate the savage into stereotypical depictions. The scenes remind us of clichéd images of voodoo, resurrect ideas of cannibal savages and animalistic ritual which indeed fuse the two – Aboriginal and animal – so that they are inseparable. Mrs Fraser, only briefly offered a speaking, or viewing, position, is dis/located, so that she is no longer the 'I' responsible for description, but becomes 'you', a second person, de/scribed. But she is nevertheless restored to her world, a centre of attention. The indigenous people, on the other hand, have disappeared. They are a ghost of barbarism that haunts the text, just as Mrs X's sufferings continue to mar her flesh. Yet the indigenous figures exist only in regard to their negative impact on the Western form. Mrs X may occasionally speak for herself, the Aboriginals never do. In the end, and while appearing to feast on Mrs Fraser, Ondaatje has in fact cannibalized the natives, has caught their 'heart still running' and has eaten them alive ... BANG in his stomach.

Notes

1 K. Schaffer, *In the Wake of First Contact: The Eliza Fraser Stories* (Oakleigh: Cambridge University Press, 1995).
2 Ibid., 178, 180.
3 D. Staines, *Beyond the Provinces: Literary Canada at the Century's End* (Toronto: University of Toronto Press, 1995), ch. 1.
4 In the case of the former, times have certainly changed. The 1995 winner of the NSW Premier's Prize for Fiction was Lily Brett for *Life's Like That*. Brett lives principally in New York. As a member of the wider judging panel I can attest to the fact that the subject of residency was never raised. Ironically, one of the fiction judges was Frank Moorhouse. For a discussion of the Moorhouse controversy see P. Washington, 'The Postcolonial, the National and Australian Cultural Studies: The Case of the Miles Franklin Award', *New Literatures Review: Factions and Fictions* 28/29 (Winter–Summer 1994–95), 129–39.
5 M. Travis Lane, 'Dream as History: A Review of *the man with seven toes*', in *Spider Blues: Essays on Michael Ondaatje*, ed. S. Solecki (Montreal: Véhicule Press, 1985), 155.
6 M. Ondaatje, *The Collected Works of Billy the Kid: Left Handed Poems* (Toronto: House of Anansi, 1970), 20.
7 For a discussion of this remote possibility see Schaffer, *In the Wake of First Contact*, 13; Y. Drummond, 'Progress of Eliza', *Royal Historical Society of Queensland Journal* 15.1 (February 1993), 16.
8 See Gerry Turcotte, ' "Coming Out of the Closet": Sexual Politics in Michael Ondaatje's *the man with seven toes*'. *La Creation Biographique/Bibliographic Creation* (Rennes: Presses Universitaires Rennes, 1997), 101-10).
9 See G. Turcotte, ' "The Germ of Document": An Interview with Michael Ondaatje', *Australian–Canadian Studies: A Journal for the Humanities and the Social Sciences* 12.2 (1994), 49–58. This is a transcript of a radio broadcast, aired on ABC Radio's *Books and Writing*, No. 42, November 1992.

10 Travis Lane, 155.

11 Again, see Turcotte, 'Coming Out of the Closet' for a more sustained analysis of this point.

12 D. Barbour, 'the man with seven toes: Michael Ondaatje's Expressionist Version of an Australian Legend', Australian–Canadian Studies: A Journal for the Humanities and the Social Sciences 10.1 (1992), 21.

13 See MacInnes' Introduction in K. Clark, C. MacInnes and B. Robertson, Sidney Nolan (London: Thames and Hudson, 1961).

14 Barbour is adamant that Ondaatje does not emphasize this aspect of the tale, arguing that 'the man with seven toes dispenses with almost everything the MacInnes quotation provides for it' (p. 33).

15 See Turcotte, 'The Germ of Document': 49–50.

16 S. Watson, 'Michael Ondaatje: The Mechanization of Death', in Spider Blues: Essays on Michael Ondaatje, ed. S. Solecki (Montreal: Véhicule Press, 1985), 160–1.

17 H. Bhabha, The Location of Culture (London and New York: Routledge, 1994), 1.

18 Schaffer, 96.

19 See Bhabha, 66–84.

20 b. hooks, Yearnings: Race, Gender, and Cultural Politics (Boston: South End Press, 1990), 58.

21 Ibid., 58.

22 See Anonymous, Narrative of the Capture, Sufferings, and Miraculous Escape of Mrs Eliza Fraser (New York: Charles S. Webb, 1837), where we are told that 'When they [the Aboriginal women] had become weary of thus tormenting me, they put into my arms the most deformed, and ugly looking brat, that my eyes ever beheld' (p. 7). For a more sustained discussion of this moment, see 'Eating the Cannibals from Within: Devouring Mrs Fraser's "Body Politic"', which was originally presented at the Politics and Poetics of the Body Conference, University of California, Santa Barbara, California, 29 April 1994. I am indebted to the 'responder' to that session, and to general audience discussion afterwards, for the shaping of those observations. The revised and expanded paper was presented at the Association for Australian Literature Conference, Adelaide, 6 July 1995 and was published in Crossing Lines: Formations of Australian Culture (ASAL: Adelaide, 1995), 165–74.

23 M. Ondaatje, the man with seven toes (Toronto: Coach House Press, 1969), 9.

24 Ibid., 10.

25 Ibid., 11–12.

26 See G. Turcotte, 'Mrs Fraser's Ravenous Appetite: The Taste for Cannibalism in Captivity Narratives', in Crossing Lines. The symposium at which the present paper was presented, of course, was yet another consumption of sorts and it is no doubt merely a lovely irony that in Greek, 'symposium' means a 'drinking-party that followed the evening meal'. I doubt this will be our last supper at the Fraser feast.

27 See K. Schaffer, 'Australian Mythologies: The Eliza Fraser Story and Constructions of the Feminine in Patrick White's *A Fringe of Leaves* and Sidney Nolan's "Eliza Fraser" Paintings', *Kunapipi* 11.2 (1989), 1–15, also reprinted as 'The Eliza Fraser Story and Constructions of Gender, Race and Class in Australian Culture', in *Women/Australia/Theory: Special Issue of Hecate* 17.1 (1991), 136–49; and Schaffer, *In the Wake of First Contact*.

28 Ondaatje, 14.

29 Ibid., 15.

30 As opposed, perhaps, to the 'natural' barbarism of the convict, where he is 'rewarded', in some accounts, with sexual favours, and perhaps even Mrs Fraser's love. This is, of course, prior to her betrayal.

31 Ondaatje, 16.

32 Ibid., 16.

33 See the woodblock illustration which accompanies the anonymous ballad, 'A Copy of the Mournful Verses', reproduced in Alexander, 1971, (p. 15) and in Schaffer, *In the Wake of First Contact*, (p. 46) and her commentary. The woodblock not only distorts the 'victims' of the putative assault by replacing the all-male crew with numerous, mostly beheaded damsels in petticoats and similarly truncated infants, but manages a smorgasbord of features, implements and costumes for the indigenous aggressors: from North American tomahawks and feathers, to Pacific Islander adornments, to Maori 'canoes'.

Chapter 11

Barbara's Eliza

Barbara Blackman

In 1977, Peter Sculthorpe invited me to write a libretto on the story of Eliza Fraser from which to derive a chamber work for piano, flute and soprano. I wrote it as a dramatic poem in five sections. The story had, in 140 years, become myth. Myth, says Joseph Campbell, is something that never happened but is always happening. A poem seeks to strike the psychic and spiritual meaning of an event in the personal terms of the writer; so here is where I stood at the time of Peter's request.

My father, Harry ('Banjo II') Patterson, a versifier and water-colourist, contributor to *Smith's Weekly*, was, in the teens and twenties of the century, a government surveyor in south-eastern Queensland. He married late and, at the end of the 1920s, soon after my first birthday, had a stroke. Realizing that he did not have long to live he took immediate action, walked out of his newly built house at Indooroopilly in Brisbane and took me and my mother to live with Aboriginal people – at Caloundra across from Bribie Island – whose way of life he preferred and whose language he spoke. We lived there in a tent for sixteen months, the time of my earliest recollections; for instance, on my third birthday my mother committed 'an act of child abuse'. She washed my hair, submerging my head in rinsing water. Blubbering, protesting, dripping water, dangling clothes, I ran out across the campsite. All the Aboriginals laughed and laughed, as did my parents. My father called my mother 'Gurra' and me 'Budgeree'.

I found out the significance of these names only much later. Olga Miller, elder of the Butchela people of Fraser Island, tells the creation myth of that region. The high spirit of creation was making the world bit by bit, making the mountains, rivers, land masses and coastlines. His woman Gurra accompanied him. When he made the coastline near Fraser Island, she declared it was so beautiful it could not be surpassed. She wanted to lie down there for the rest of time. The Creator said she could not do this as there was much more earth and sea to be made. She insisted. He said that she must stay not in spirit form but as part of his work. He ordered her to step into the sea and lie down. He made her into the Great Sandy Island and marked their parting with high cliffs of rainbow-coloured sands. This could be the origin of my father's name for my mother and 'Budgeree'/Budchelee, meaning little female person, for me.

So, after that, I had the childhood of an only child with many dolls as companions, dolls of all sorts, from a glamorous Shirley Temple to exotic Japanese and Fijian costume dolls, including two rag dolls so decrepit, so past their 'use-by date' that they had been dubbed Spring Hill Liz and Liza Fraser. (Spring Hill was the hillside slum area of Brisbane.) But these were my favourites at bedtime. My mother, seeing a woman in the street who was dirty and dishevelled would say, 'There goes Eliza Fraser' just as, on seeing a dishevelled room, she would say, 'It looks like the wreck of the Hesperus'. These two dolls did not move with us to the city in 1937.

In 1947, Sidney Nolan came up to Brisbane from Melbourne for the first time, falling in with the Barjai-Miya group of young avant-garde writers and painters led by Barrett Reid, who, through his contacts with *Angry Penguins* magazine which John Reed edited along with Max Harris, had been to Melbourne and met John and Sunday Reed. Nolan had just severed his life with the Reeds at Heide and was looking about. He went with a young painter Joy Roggenkamp and her brother to their home ground of Magnetic Island out from Townsville. He returned just as the Queensland poet Judith Wright and her husband, philosopher Jack McKinney, were back from a trip to Fraser Island. They were all talking about the place, about Eliza Fraser and about the grace of the timber workers treading the logs as they brought them down river. Sid and Barrie decided to go over to the island. Sid became entranced by the story of the shipwrecked, degraded woman and the fleeing convict rescuer and painted his first Mrs Fraser series. I think Judith must have got together the money for this trip because he gave her two of the paintings, a figure rising from a swamp and a woman crouching on the seashore. These hung in the main room and back bedroom of the McKinney house on Mount Tamborine for over ten years and were familiar to Charles and me (painter Charles Blackman, my former husband) on our frequent sojourns there in the 1950s.[1]

In January 1966, just before we left London, Dr H.C. (Nugget) Coombs told us of a scheme to dream up an opera about Eliza to open the Sydney Opera House. For this purpose an expedition was mounted, bringing together Patrick White the scenario writer elect, Peter Sculthorpe the composer elect, Sidney Nolan the scene designer elect and Robert Helpmann the dancer and choreographer elect. Such drama ensued that clearly the Opera House would be too small a venue for such a combination of forces. The opera was abandoned, but Patrick brooded on the theme and ten years later produced his novel *Fringe of Leaves*; Peter sat on the idea; Sidney went on drafting new thoughts for years to come; and Robert gave up the idea of giving birth to a baby in the surf.

However apocryphal the story, the novel and music did surface ten years or so later.

I went to Fraser Island only once. In mid-1969, after Charles opened his large exhibition of 40 paintings and 40 drawings at Bonython Gallery in Sydney to mark his fortieth year, we went there for a honeymoon holiday and stayed at probably the first resort, island style. Spurred on by our enthusiasm, embroidered with the Eliza story, our Melbourne friend Hal Hattam, gynaecologist and painter, went there with his wife and painted a series which was subsequently widely exhibited. Indeed, one of them, a Fraser Island landscape, hangs in the entrance hall of my present house.

In the 1960s, Hal and Kate Hattam played something of the role in Melbourne that the Reeds had played in the 1940s, and which Georges and Mirka Mora in their 9 Collins Street studio and later Balzac restaurant, did in the 1950s. Hal, as John Reed in his time and Georges Mora in his, was President of the Contemporary Art Society. He and Kate were people of great style, generosity, curiosity and hospitality. Their grand house in South Yarra became the centre of gravity for academics and artists. Their generosity was in terms of time, patience and the 'open house' they provided, with restraint of judgement and openness to all critical argument. Hal was a distinguished gynaecologist and surgeon. He stood by crises in friends' lives with all the cool-headedness, patience and endurance he brought to his patients. He delivered babies for all the artists' wives and his walls filled with their gratitude of paintings.

Tim Burstall, who would later direct the film *Eliza Fraser* (1976), was a frequenter of the Hattam house and had been in London when we – Blackmans, Boyds, Percevals – were there. He had met Suzannah York through her purchase of our paintings. Eliza Fraser was much discussed and Tim saw in the story a chance to seduce Suzannah into making the film and thus extending their relationship. Indeed, the opening scenes of his film *Eliza Fraser* were shot in the Hattam's house. (In due course Tim was married in that house, but not to Suzannah York.)

It was with this background and with my childhood acquaintance with the countryside north of Brisbane, and my childhood and teenage holidays on the beaches north of Caloundra, that I welcomed the Eliza libretto commission when approached by Peter Sculthorpe. I read as research Michael Alexander's book *Mrs Fraser on the Fatal Shore*, first published in 1971 and reprinted in 1976. I took from it what imagery I felt was apt. I was in no way in search of the true story any more than of the true geography. In the calling of the tribes section of the libretto I deliberately used the Aboriginal place names as familiar to me as the names of railway stations, beach sites and the Glass House mountains. Otherwise I tried to stick to the Alexander book as reference but with one outstanding difference, unintentional but interesting in origin.

The Great Sandy Island tribe are the Butchella/Badtjala people, but I have called them the Kabi people, a name that had surfaced from my earliest childhood, replacing the researched fact. My mother's grandparents, George and Emma Poole, travelled from the Forest of Dean in England in the late 1850s and settled seven miles out of Kilcoy in the direction of Toogoolawah, inland and south of Fraser Island. They had – even when I knew the place in the 1930s – a slab hub and simple red unclad timber house on Neara Creek, distinguished only as being the end of the mail run. This, and not Fraser Island, is Kabi Kabi country. It must have been this knowledge, long buried in memory, that materialized when I wrote the piece.

Peter Sculthorpe and I discussed at length our perception of Eliza. I envisaged her in terms of a woman's view from the inside. I was concerned with her bodily experience and the effects I supposed it might have had on her mind. Peter had his vision of the contour of the work: first movement – the sea-rocking, lullaby rhythm of shipwreck and childbirth; second movement – the narrative and sense of threat of the island; third movement – a mounting dramatic section building up to an explosion, a scream into hysteria; fourth movement – a dream state, pastoral; fifth movement – a staccato interruption of the rescue leading into a postlude at the Hyde Park fair.

I carried this through in my own terms. For me, the kernel of the poem was in the reference to the reincarnation beliefs of the Aboriginal people signified in a mystique that the spirits of the dead, seen to rise in pale smoke as their bodies were burned, could return as spirits or ghost people. I made the central drama a corroboree spectacle in which the island 'she ghost', Mrs Fraser as apparition, was brought to a meeting, or mating, with a 'he ghost', an escaped convict living with a neighbouring tribe on the coast. The experience so traumatizes Eliza that she goes into a comic-tragic English charade, addressing the black people as though she were their protector, their rescuer of European niceties. In her subsequent self-protective delirium she transforms the English convict into a dream lover, giving me the chance to use my love of that familiar landscape of early childhood. The rude awakening of the rescue shocked Eliza out of any sense of gratitude to the convict. The Hyde Park scene was then an irony of reconciliation.

I published this poem suite in *Quadrant* magazine in April 1977 as a forerunner to the Sculthorpe work. It was accompanied by a photograph of a Fraser Island saga diorama done by Charles Blackman in sand tray fashion with little figurines, as used by sand play therapists.

As Peter worked on the piece, he would come round to our house and play passages on the piano, building around a ballroom dance piece popular in the 1830s. Gradually he drew out of my libretto a poignant Eliza, particularly in the final scene, by using a first-person rather than my third-person narrator. My text, in performance, runs to about ten minutes, whereas the Sculthorpe music with its cadenzas and music passages, the several flutes used, the piano played from without and within, the full soprano range called into action, lasts for about twice that time. Peter wanted to call the piece 'Mrs Fraser Sings'. I objected on the grounds that Mrs (Tammie) Fraser was then the Lady of the Lodge in Canberra and 'Tammie's in Love' a popular song. I stuck to my title of 'Eliza Surviva' [*sic*] and he compromised with 'Eliza Fraser Sings'.

Our Eliza came on the scene in a double first performance on 1 July 1978 at the Seymour Centre under the baton of Vincent Plush. The first half of the programme was a dramatic performance of 'Eliza Surviva' spoken by actress Gillian Jones, accompanied by electronic music. She wore a drab garment – garbage bin trench coats then being popular with the young – and the scene was a spaghetti of electric cords. The calling of the tribes for the corroboree scene was put on loop and echoed round and round the room with growing intensity and menace. Echoes and fades were used with effect for the repetitions of the '*Stirling Castle*, Captain Fraser' refrains. After an interval the Sculthorpe music theatre piece for trio was performed by the Seymour Group. The contrast effect was sensational. Unfortunately, as far as I know, it has not been performed in this way since.

The next performance was in Melbourne on 3 September 1978, an item among three in a programme that ran for several nights. It was a production of the Lyric Opera Company of Victoria. There have been several other performances, notably in the Recording Room at the Sydney Opera House in September 1988, one item in a programme of three. The only recording has been the Vox Australia, from the Australia Music Centre, in 1995; but this omitted the whole central section, giving only twelve minutes of the work. Again the CD was shared among three items.

I have been asked if now, twenty years later, I would want to change anything. I think the question implies the change of attitude brought about by the Women's Movement and the Aboriginal Land Rights political changes. I cannot see that either of these influences has anything to do with my response to Eliza as woman and as myth. I think she and the Badtjala people were a bewilderment to each other, a trespass and a trauma, a source of misunderstanding and thus misreporting and mythologizing. The misrepresentations and fact foraging will go on. When a story touches the archetype so deeply that it becomes diffused in mysteries, it has inherently the power to draw explorers and creative interpreters into its spell. The more Eliza Fraser becomes mirage, the more she will be seen as this woman or that, in every mirror image of the searcher.

Eliza Surviva

Barbara Blackman

Part 1: Shipwreck and Childbirth

> List to the ship wreck –
> Mishap when reef struck,
> Strangling embrace of the reef-ribboned sea.
> > *Stirling Castle*, Captain Fraser.

> Crew all they leave her,
> Cruel the lee shore,
> Stranded in boats in the great griefless sea.
> > *Stirling Castle*, Captain Fraser.

> *'I was the wife of the Captain.*
> *I saved the life of the Captain'.*

> Six days of bailing,
> Thirst-crazed and ailing
> Straggling on south in the lost lonely sea.
> > *Stirling Castle*, Captain Fraser.

> Sea-drift, dispirited,
> Landfall – of cannibal,
> Staggering ashore – to risk slavery.
> > *Stirling Castle*, Captain Fraser.

> *'I was with child to the Captain.*
> *I gave birth to the child of the Captain'.*

> Slumped in the scuppers
> Swooning her womb away,
> She gave birth to a baby, drowned instantly.
> > *Stirling Castle*, Captain Fraser.

157

Sand dune and spinifex,
Spear thrown by savages,
Stripped and exposed
To their black savagery.

Stirling Castle, Captain Fraser.

Part 2: On the Island

Island and Tribe land,
Sandy, a salt land
Swamp at the centre,
Spume on the sea
         in the land of the Kabi.

Mists on the shoreline,
Myths of the story time
Spirits of dead men
Pale as they burn them
Rise and return then
As white men among them
         in the land of the Kabi.

White men are shared out,
White women stared at,
Their nakedness jeered at,
Spat at and speared at,
         in the land of the Kabi.

Twig bed and scrap food,
Catch crab and fetch wood,
Her white skin they blacken
With tribal marks pattern
Beat her but leave her
Her tar-smelling head-dress
         in the land of the Kabi.

'*Finally I gave them*
My chest of lace and linen,
Wrapped myself in seaweed
Still wearing my sou'wester'.

Sweet from the honey hive
Must give to the chief men,
Milk sap of breast
Must give to the vilest
Child of the tribe
And carry him on her,

Sees once her husband,
Speaks and they spear him

'My dear, how you neglected me
On the sands a month ago.
Did you say that you expected me
Immediately to follow?'
                in the land of the Kabi.

Part 3: Corroboree

Cootharaba Cootharaba
To Kabi the Wa Wa
Tribes come from near and far
From Noosa, Mooloolaba,
Caboolture, Cooloola,
Maroochy Mooloolah,
From Buderim Bungunyah Mundubra,
Nambour, Caloundra,
Tewantin, Toogoolawah –
          To come to Cootharaba
              To Kabi Corroboree
        The She Ghost to see.

          Cootharaba Cootharaba
        Tribes loom their moon miles
            To gather to Wa Wa.

Tibragagan Tibragogan
Kin Kin, Urangen,
Yandina, Kandanga,
Bly-Bly and Woombye,
Cooroy and Coolum,
Majimba, Ninderry,
Beerburrum and Beerwah
          To come to Cootharaba
           To gather at Wa Wa
           To Kabi Corroboree
        The She Ghost to see.
Round as a show ground
Make bora to ring her,
Entrance at one end
From bower to bring her.
Chanting and stamping
Fire brands fling her
          the She ghost to see.

Ritual ridicule
Spectacle spiritual
Woman among us
Returned from a world
Believed but beyond us
Appearingly real to us –
Touch her and pinch her
Fire her and flesh her
                              the She ghost to see

From far Kabi country
Come men of Eumundi
From mountain and forest
By water and far coast
                              to bring her their He Ghost.

When he takes her in his swarthy arms
Her scorched and scourged body
She sees beneath his rhythms
The scars of his floggings,
She feels beneath his brutings
The bites of his leg irons
And knows that her He Ghost Was Englishman once.

'Had I been here in my English dress
To tend to you in your distress,
I could have brought you midwifery
Hygiene and laundry,
Haute cuisine and embroidery
Hospital rules and good husbandry.
I could have taught you to ballroom dance
Delivered you all from your ignorance!'

Part 4: Dream Sequence

As I lie in my distress
I dream him man of English dress
Dream he comes by night as cover
Leads me out each dawn as lover.

Where only the whip birds lash
Only the bunyah nuts crack
No savage or soldier pursues
Along our sandy track.

The gums are wild with fruits
The gullies fresh with water.
My body flowers again in the caress of a love

Never shall the forest's
Ecstatic leaflight end
For we shall fly forever
To cliffs of rainbow sands.

Days of their starving me
Nights of their beating me
Tortures not hurting me
Now that the dream is me.

Part 5: Rescue

Comes the rescue,
            comes the boat crew,
            Comes to claim me
            One that names me.

            'here's a cloak
            A petticoat.
            Come with me
            to the Military'.

            Aged in my agony
            Exit from ecstasy
            Wrecked in reality
            Freak female property.

They do not see my lover
In ghost gums where he stands,
Or know he holds for ever
My sunlight in his hands.
                        Cootharaba Cootharaba
                        Gather at Wa Wa
                        Come to Corroboree
                        She Ghost to see.

Postlude
Come to the booth Rah-rah!
Come to the show!
Roll up whoe'er you are
Strange sight to see!

Eliza Surviva!
Late from Australia
Lady Adventurer
Hear her for sixpence.

Eliza surviva
Hear her adventures
Shipwreck and ravages
Sav-ed from savages.
Hear her for sixpence
            Stirling Castle, Kabi country.
            Come to Wa Wa, Captain Fraser.

Barbara Blackman
for a libretto for Peter Sculthorpe.
First published in *Quadrant* 1977.

Chapter 12

A blast from the past

Fiona Foley

In Aboriginal Australia there are six major seasons in the yearly cycle. It was during the Aboriginal seasonal calendar of Midawarr (the fruiting season) that the journey unfolds.

I was airshipped to Germany along with a number of other Australians, both indigenous and non-indigenous, during March 1995. The international guests attending the Eliza Fraser symposium in Germany were treated to a field trip. From West Berlin further into the East on a train threading its way through a scene similar to Spielberg's *Schindler's List*, the destination that day was the Leipzig Museum and the collection of the renowned German naturalist, Amalie Dietrich. It soon became apparent that there was another ominous narrative seeking its own brand-new day. For the two indigenous people in the guided tour there were flashbacks to a feature article on the front of the Australian *Bulletin* of 12 November 1991, where Dietrich was also known as 'The Angel Of Black Death'.[1]

Amalie Dietrich, naturalist and collector, began work in the State of Queensland, Australia in 1863 and continued until 1873. The Leipzig Collection comprises more than 130 pieces of material culture and eight skeletal remains from Queensland, five male and three female, as well as a male skull from the city of Rockhampton. Subsequently and somewhat coincidentally, all the skeletal remains were destroyed during the bombing of the museum during the Second World War.

Amalie Dietrich was also known to have offered a financial incentive to local settlers in return for the shooting of healthy Aboriginal specimens for the assembled collection of shipping magnate Godeffroy and his recently established museum.

Aboriginal bones were used to support the new scientific theory of our supposed racial inferiority. This was based on Darwinian evolutionary theory, and is not unlike the situation in the 1920s, when similar racist theories emerged through the National Socialist movement and were embraced by Adolf Hitler.

The new export industry in Australian colonies were the shipments of Aboriginal skulls. It is estimated that between 5000 and 10,000 Aboriginal bodies were a part of the international scientific trade.

However, the insidious new science of the twentieth century is one that is not based on the physical but the intellectual. What has horrified me the most in this decade is the pervasive colonization of the intellect. Not content to be the body snatchers as were their forebears, the *nouveaux* colonialists colonize our indigenous intellect.

In my situation as a Badtjala woman from the largest sand island in the world, Fraser Island, Australia, I see this *nouveau* colonization taking place through three avenues: first through the reconstruction of colonists' narratives nationally; second through language when using maligned buzz-words such as hybridization, reconciliation and mediation; finally, I see this taking place through academia where Aboriginal people are informants in the extensive research carried out by non-Aboriginal people obtaining their PhD qualifications.

The dubious status of Australian academia not accrediting Aboriginal informants also parallels the role of indigenous women on this continent. The status of Aboriginal women was especially complex, at times bordering on treacherous liaisons for reasons of economic survival. They played a major role at the frontier, making significant contributions in the workforce. This included stock-riding, mustering, shepherding, housework, cooking, washing and acting as nursemaids, to list but a few occupations.

The thirst to conquer was also on another footing which was not often written about but is touched on in the Henry Reynolds publication *With the White People*, when he alludes to other ephemeral happenings, such as the actions of the 'sex hungry' male 'occupational force'.[2] Aboriginal women were usually objects of desire and Anglo-Australian males could forcibly unleash their brutal lust and sire illegitimate offspring. The double context of this was the unspoken taboo of Aboriginal women never being elevated to the status and inner sanctum of marriage. Therefore, the complex dichotomy always placed the black woman on the lowest rung of the economic ladder.

Butting up against the virtues of women on the frontier was the need to create strong historic females in our national identity. The dilemma is that (as an indigenous woman) I cannot recall one Aboriginal heroine. The unresolved puzzle concerning the Australian Heroine is the fact that she could never be black. The narrative has always puzzled me: why is it that the heroine could only be white? – the white damsel in distress battling against the harsh forces of nature and native savages. Her black counterpart has not left a single mark in Australian literature, yet in this landscape her skeletal remains at Lake Mungo have been carbon dated in the region of 30,000 years.

The supposed heroine in my immediate adulthood is the elusive narrative of Eliza Fraser. The constant public mythologizing has lionized Mrs Fraser as a national and international heroine. In 1836 she was marooned for five weeks on Fraser Island and her saga has been allowed to continue throughout two centuries. Mrs Fraser's incarceration on the island would, in turn, imprison the traditional owners of Fraser Island, the Badtjala. The absence of a dialogue with the Badtjala has irrevocably damaged and put this people to rest. I often wonder when she too will be put to rest.

Within my retrieval of Badtjala archival material there was a mysterious and striking image of one of my forebears (Figure 12.1). Her gaze was averted. No name. No birth. No death. The signifier in this instance is one black-and-white photograph held in the John Oxley Library, Brisbane. The real heroine of my narrative is nameless, black and defiant. She has not had a serious quarrel with the truth, unlike Mrs Fraser. She does not appear in a Patrick White novel or in a Sidney Nolan painting.

In bell hooks' book, *Black Looks*, I think of this quote when I reflect on my photographic series titled, 'Native Blood': 'She conquers the terror through perverse re-enactment, through resistance, using violence as a means of fleeing from a history that is a burden too great to bear.'[3] The thought arises of all the unnamed Black women around the world, their unrecorded births and deaths. These marginalized women of historic deeds and their lives have never been recorded. Yet they live on in our collective memories.

The women who are often nameless in this country for the space they have reclaimed, often on behalf of the communities they come from, are largely indigenous. These women I speak of include Shirley Foley for her wisdom and foresight to reclaim land on Fraser Island and introduce Badtjala language programmes designed especially for children into the Hervey Bay community. She is currently the Co-ordinator (zone two) of the Central Queensland Language Programme and has completed a Badtjala dictionary.

Artist Bunduk Marika is noted for her determination to bring leading Australian architect Glenn Mercutt to her community of Yirrkala to institute economical contemporary architecture suitable for northern monsoonal weather, and her regeneration of native plant species in Yirrkala.

The women of Maningrida have shared their knowledge and travelled for weaving cultural exchanges with Aboriginal women from Queensland and South Australian communities. In the twentieth

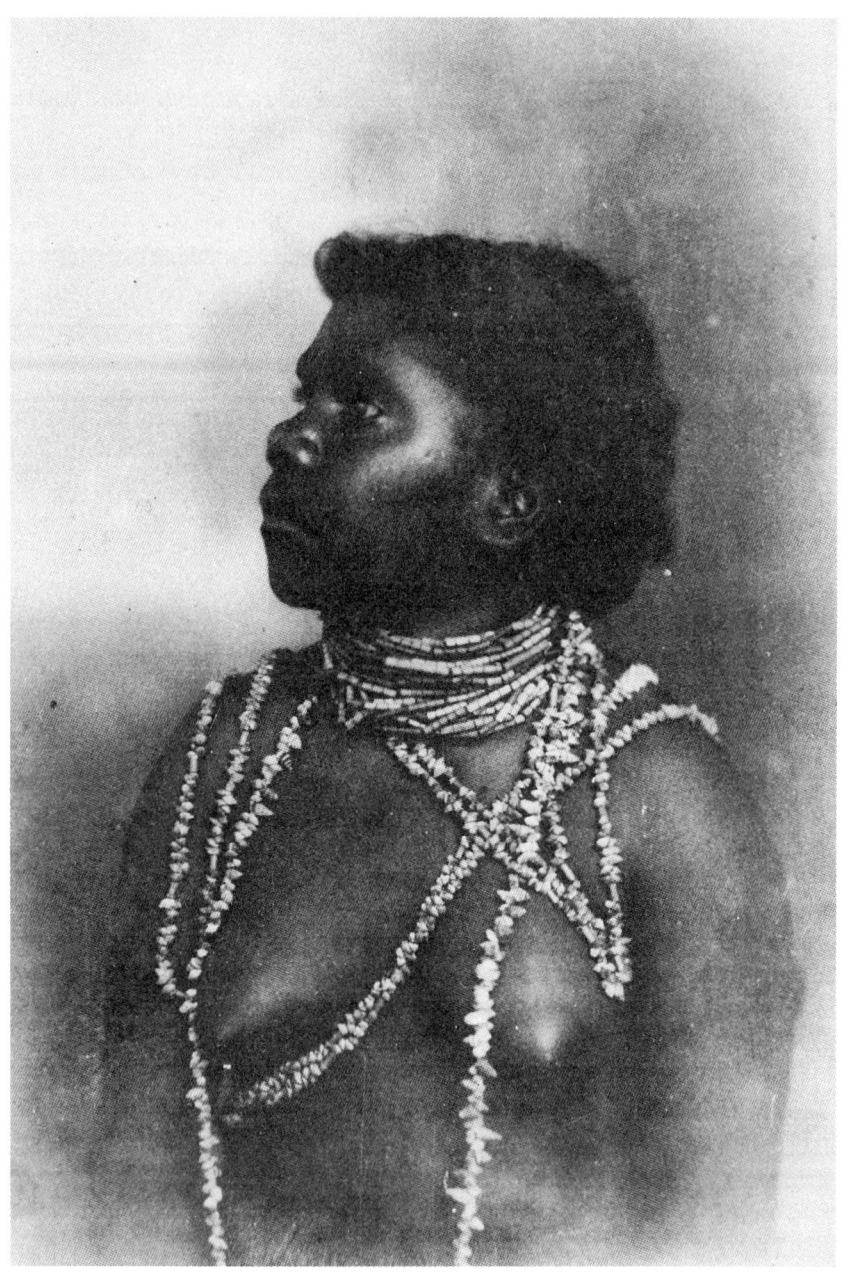

Figure 12.1 A member of the Badtjala. Collection: John Oxley Library, Brisbane.

century these women are continuing traditional and innovative weaving practices.

The women of Hindmarsh Island must be remembered for standing their ground concerning Aboriginal women's religious rites and defying the development of a bridge, the South Australian Government and a Royal Commission. These women retain their knowledge of women's secret ceremony of this tract of land and sea. They challenged the patriarchy of our Australian parliament and judicial system.

We applaud the strength of women from Central Australia who conduct business ceremonies from 60,000 years of religious practices in the age of the Internet and the information super highway. In arid country and in secret places, times governed by the seasons and lunar phases, hundreds of invited Aboriginal women gather to maintain their traditional ties to land and kinship responsibilities.

Women have effected a difference through sharing secret/sacred knowledge and objects. The positive outcome is a coming together clearly evolving a change in a verbal and non-verbal discourse between indigenous women of this continent. Hence, linked to this is an immense appreciation of cultural leaders, most of whom, for me, are Aboriginal women from the various nations within Australia.

Yet twice this year I have had to contend with the maligned English heroine Eliza Fraser, both in Australian academia and German theatre. Not one of the above indigenous women has had a symposium created around her life or is likely to in the foreseeable future.

So to recast the heroine a perverse re-enactment takes place: the Black heroine of yore. The heroine in this instance is Badtjala. The only way I could come close to her was to recast her in my image. The skirt I wear in the photograph titled 'Native Blood' is from Maningrida. Like the shell and reed necklaces, these objects were made by Aboriginal women coming from a remote Australian community. The red, black and yellow hand-painted platform shoes symbolize the Aboriginal land rights flag.

Unlike my forebears, my discarded symbols may possibly leave a mark on this urban landscape. The viewers have to draw their own conclusions. Yet I live in hope that my heroine could be your heroine, as she defies all odds with an unspoken eloquence of spunk.

As the history of this continent has been written by the victors, the dominant discourse has tended to be a clearly spelt out colonialist narrative, which is linear, rather than dealing with complex histories which overlap spatial shifts in time. There has been an effective silencing.

For some it begins with the doctrine of *terra nullius* in 1788, a Latin term meaning 'empty land'. From 1788 until 1992 this false doctrine was in place concerning the indigenous populations. However, for the

Badtjala it begins in 1836 with the shipwreck of the *Stirling Castle* and the first English woman to come ashore at Fraser Island. A conspicuous absence is entered by an unsuspecting nation of Badtjala. The psychological impact was great and did not afford the Badtjala a voice until 1964, with the publication written by my great-uncle Wilfie Reeves titled *The Legends of Moonie Jarl*.

What does this deafening SILENCE say to me? One hundred and twenty-eight years of a history ruptured or six generations of a people without records of their existence except on mission files? The messages are fraught with contradictory facts and public mythologizing.

At a regional level the jarring of symbols also resounded a few years ago at a site on Fraser Island at Poyungan Rocks, or if you were to say it in Badtjala it would be Boyungan. This particular shell midden is 1500 years old and contains layers of wah wong mollusc. Cutting through the middle of the oldest recorded midden site on the island is a road for four-wheel drive vehicles used by local residents to access the beach and various common throughfares.

The static image invokes a memory of a severed history imbued with an immense sense of loss that has occurred through subtle and overt acts of physical and cultural genocide. In stark contrast, the artefact, in this case Badtjala cultural material collected and housed in the state museums such as the South Australian Museum, bear heavily on access to knowledge for my generation of indigenes.

These objects have become so valued and precious because of their scarcity that they are protected through museum policy and government acts. Although the custodial guardians still inhabit this continent, they do not retain the right to house and use them in the passing down of knowledge. At best, an appointment is made with the relevant institution and the artefacts can be held and photographic records made available to the Badtjala people on request. In turn these same objects will assist to legitimize a race of people when they choose to seek native title on Fraser Island.

Banjo Owens, or Buthung, was a well-known Badtjala man who was a resistance fighter. In the 1930s he maintained a one-man vigil to reside on Fraser Island. The problem was that the Badtjala had been forcibly removed from Fraser Island in 1904. Law enforcement officers of the day also saw it as their duty to abide by the previous ruling.

Banjo would row over to Fraser Island to hunt, fish and set up camp, only to be tracked down by the local constable, taken back in his dinghy and brought back to the mainland of Hervey Bay. His dinghy would be chained up to a monumental gum-tree. But the clever Buthung would only return to the site with an axe to cut down the trunk and lift the padlocked chain over the stump. He would jump into his dinghy and once again return to the island. And the saga would continue in this vein. Banjo's stance, however, does not negate the continuous link other Badtjala clans have had in maintaining a custodial right, through their unrecorded yet frequent visits to the island.

The season is now Barra mirri (the growth season) and the end of the journey draws closer. With successive generations of Badtjala, fortunately for my indigenous peers, we have been afforded a voice – sometimes in mainstream spheres, at other times in our local communities. As modern subversives the oars for the dinghy are still close at hand. The challenge is in how we use our Aboriginal heroes and heroines.

This brings me to Marcia Langton's paper presented at the Global Diversity Conference, Sydney, 1995. In 'Representations and Indigenous Images', Langton states:

> These icons of Aboriginality are produced by Anglo-Australians, not in dialogue with Aboriginal people, but from other representations, such as the noble savages or the dying race. They are inherited, imagined representations that date to the days of the colony.[4]

What has tended to take place through the writings of Australian historians and academics is a gross romanticization of life in the colony based on British ignorance of the complex systems of Aboriginal languages, kinship, religion, art and science. Overwhelmingly we see a glaring absence of a dialogue not only between the indigenous populations but also between the colonized and the colonizer, yet the populations of Australia spoke over 250 different languages and 700 separate dialect groups have been recorded. Many Aboriginal people were multilingual, able to speak and understand many different languages as well as English.

Sadly, it is rare for Anglo-Australians to understand or speak one word of an Aboriginal language, let alone a phrase or sentence structure. Yet our indigenous children are indoctrinated to read, write and converse in the dominant language, possibly making our systems of complex grammar defunct, as the decline of our native languages is in a serious state of retrieval and maintenance nationally. The power of language is a daunting phenomenon, its treachery reordering the subordination of the colonized.

The great chain of Australian history begins for the Eora in 1789 around the legs of the first prisoners of war, Bennelong and Colbee. Governor Arthur Phillip ordered the kidnap of two Aboriginal men. Their significant roles were as interpreter to translate English into Eora and vice versa.

On 27 November 1789, Bennelong and Colbee were brought back to Government House. They were washed, shaved, clothed and more importantly shackled by the legs. The writings of Frantz Fanon echo loudly across continents when he says, 'The practice of violence binds them together as a whole, since each individual forms a violent link in the great chain, a part of the great organism of violence which has surged upwards in reaction to the settler's violence in the beginning'.[5] The paradigm is at play again today, bringing together the Aboriginal peoples, the Australian Government and the British Monarchy.

Pemulwuy, one of Australia's first subversive activists, was an Eora man who carried on a war for fourteen years. He fought the British regime from Lane Cove to Toongabbie and Parramatta. This region is better known as the city of Sydney. He was responsible for the phrase 'Tyerabarrbowyaou' which means, 'I shall never become a white man'. What Pemulwuy was saying in effect was that he could never fence off land like the settlers. The boundaries are governed by natural phenomena such as tidal estuaries, water courses, rocky outcrops and mountain ranges.

Aboriginal informants, who were often written out of history altogether, have never been credited for the roles they have played in shaping this country's economy and development as a nation. Early colonialists, escaped convicts, settler historians and in 1897 the government-appointed Protectors of Aborigines were the earliest recorders of a dialogue between the indigenous populations and the colonizers. Paradoxically, it is these early and scant documents that are a pivotal key in the location of a disjointed inheritance. A dialogue was initiated; however, the frontier was to switch strategy on numerous occasions.

In the State of Queensland the larger scenario contains true guerilla warfare. From 1848 the regime of 'dispersal' came into force and continued for the next three decades. Violence was the backdrop with the use of the native police from southern states and overly zealous officers. The duty of 'dispersal' was a deceptive term used in official reports to underscore what truly took place: massacres. Today we use the term 'ethnic cleansing'. It was then commonly believed that the path was smoothed for the demise of a 'dying race'.

As the frontier continued north and west there was an increasing need for Aboriginal labour. Charles D. Rowley speaks of a new pact for economic survival of the new arrivals; 'professed morality in a settler democracy can be moulded by economic interest and the need to cover up awkward facts.'[6] Aboriginal labour was cheap and payment was usually made in the form of alcohol, opium, tobacco, one blanket, food, sometimes clothes. Aboriginal people provided labour for the mining fields, sugar plantations, pastoralists, timber and pearl industries.

Jimmy Governor reminds me of the Aboriginal subversive activists such as Pemulwuy and Banjo, men who stood outside the law; Aboriginal heroes who sought justice in their lifetime. Jimmy Governor (1875–1901) dared to go against the social order of the day and married a white woman, Ethel Page, aged 16. The unspoken politics of sexual tensions in the colony come into play in Governor's life. He was subsequently hanged in Paddington, Sydney.

Although illicit intercourse with native women on a casual or semi-permanent basis was common, the same could not be said for an Aboriginal man and a white woman. Constant slighting remarks were made to both husband and wife. In reprisal for racist taunts during July 1890, Governor committed murder at the Mawbey homestead. For fourteen weeks Governor and his brother became bushrangers.

Brian Davies, through historical accounts of events in *The Life of Jimmy Governor*, makes an astute observation of society in Australia during the turn of the century.

> They had shed their own criminal past of convict forebears. They had built town, steeple and school where, as they perceived it, only barbarism had existed. They had every right to congratulate themselves ... and to expect subsequent centuries to remember and acknowledge them. They were not unmindful that what they laid down then, would be their own memorial in the future and they built well.[7]

The subject of memorials brings to mind the Australian national holiday held annually on 25 April, Anzac Day, where we remember our fallen soldiers of past wars, except of the very first war. It is a luxury that has never been afforded to the first Australians who died defending this land.

In the state of Queensland alone, Henry Reynolds writes that

> There is no telling the size of the Aboriginal deathtoll from overt violence, guestimates of 15,000 have been made – based rather roughly upon a rule of thumb that white frontiersmen established a kill ratio of fifteen or twenty to one against the Aborigines. For comparison sake, this is more than the number of Queenslanders killed and injured at the Sudan, the Boer War, and Korean War and the Vietnam War combined.[8]

What were the casualties of the other states and territories?

In the well-known text *The Black Aesthetic*, in particular the chapter by Larry Neal, 'The Black Arts Movement', he speaks of Brother Knight calling for a new black aesthetic; he realizes, 'we must create a new history, new symbols, myths and legends'.[9] This philosophy has heralded a new visual language and curatorship direction within Aboriginal Australia.

What has taken place for the first time are three significant public sculptures that pay tribute to our indigenous fighters. During the

Bicentennial year 1988, Djon Mundine conceived and curated 'The Aboriginal Memorial' which was installed at the Sydney Biennial and is on permanent exhibition at the National Gallery of Australia, Canberra. Ramingining artists and the surrounding communities worked towards collating 200 hollow log coffins in a tribute to all Aboriginal people in this country who have died defending Australia.

The year 1995 ushered in the second tribute to a specific nation of Aboriginal people, the Eora. This public sculpture, titled 'Edge of the Trees', is a collaboration between Janet Laurence and myself. This sculpture stands in the forecourt of the Museum of Sydney, the previous site of the first Government House. The single most striking aspect of this work is the haunting use of the Eora language both in the written context and the spoken word on compact disc. It must be noted that the political significance of the work is that it is the oldest retrieval of an Aboriginal language since colonization in Australia.

At a site along the Brisbane River, artist Ron Hurley completed a sculpture titled 'Geerabaugh, Midden'. The six timber columns and cast aluminium represent the six nations which shared an aspect of the one creation story concerning the rainbow serpent ceremony held at Coolum as told by Willie McKenzie. There is a haunting visual presence taking shape along the eastern half of this continent.

Through our memorials that pay tribute to Aboriginal people we have much to celebrate as a nation on the verge of maturity. The irony of the settler culture has brought about many double contexts and unanswered questions such as the Eliza Fraser saga. As a Badtjala artist reflecting on the past two centuries, the intensity of the gaze has increased. It is the omnipresent Aboriginal gaze which reflects your colonial gaze. What I see mirrored in the exclusive gaze of race is an inarticulate consumption of guilt, an awkward Australia.

Notes

1 D. Monaghan, 'Angel of Black Death', Cover Story, *Bulletin* with *Newsweek*, 12 November 1991, 31, 38.

2 H. Reynolds, 'VI Black Pioneers', in *With The White People* (Melbourne: Penguin, 1990), 214.

3 b. hooks, 'Representations of Whiteness', in *Black Looks* (Boston: South End Press, 1992), 176.

4 M. Langton, 'Representations and Indigenous Images'. Paper presented at the Global Diversity Conference, Sydney 1995.

5 F. Fanon, 'Concerning Violence', in *The Wretched of the Earth* (Harmondsworth: Penguin, 1967), 73.

6 C.D. Rowley, 'The Queensland Frontier, 1859–1897', in *The Destruction of Aboriginal Society: Aboriginal Policy and Practice, Vol. 1* (Canberra: Australian National University Press, 1970), 175.

7   B. Davies, 'The Beginning', in *The Life of Jimmy Governor* (Sydney: Ure Smith, 1979), 18.

8   T. Hardy, '"The Owl and the Eagle": The Significance of Race in Colonial Queensland', *Social Alternatives* 5.4 (1986) 18).

9   L. Neal, 'The Black Arts Movement', in *The Black Aesthetic*, ed. G. Addison Jr (New York: Anchor Books & Doubleday, 1971), 258.

Bibliography

Abrams, P. *Historical Sociology*. New York: Cornell University Press, 1982.

Abrams, P. *The Origins of British Sociology 1834–1914*. Chicago: University of Chicago Press, 1968.

Aldridge, H. Letter in A.W. Howitt, The Ngarigo File. Howitt Papers, State Library of Victoria, Box 8.

Alexander, M. *Mrs Fraser on the Fatal Shore*. London: Michael Joseph, 1971.

Alexander, P., Hutchinson, R. and Schreuder, D. *Africa Today*. Canberra: Humanities Research Council, 1996.

Anonymous. 'A Copy of the Mournful Verses'. Seven Dials: J. Catnach, 1938 (British Museum).

Arnold. J. and Ross, J. *1934: A Year in the Life of Victoria*. Melbourne: State Library of Victoria, 1984.

Atwood, B. and Arnold, J. *Power, Knowledge and Aborigines*. Melbourne: La Trobe University Press, 1993.

Australian Fraser Island Environmental Inquiry – Final Report. Canberra: Australian Government Publishing Service, 1976.

Barbour, D. '*the man with seven toes*: Michael Ondaatje's Expressionist Version of an Australian legend'. *Australian–Canadian Studies: A Journal for the Humanities and the Social Sciences* 10.1 (1992).

Barbour, D. *Michael Ondaatje*. New York: Twayne, 1993.

Barrett, C. *White Blackfellows*. Prahran: Hallcraft, 1948.

Basedow, H. *The Australian Aborigines*. Adelaide: F.W. Preece and Sons, 1929.

Basedow, H. 'Burial Customs in the Northern Flinders Ranges'. *Man* 13 (1913).

Baxter, J. Report to Foster Fyans at Moreton Bay. 6 September 1836. AONSW SZ976, COD 183.

Bhabha, H. *The Location of Culture*. London and New York: Routledge, 1994.

Blackman, B. 'Eliza Surviva'. *Quadrant* 21.2 (April 1977).

Broadsheet. *Wreck of the Stirling Castle*. London: J. Catnach, 1838.

Brink, A. *An Instant in the Wind*. London: Fontana, 1976.

Brink, A. *Mapmakers: Writing in a State of Siege*. London: Faber & Faber, 1983.

Brown, H. 'Nolan's Journey to Paradise'. *Weekend Australian Magazine*, 21–22 October 1989.

Burrow, J. *Evolution and Society*. Cambridge: Cambridge University Press, 1966.

Carter, M. *Framing Art: Introducing Theory and the Visual Image*. Sydney: Hale and Iremonger, 1990.

Carter, P. *The Road to Botany Bay: An Essay in Spatial History*. London and Boston: Faber & Faber, 1987.

Carter, P. *The Sound In-Between: Voice, Space and Performance*. Strawberry Hills, NSW: New South Wales University Press, 1992.

Carter, P. and Malouf, D. 'Spatial History'. *Textual Practice* 3.2 (1989).

Chambers, T. after S. Parkinson, 'Two of the Natives of New Holland advancing into combat', from Parkinson's *Journal of a Voyage to the South Seas*, 1773.

Chapman, M., Gardner, C. and Mphahlele, E. (eds) *Perspectives on South African English Literature*. Johannesburg: Ad. Donker, 1992.

Clark, J. 'Convulsion and Calm: Death in the Afternoon', in *Creating Australia: 200 Years of Art 1788–1988*, ed. D. Thomas. Adelaide: International Cultural Corporation of Australia/Art Gallery of South Australia, 1988.

Clark, J. *Sidney Nolan: Landscapes and Legends*. Cambridge/Melbourne: Cambridge University Press, 1987.

Clark, K., MacInnes, C. and Robertson, B. *Sidney Nolan*. London: Thames and Hudson, 1961.

Coetzee, J.M. *White Writing: On the Culture of Letters in South Africa*. New Haven and London: Yale University Press, 1988.

Coleman, P. *Australian Civilization*. Melbourne: F.W. Cheshire, 1962.

Collins, Lt. Col. D. *An Account of the English Colony of New South Wales*, ed. B. Fletcher. Facsimile edition 1798–1802; London: A.W. Reed, 1975.

Condorcet, Marquis de. *Esquisse d'un tableau historique des progres de l'esprit humain* (1795). Paris: Masson, 1822.

Corbin, A. *The Lure of the Sea*. London: Penguin, 1995.

Cunningham, P. *Two Years in New South Wales*. London: Henry Colburn, 1828.

Curr, E.M. 'Great Sandy or Fraser Island'. *The Australian Race*, vol. 3, ed. E.M. Curr. Melbourne: Government Printer, 1887.

Curtis, J. *The Shipwreck of the Stirling Castle*. London: George Virtue, 1838.

Daniel, G. *A Short History of Archaeology*. London: Thames and Hudson, 1981.

Darian-Smith, K., Poignant, R. and Schaffer, K. *Captured Lives: Australian Captivity Narratives*. London: Sir Robert Menzies Centre for Australian Studies, 1993.

Davidson, I., Lovell-Jones, C. and Bancroft, R. *Archaeologists and Aborigines Working Together*. Armidale: University of New England Press, 1995.

Davidson, J. 'Beyond the Fatal Shore: The Mythologisation of Mrs Fraser'. *Meanjin* 49.3 (1990).

Davidson, J. Interview with André Brink. *Overland* 94.5 (1984).

Davies, B. *The Life of Jimmy Governor*. Sydney: Ure Smith, 1979.

Davison, L. *The White Woman*. St Lucia: University of Queensland Press, 1994.

Devitt, J. 'Fraser Island: Aboriginal Resources and Settlement Pattern'. Unpublished BA (Hons.) thesis, University of Queensland, 1979.

Driver, D. 'Women and Nature, Women as Objects of Exchange: Towards a Feminist Analysis of South African Literature', *Perspectives on South African English Literature*, eds M. Chapman, C. Gardner and E. Mphahlele. Johannesburg: Ad. Donker, 1992.

Drummond, Y. 'Progress of Eliza'. *Royal Historical Society of Queensland Journal* 15.1 (February 1993).

Dutton, K.R. *The Perfectible Body: The Western Ideal of Physical Development*. London: Cassell, 1995.

Dwyer B. and Buchanan, N. *The Rescue of Eliza Fraser*. Noosa: Noosa Graphica, 1986.

Elkin, A.P. 'Anthropology in Australia: Chapter One'. *Mankind* 5.6 (1958).

Evans, R. and Walker, J. ' "These strangers, where are they going?" Aboriginal–European Relations in the Fraser Island and Wide Bay Region 1770–1905'. *University of Queensland, Anthropology Museum, Occasional Papers in Anthropology* 8 (1977).

Fanon, F. *The Wretched of the Earth*. Harmondsworth: Penguin, 1967.

Final Discussion Paper Volume III: Issues. Commission of Inquiry into the Conservation, Management and Use of Fraser Island and the Great Sandy Region. Brisbane: Queensland Government Printer, 1990.

Flinders, M. *A Voyage to Terra Australis 1801, 1802, 1803*. 3 vols. London: G and W. Nichol, 1814.

Foley, F. 'Urban Art', in *Aboriginal Art and Spirituality*, ed. R. Crumlin. Victoria: Collins Dove, 1991.

Foley, F. 'Author's Introduction', in *Tyerabarrowaryaou: I Shall Never*

Become a White Man, curated by F. Foley and D. Mundine. Sydney: Museum of Contemporary Art, 1992.

Foley, S. *The Badtjala People*. Hervey Bay: Thoorgine Educational and Cultural Centre Aboriginal Corporation Inc., 1994.

Foucault, M. *The Order of Things: An Archaeology of the Human Sciences*. London: Tavistock, 1970.

Frankland, K. 'Booral: Preliminary Investigation of an Archaeological Site in the Great Sandy Strait Region, Southeast Queensland'. Unpublished BA (Hons.) thesis, The University of Queensland, 1990.

Fraser, E. 1836, Public Archives of NSW, File No. SZ 976.

Graham, J. A Memorandum of the Real Facts. 4 January 1837. AONSW 4/2325.4, in *Brisbane Town in Convict Days*, J.G. Steele. St Lucia: University of Queensland Press, 1987.

Gray, S. *Southern African Literature: An Introduction*. Cape Town: David Philip, 1979.

Hardy, T. ' "The Owl and the Eagle" ': The Significance of Race in Colonial Queensland'. *Social Alternatives* 5.4 (1986).

Hassall, A.J. 'The Lives of Adamastor', in *International Literature in English: Essays on the Major Writers*, ed. R.L. Ross. New York and London: Garland, 1991.

Hassall, A.J. 'The Making of a Colonial Myth: The Mrs Fraser Story in Patrick White's *A Fringe of Leaves* and André Brink's *An Instant in the Wind*'. *Ariel* 18.3 (1987).

Hill, B. *Ghosting William Buckley*. Melbourne: Heinemann, 1993.

Hobbes, T. *Leviathan* (1651). Baltimore: Penguin, 1968.

hooks, b. *Black Looks*. Boston: South End Press, 1992.

hooks, b. *Yearnings: Race, Gender, and Cultured Politics*. Boston: South End Press, 1990, 58.

Hughes, R. *The Art of Australia*. London: Penguin, 1966.

Isaacs, J. *Aboriginality: Contemporary Aboriginal Paintings and Prints*. Brisbane: University of Queensland Press, 1989.

Isaacs, J. 'Fiona Foley on Aboriginality in Art, Life and Landscape'. *Art Monthly* (May 1990).

Johnson, T. 'Paying the Rent', in *What is Appropriation?*, ed. R. Butler. Brisbane: Institute of Modern Art/Power Publications, 1996. Reprinted from *Stories of Australian Art* (exhibition catalogue). London: Australia Institute, 1988.

Josipovici, G. 'Dreams of Mrs Fraser', in *Steps: Selected Fiction and Drama*. London: Carcanet, 1989.

Kossew, S. *Pen and Power: A Post-Colonial Reading of the Novels of J.M. Coetzee and André Brink*. Amsterdam and Atlanta: Rodopi, 1996.

Kossew, S. 'Re/presenting the Afrikaner: André Brink and the Politics of Representation', in *Africa Today*, ed. P. Alexander, R.

Hutchinson and D. Schreuder. Canberra: Humanities Research Council, 1996.

Kucklick, H. *The Savage Within: The Social History of British Anthropology, 1885–1945*. Cambridge: Cambridge University Press, 1991.

Langevad, G. *Some Original Views Around Kilcoy: Book 1. The Aboriginal Perspective*. Queensland: Archaeology Branch, 1982.

Langton, M. 'Representations and Indigenous Images'. Paper presented at the Global Diversity Conference, Sydney 1995.

Lattas, A. 'Primitivism, Nationalism and Individualism in Australian Popular Culture', in *Power, Knowledge and Aborigines*, eds B. Atwood and J. Arnold. Melbourne: La Trobe University Press, 1993.

Laudan, R. Review of Paolo Rossi's *The Dark Abyss of Time: The History of the Earth and the History of Nations from Hooke to Vico. Philosophy of Science* 52 (1985).

Lauer, P.K. 'Ethnohistorical Observations on Fraser Island' (1975). Ms. submitted to the Fraser Island Environmental Inquiry, Exhibit No. 543. Australian Archives, Canberra, A3911 Series.

Lauer, P.K. 'The Museum's Role in Fieldwork: The Fraser Island Study'. *University of Queensland, Anthropology Museum, Occasional Papers in Anthropology* 9 (1979).

Lauer, P.K. 'Report on a Preliminary Ethnohistorical and Archaeological Survey of Fraser Island'. *University of Queensland, Anthropology Museum, Occasional Papers in Anthropology* 1 (1977).

Layton, R. (ed.) *Who Needs the Past? Indigenous Values and Archaeology*. One World Archaeology 5. London: Unwin Hyman, 1989.

Leed, E. *The Mind of the Traveler: From Gilgamesh to Global Tourism*. New York: Basic Books, 1991.

Lynn, E. 'The Painting of Ned Kelly', in *Sidney Nolan's Ned Kelly: Paintings and Drawings from the Collection of the Australian National Gallery*. Canberra: Australian National Gallery, 1985.

MacInnes, C. *Sidney Nolan*. London: Thames and Hudson, 1961.

McNiven, I.J. 'Ethnohistorical Reconstructions of Aboriginal Lifeways along the Cooloola Coast, Southeast Queensland'. *Proceedings of the Royal Society of Queensland* 102 (1992).

McNiven, I.J. 'Prehistoric Aboriginal Settlement and Subsistence in the Cooloola Region, Southeast Queensland'. Unpublished Ph.D. thesis, The University of Queensland, 1990.

McNiven, I.J. *'Relics of a By-gone Race'? Managing Aboriginal Sites in the Great Sandy Region'*. Ngulaig Vol. 12. St Lucia: Aboriginal and Torres Strait Islander Studies Unit, The University of Queensland, 1994.

McNiven, I.J. 'Sandblow Sites in the Great Sandy Region Coastal Southeast Queensland: Implications for Models of Late Holocene Rainforest Exploitation and Settlement Restructuring'. *Queensland Archaeological Research* 9 (1992).

McNiven, I.J. 'Shell Middens and Mobility: The Use of Off-site Faunal Remains, Queensland, Australia'. *Journal of Field Archaeology* 19.4 (1992).

McNiven, I.J. 'Teewah Beach: New Evidence for Holocene Coastal Occupation in Southeast Queensland'. *Australian Archaeology* 33 (1991).

McNiven, I.J. and Russell, L. 'Place with a Past: Reconciling Wilderness and the Aboriginal Past in World Heritage Areas'. *Proceedings of the Royal Historical Society of Queensland* 15.11 (1995).

McNiven, I.J. and Russell, L. ' "Strange Paintings" and "Mystery Races": Kimberley Rock Art, Diffusionism and Colonial Constructions of Australia's Aboriginal Past'. *Antiquity*, 71 (1997), 801-9.

Malina, J. and Vasicek, Z. *Archaeology Yesterday and Today.* Cambridge: Cambridge University Press, 1990.

Marr, D. *Patrick White: A Life* (1991). Sydney: Vintage, 1992.

Mathew, J. *Two Representative Tribes of Queensland.* London: T. Fisher, Unwin, 1910.

Melville, R. *Sidney Nolan: Paradise Garden.* London: R. Alistair McAlpine Publishing, 1971.

Meston, A. *Report on Fraser Island.* Queensland Legislative Assembly, 1905.

Miller, O. *Fraser Island Legends.* Brisbane: Jacaranda Press, 1993.

Monaghan, D. 'Angel of Black Death'. Cover Story. *Bulletin* with *Newsweek*, 12 November 1991.

Morris, M. 'Two Types of Photography Criticism Located in Relation to Lyn Silvermann's Series', in *The Pirate's Fiancée*. London: Verso, 1988.

Mundwiler, L. *Michael Ondaatje: Word, Image, Imagination.* Vancouver: Talonbooks, 1984.

Neal, L. 'The Black Arts Movement', in *The Black Aesthetic*, ed. G. Addison Jr. New York: Anchor Books and Doubleday, 1971.

Obeyesekere, G. *The Apotheosis of Captain Cook: European Mythmaking in the Pacific.* Princeton: Princeton University Press, 1992.

Ondaatje, M. *The Collected Works of Billy the Kid: Left Handed Poems.* Toronto: House of Anansi, 1970.

Ondaatje, M. *Coming Through Slaughter.* Toronto: House of Anansi, 1976.

Ondaatje, M. *The English Patient.* Toronto: McClelland and Stewart, 1992.

Ondaatje, M. *In the Skin of a Lion*. Toronto: McClelland and Stewart, 1987.

Ondaatje, M. *the man with seven toes*. Toronto: Coach House Press, 1969.

Ondaatje, M. *Running in the Family*. Toronto: McClelland and Stewart, 1982.

O'Regan, T. 'Cinema Oz: The Ocker Films', in *The Australian Screen*, eds T. O'Regan and A. Moran. Ringwood, Victoria: Penguin, 1989.

Otter, C. 27 August 1836. AONSW SZ976, COD 183.

Pagden, A. *Europeans' Encounter with the New World*. New Haven: Yale University Press, 1993.

Pagden, A. *The Fall of Natural Man: The American Indian and the Origins of Comparative Ethnology*. New York: Cambridge University Press, 1982.

Pascall, G. 'Eliza's on the Rocks'. *The Australian*, 18 December 1976.

Pollock, G. 'Trouble in the Archives'. *Women's Art Magazine* 54 (September/October 1993).

Pratt, M.L. *Imperial Eyes: Travel Writing and Transculturation*. New York: Routledge, 1992.

Petrie, C.C. *Tom Petrie's Reminiscences of Early Queensland*. Brisbane: Watson, Ferguson & Co., 1904.

Pulleine, R.H. 'The Tasmanians and Their Stone-culture'. *Report of the Nineteenth Meeting of the Australasian Association for the Advancement of Science (Australia and New Zealand)*, ed. C.E. Lord. Hobart: Government Printer, 1929.

Reeves, W. and Miller, O. *The Legends of Moonie Jarl*. Brisbane: Jacaranda Press, 1964.

Reynolds, H. *With The White People*. Melbourne: Penguin, 1990.

Ross, J.W. 'André Brink', in *Contemporary Authors*. Detroit: Gale, 1982.

Ross, R.L. (ed.) *International Literature in English: Essays on the Major Writers*. New York and London: Garland, 1991.

Rousseau, J.J. *First and Second Discourses* (1762). New York: St Martins, 1964.

Rousseau, J.J. *The Social Contract* (1755). New York: Dutton, 1938.

Rowley, C.D. *The Destruction of Aboriginal Society: Aboriginal Policy and Practice, Vol. 1*. Canberra: Australian National University Press, 1970.

Russell, H.S. *The Genesis of Queensland*. Sydney: Turner & Henderson, 1888.

Russell, L. '(Re)Presented Pasts: Historical and Contemporary Constructions of Australian Aboriginalities'. Unpublished Ph.D. thesis, The University of Melbourne, 1995.

Russell, L. and McNiven, I.J. 'Monumental Colonialism: Megaliths and the Appropriation of Australia's Aboriginal Past'. *Journal of Material Culture*, 3 (3), 1998.

Said, E. *Orientalism*. New York: Pantheon, 1978.

Saurin, J. 'Aboriginal Spirit and "Look"'. Exhibition review, Arts section, *Sydney Morning Herald*, 1991.

Schaffer, K. 'Captivity Narratives and the Idea of "Nation"'. *Captured Lives: Australian Captivity Narratives, Working Papers in Australian Studies*, Nos. 85, 86 and 87, ed. K. Darian-Smith, R. Poignant and K. Schaffer. London: Sir Robert Menzies Centre for Australian Studies, 1993.

Schaffer, K. 'The Eliza Fraser Story and Constructions of Gender, Race and Class in Australian Culture'. *Hecate* 17.1 (1991).

Schaffer, K. 'Eliza Fraser's Trial by Media'. *Antipodes* 5.2 (1991).

Schaffer, K. *In The Wake of First Contact: The Eliza Fraser Stories*. Cambridge: Cambridge University Press, 1995.

Simpson, S. Narrative of David Bracewell. Enclosure with letter to Colonial Secretary dated 30 May 1842. 'Some Original Views around Kilcoy. Book 1 – The Aboriginal Perspective', ed. G. Langevad. *Queensland Ethnohistory Transcripts* 1.1 (1842).

Sinclair, J. *Fraser Island and Cooloola*. Willoughby: Weldon, 1990.

Sinclair, J. and Corris, P. *Fighting for Fraser Island: A Man and an Island*. Alexandria: Kerr, 1994.

Solecki, S. 'Point Blank: Narrative in Michael Ondaatje's *the man with seven toes*'. *Canadian Poetry* 6 (Spring/Summer 1980).

Staines, D. *Beyond the Provinces: Literary Canada at the Century's End*. Toronto: University of Toronto Press, 1995, ch.1.

Steele, J.G. *Brisbane Town in Convict Days: 1824–1842*. St Lucia: University of Queensland Press, 1987.

Stocking, G.W. (ed.) *Observers and Observed: Essays on Ethnographic Fieldwork*. Madison: University of Wisconsin Press, 1983.

Thomas, M. *Lick My Black Art*. Exhibition catalogue. Sydney: Australian Centre for Contemporary Art, 1993.

Thompson, C.H. and Moore, A.W. 'Studies in Landscape Dynamics in the Cooloola-Noosa River Area, Queensland. 1. Introduction, General Descriptions and Research Approach'. *CSIRO Division of Soils, Divisional Report* 73 (1984).

Torgovnik, M. *Gone Primitive: Savage Intellects, Modern Lives*. Chicago: University of Chicago Press, 1990.

Travis Lane, M. 'Dream as History: A Review of *the man with seven toes*', in *Spider Blues: Essays on Michael Ondaatje*, ed. S. Solecki. Montreal: Véhicule Press, 1985.

Trigger, B.G. *A History of Archaeological Thought*. Cambridge: Cambridge University Press, 1989.

Turcotte, G. ' "Coming Out of the Closet': Sexual Politics in Michael Ondaatje's *the man with seven toes*'. *La Creation Biographique/ Bibliographic Creation*, Rennes: Presses Universitaires Rennes, 1997.

Turcotte, G. 'Eating the Cannibals from Within: Devouring Mrs Fraser's "Body Politic" ', in *Crossing Lines: Formations of Australian Culture*, ed. P. Butterss, C. Guerin and A. Nettelbeck. Adelaide: ASAL, 1995.

Turcotte, G. ' "The Germ of Document": An Interview with Michael Ondaatje'. *Australian-Canadian Studies: A Journal for the Humanities and the Social Sciences* 12.2 (1994).

Voltaire, F.M. *Essai sur les moeurs et l'esprit des nations*. Paris: Chez Werdet et Lequien Fils, 1745.

Warner, M. *Monuments and Maidens*. London: Wiedenfeld & Nicolson, 1985.

Washington, P. 'The Postcolonial, the National and Australian Cultural Studies: The Case of the Miles Franklin Award', *New Literatures Review: Factions and Fictions* 28/29 (Winter–Summer 1994–5.

Watson, D. *Caledonia Australis: Scottish Highlanders on the Frontier of Australia*. Sydney: Collins, 1984.

Watson, S. 'Michael Ondaatje: The Mechanization of Death', in *Spider Blues: Essays on Michael Ondaatje* ed. S. Solecki. Montreal: Véhicule Press, 1985.

Wharton, W.J.L. (ed.) *Captain Cook's Journal During His First Voyage Round the World Made in H.M. Bark 'Endeavour' 1768–71. A literal transcription of the original MSS.* London: Elliot Stock, 1893.

White, P. *Flaws in the Glass*. London: Jonathan Cape, 1981.

White, P. *A Fringe of Leaves*. London: Jonathan Cape, 1976.

Williams, F. *Written in Sand: A History of Fraser Island*. Brisbane: Jacaranda Press, 1982.

Williamson, D. *Eliza Fraser*. Melbourne: Sun Books, 1976.

Wilton, R. ' "Things Happened": Narrative in Michael Ondaatje's *the man with seven toes*'. *Canadian Literature* 137 (Summer 1993).

Wyk Smith, M. van ' "What the waves were always saying": *Dombey and Son* and Textual Ripples on an African Shore'. Unpublished ms.

Youlden, H. 'Shipwreck in Australia'. *Knickerbocker* 41.4 (1853).

Index

Page numbers in italics refer to illustrations.
'EF' is used as an abbreviation for references to Eliza Fraser.